Khizr Tiwana, the Punjab Unionist Party and the Partition of India

The Proud Premier of the Punjab

Khizr Tiwana, the Punjab Unionist Party and the Partition of India

Ian Talbot

Routledge
Taylor & Francis Group
LONDON AND NEW YORK

First Published 1996
by Curzon Press

2 Park Square, Milton Park, Abingdon, Oxon OX14 4RN
711 Third Avenue, New York, NY 10017, USA

Routledge is an imprint of the Taylor & Francis Group, an informa business

First issued in paperback 2016

Copyright © 1996 Ian Talbot

Typeset in Sabon by LaserScript Ltd, Mitcham

All rights reserved. No part of this book may be reprinted or reproduced or
utilised in any form or by any electronic, mechanical, or other means, now
known or hereafter invented, including photocopying and recording, or in any
information storage or retrieval system, without permission in writing from
the publishers.

Notice:
Product or corporate names may be trademarks or registered trademarks, and
are used only for identification and explanation without intent to infringe.

British Library Cataloguing in Publication Data
A catalogue record for this book is available from the British Library

ISBN 13: 978-0-7007-0427-9 (hbk)
ISBN 13: 978-1-138-99290-0 (pbk)

Contents

Preface	vii
Foreword	ix
Dr. L.M. Singhvi. Indian High Commissioner in the UK	
List of Abbreviations	xiii
Introduction	1

Part One   Inheritance

1 The Tiwanas of Shahpur	12
2 Father and Son	36
3 The Unionist Party	51

Part Two   The Pinnacle of Power

4 Apprentice to Power	67
5 Inheriting the Crown	83
6 Leader in War and Peace	99

Part Three   The Passing of a World

7 Sailing in Two Boats	111
8 'Pakistan Zindabad'	129
9 General Without an Army	145
Epilogue	167
Conclusion	177
Glossary	182
Select Bibliography	184
Index	190

Preface

The mid-1990s provide a good vantage point for a reconsideration of the Punjab Unionist Party and its last leader, Khizr Hayat Khan Tiwana. Khizr remains a little studied and much misunderstood figure who fits uneasily in both Indian and Pakistani historiography of the freedom movement against the Raj.

This volume argues that his career deserves serious evaluation not just because of the rapid approaching golden jubilee of the partition of India which he so steadfastly opposed. But because of the insights it provides into the ability of consociational devices to maintain stability in highly segmented socities. Indian and Pakistani experiences of recent communal and ethnic conflict call for a serious examination of the prescription of consociational power-sharing. The Unionist experience of the 1940s provides a key historical case study for such an evaluation. Khizr's career is likely to become of increasing interest in the emerging debate on consociationalism.

This work has grown out of a number of years study of the Punjab and its peoples and the emergence of Pakistan. I am deeply indebted to a large number of people who have helped and encouraged me during this period. Thanks go to such doyens of Punjab history as Clive Dewey, Craig Baxter, Iftikhar Malik and David Gilmartin. I also owe an immense debt to Francis Robinson who introduced me to research on South Asia more years ago now than I care to remember.

I am much obliged for the work of the Librarians and Staff of The India Office Library, Nehru Memorial Museum and Library, Southampton University Library, Chicago University Library and the South Asia Institute Library, Heidelberg University. I must thank Dietmar Rothermund for his kind invitation to work in the latter institution.

vii

I am especially grateful to my friend and colleague Gurharpal Singh who encouraged me to delve into the literature on consociationalism and political accommodation. This interest was further stimulated by a chance meeting with Arend Lijphart at the India International Centre in New Delhi.

Mr. K.V.F. Morton, Mr.C.H. Barry, Mr. R.A.F. Holroyd, Alan Campbell-Johnson, Stuart Abbott, Swaran Singh, Azim Husain, Barkat Hayat, Narinder Saroop and Justice Kalwant Singh Tiwana all gave generously of their time during the preparation of the manuscript. Dr Manohar Sondhi, Pran Neville and Bikram Singh acted as the perfect hosts during a brief visit to New Delhi. I must especially thank Nazar Tiwana for the great trouble he has taken in helping me with my research and for his frienship and gracious hospitality. Finally, I am grateful for the comments of numerous colleagues over the years. Any errors of fact or omissions are my responsibility alone.

Coventry, May 1995
Ian Talbot

Foreword

Dr. Ian Talbot's study "Khizr Tiwana, the Unionist Party and the Partition of India" reflects on the well known maxim of Carlyle that history is a series of innumerable biographies. In a similar vein, Emerson had observed that there was probably no history, only biography. Dr. Talbot's study however is not only political biography and history, it is much more. It is an inter-disciplinary study which also has the advantage of being an absorbing narrative of the life and time of Sir Khizr Hayat Khan Tiwana, a biography which constitutes the stuff of history and political sociology without which the traumatic event of the partition of India in 1947 can never be fully comprehended.

Describing the backdrop of Sir Khizr's patrimony and political inheritance, his ascendancy to the premiership of Punjab and the tragic denouement of the frustration of Unionist politics in Punjab which paved the way for the partition of India, Dr. Talbot has made a significant contribution to the study of an extremely complex and difficult period in the history of modern undivided India which becomes increasingly obscure with the passage of time. I believe that the history of that period has not ceased to be relevant. Indeed, it has some valuable lessons and insights to offer even at this distance of time if we are disposed to fathom the social and psychological depths of that era which drew to a close with the partition of India but which appears to have transmitted some of its genes to the post-partition era both in India and Pakistan.

Dr. Talbot's study throws considerable light on the dynamics and deadlocks in the pre-partition politics of the Punjab. Its strength is its biographical focus which provides an authentic understanding of the ground realities of class, caste, religion and politics. The story of the Tiwanas of Shahpur, culled and woven painstakingly and objectively by Dr. Talbot, is the story of an important landowning family and its influence and power in the first half of the twentieth century. In a fascinating narrative, the author not only profiles the personal disposition, educational background and political ideas of Sir Khizr but also delineates the matrix which shaped Sir Khizr's life and outlook and the forces with which he had to contend.

Dr. Talbot's biography of Sir Khizr is divided in three parts, Inheritance, Pinnacle of Power and the Passing of a World. Each part is engaging in its own way and tells the story of a phase in the life of Khizr Tiwana as indeed of the changing political scene in India. The last part of the book, The Passing of a World, reads somewhat like a Greek tragedy and Sir Khizr emerges as a tragic hero cast adrift by the ruthless forces of religious communalism unleashed by the Muslim League in India which left Sir Khizr in the predicament of being a "General without an Army".

A scion of a prominent landowning family with a conspicuous history of loyalty to the Raj, Sir Khizr was not really a political animal. He was a pragmatist. He was too much the patron-aristocrat to be a demagogue and a rabble rouser. He was not a mass leader but a practical administrator who wanted to do good for his people in the spirit of *noblesse oblige*. He stepped into the shoes of the Unionist Premier of the Punjab, Sir Sikander who died suddenly at the age of fifty in 1942. On that occasion, Sir Khizr declared: "The best way to perpetuate the memory of the departed leader is to continue the work which was dear to heart, *namely protection of communal harmony and unconditional support for the prosecution of the war*" (emphasis added). He pursued those two objectives singlemindedly during his term of office but Sir Khizr's goal of communal harmony and the idea of a working coalition based on composite culture, however, proved to be too ad-hoc and quite unequal to the crusading battle cry of religious separatism spearheaded by the Muslim League. As Sir Bertrand Glancy, Governor of the Punjab who had genuine affection for Sir Khizr said in a perceptive 'end of the term report', "Khizr has no inclination to imitate Congress tactics and clamour for the independence of India nor abase himself to Jinnah and cry aloud for Pakistan. The pro-Zamindar campaign of the Unionist Party with its concomitant agrarian legislation has for the present more or less exhausted itself."

Sir Khizr's liability in the Unionist legacy was his predecessor's

Foreword

pact with Jinnah's Muslim League under which national politics were ceded to the League in exchange for the autonomy of the Unionist pattern of power-sharing) e.g. with Jats under Sir Chotu Ram) in the Punjab. The Unionists were closer to the National Congress in their rejection of narrow and divisive communalism, but they did not join hands in time to provide a common front against the League. When the Muslim League became more strident and more fanatical in its separatist demands, and when it gained somewhat wider public support among the Muslims of Punjab, the integrity and the autonomy of Sir Khizr's party came under serious threat. Had the Unionist coalition had a stronger ideological element and a wider democratic base, had they been able to modify their image "as a party of the landed aristocracy", they could perhaps have forged a strong and timely alliance with the Congress Party and the Akali Dal in 1945 and might conceivably have successfully stemmed the tide of communal frenzy, mistrust and violence. But that was not to be. The Unionist setback finally paved the way for the partition of India and its tragic consequences.

In a sense, Sir Khizr's politics in the Punjab is a forgotten chapter; in another sense, the Unionist politics of inter-communal accommodation is relevant not only in Indian and Pakistani Punjabs but both in India and Pakistan. That chapter is particularly a poignant reminder of the difficulties of dealing with the politics of fanaticism and separatism, which keep erupting even after the partition. Sir Khizr had many forebodings in respect of the partition based on religion and many of them have unfortunately come true.

Sir Khizr was a man of moderation. He would have heartily endorsed the Buddhist idea of the middle path or the maxim of Cleobulus of Lindus, one of the seven wise men of ancient Greece that moderation is best. The Latin maxim **optimus modus** would be an expressive epitaph on Sir Khizr's gravestone. His moderation in politics could have provided a durable solution in the long run, but then the short run notoriously has an edge over the long run in politics. Human beings are easily swayed by momentary impulses, more so by emotive appeals in the name of religion. The political lesson of Sir Khizr's biography is to beware of that fault line in human nature.

Cicero described history as the Witness of Times and the Light of Truth, but to turn the light of truth to decode the signals of the

Khizr Tiwana, the Punjab Unionist Party and the Partition of India

history is not an easy task. That is why, historical interpretation moves from crossroads to crossroads. Dr. Talbot's study will also inevitably pass through many crossroads but I am confident it will be regarded as a worthy witness of the life and time of Sir Khizr and will throw considerable light of truth on Sir Khizr's personality and his successes, failures, hopes and disappointments.

I applaud Dr. Talbot's work and my friend Nazar Tiwana's single-minded devotion to the memory of his father. I would like to recall and adapt for my foreword to Dr. Talbot's book what Pliny the Younger had said in the Epistles: "I hold it a noble task to rescue from oblivion those who deserve to be remembered." Dr. Talbot deserves to be congratulated for performing such a noble task and for putting Sir Khizr's life and message in perspective.

Abbreviations

The following abbreviations are used in the notes to the text.

FMA   Freedom Movement Archives
IOL   India Office Library
FR   Fortnightly Report
NAI   National Archives of India
QEAP Quaid-i-Azam Papers
SHC   Shamsul Hasan Collection
TP   *Transfer of Power* series

Introduction

Pakistan's creation depended on the Punjab. The region's large Muslim population,[1] agricultural wealth and even more importantly its strategic position as the 'land-gate' of the Indo-Gangetic Plain[2] made it crucial to the viability of a North Indian Muslim homeland. Indeed, Jinnah called Punjab the 'corner-stone' of Pakistan. Yet its politics were dominated by the cross-communal Unionist Party. This grouping of predominantly Muslim Rajput and Hindu Jat landowners had been founded in 1923. Malik Khizr Hayat Khan Tiwana was its last leader. He played a key role in limiting the Muslim League's influence in the Punjab from 1942–7. Khizr countered the Pakistan demand with his own vision of a United Punjab within a decentralised federal India.

Khizr clashed publicly with Jinnah in 1944. The Punjab Muslim League thereafter waged an increasingly vitriolic campaign against him. Khizr was denounced as a 'quisling' and 'kafir.' Mock funerals were held outside his official residence and during the last weeks of his Premiership he was greeted everywhere with black flag protest demonstrations.

Much has been written about the rise of the Punjab Muslim League.[3] Khizr and the Unionists have been largely neglected. Their eventual eclipse is seen as an inevitable part of the wider circumstances of the transfer of power. For most Pakistani nationalist writers, Unionism forms a mere footnote to the triumphant progress of Muslim separatism.[4] But such nationalist approaches leave a number of important questions unanswered. Why for example did the great transformation in the Muslim League's fortunes occur so late in the Punjab? Moreover, why did Khizr not expediently ally himself with the League once it was clear that the British were leaving?

Such 'progressive' Pakistan writers, as Imran Ali and Tariq Ali, find Khizr an equally unappetizing figure. He represents the unholy alliance between the feudalists and the colonial state which perpetuated the gulf between the rural rich and poor. According to this reading of history, Khizr personifies the loyalism of a class, whose influence was shored up by the British who amply rewarded it with property and titles.[5] Imran Ali, for example merely lumps the Tiwanas along with other 'agrarian magnates' who benefited from the 'distorted' agricultural development under Imperial rule. The resulting retardation of nationalism, weak civil society and 'under-development' continue in his opinion to exert baleful effects on contemporary Pakistan.[6]

Indian writers are similarly unenthusiastic about the Unionist period, despite Khizr's coalition with the Punjab Congress in 1946–7. This interlude has failed to erase memories of his earlier hostility to the nationalist cause. In one of the opening debates in the newly formed Punjab Legislative Assembly in 1937, the immensely wealthy but 'progressive' Congress President Mian Iftikharuddin, dubbed the Unionists 'mercenaries' who were not only going against the interests of India, 'but all the democratic countries in the world.' This view was maintained as late as August 1945, when the Muslim nationalist Khan Abdul Qaiyoom characterised Khizr's ministry as a 'diehard and reactionary regime.' Nehru echoed this during his election tour of the Punjab in November, when he observed that the Unionist Party, 'merely mirrored the image of the British Government.'[7] A similar outlook had encouraged such Punjabi Communists as Daniyal Latifi to throw in their lot from 1944 onwards with the more 'progressive' Muslim League in order to overcome the 'reactionary' Unionists.[8]

i

Khizr was born on 7 August 1900 in Chak Muzaffarabad, the home of his Mother's section of the Tiwana 'tribe.' The Muslim Tiwanas had entered the **thal** area of Shahpur nearly seven centuries earlier. During the course of a violent history, they had become not only the leading landholding 'tribe' in the region, but in the whole of the West Punjab. The Tiwanas' prominence stemmed from their superb horsemanship. The Tiwana cavalry continuously swept aside their more numerous Awan, Baloch and Gheba foes.

Khizr's parents were first cousins, the preferred type of marriage

Introduction

arrangement for the West Punjab Muslim elite. His mother, Fateh Khatun was unlettered and fluent only in Punjabi. Khizr was closer to her than usual, because of his father Umar's prolonged absences in Delhi and London on Government business. Fateh Khatun remained at Kalra during these periods, as Umar only travelled with his younger second wife.

Fateh inherited property from her father, Malik Fateh Khan as she had only one brother.[9] Its rental income meant that she was a woman of considerable financial independence. Although the property was controlled by her managers, she occasionally went out to the villages to discuss matters with the tenants. Khizr's close attention to the running of the Kalra estate in the 1920s undoubtedly stemmed from his mother's influence. During one such tour, he established a liaison with the wife of one of his tenants.[10] Fateh Bibi became his mistress and he eventually married her, although this was kept a secret from Umar for many years.

Fateh Khatun was a pious woman especially devoted to Sufism. She was the first member of her branch of the family to become a **murid** (disciple) of Pir Golra, Syed Mehr Ali Shah. She visited the **pir** three or four times annually, travelling by tonga from the railway station to the shrine situated at the foot of the Margalla hills on the last leg of the journey. When Fateh Khatun journeyed with Khizr and her grandson Nazar to Simla in the summers of 1935–6 she ensured that they went by the Rawalpindi rather than the more direct Jammu route so that she could pay her respects at Golra Sharif. On the latter visit, one morning following the end of the **qavvali** ceremony, she asked the **pir** to pray for Khizr's success in the forthcoming provincial elections. Pir Golra predicted that her son would become a Minister. When she asked what future would lie in store for her grandson Nazar, he replied that the boy would become a Governor one day. This unfulfilled prediction became a family joke in later years.[11]

Syed Mehr Ali Shah had transformed Golra into a large religious complex[12] from which he spread his influence among the West Punjab 'tribal' elites. Umar stood aloof from this network,[13] but Khizr often visited Golra. He was far more devout than his father, who drank quite heavily until he went on **haj** in 1935. He would pray five times a day whether in Lahore, London or New York and after Asr prayers would sit with prayer cap firmly fitted and recite verses from the Quran.[14] Despite this devotion, he never, however displayed bigotry or communal bias of any kind. This was as true of his private as public dealings.

3

Significantly, Khizr sought the cure from a pir for an anal fistula which he developed in the early 1930s. This prevented him from riding or playing polo. He also suffered the indignity of having to use a rubber cushion in his office and car and at home. Conventional medical treatment in Europe in 1935 failed to do the trick, although x-rays revealed the extent of the problem. Khizr finally overcame this by using a 'miracle cure' of an oil based ointment provided by a Mianwali pir.[15]

ii

The Punjab into which Khizr was born was an old and distinctive society which had been greatly influenced by its frontier situation and subsequent turbulent history. The Raj it is true had introduced the Pax Britannica and attempted to establish the region as a model of agricultural stability and prosperity.[16] But the impress of the past was seen in the weakness of the caste system in the attachment to land as a symbol of power and in the creation of the 'martial races'. The Tiwanas themselves based their izzat on fighting prowess. This had first brought them to prominence in their barren thal locality. The British introduction of irrigation and opening of military opportunities for the Punjabi Rajput 'martial castes' had greatly consolidated their wealth and influence.

The two overriding characteristics of the colonial Punjab were its rural nature and the co-existence of vigorous Muslim, Hindu and Sikh communities. Around two thirds of the total population was dependent on agriculture for its livelihood. British rule had introduced large irrigation projects in the south west Punjab, the so-called canal colony developments had converted the province into a major exporter of grain and cotton. They had also intensified intra-regional variations in agricultural performance. Development throughout the British era was agriculturally rather than industrially centred.[17] The overall pattern of landlordism in the West Punjab, and peasant proprietorship in the central and eastern areas remained largely unaltered.[18]

Punjab's agrarian diversity was parallelled by its communal composition. Whilst the West Punjab was overwhelmingly Muslim, Hindus and Sikhs together outnumbered the Muslims in the central and eastern regions.[19] The Sikhs, whose faith originated in the Punjab had of course only risen to political prominence in the wake of their military prowess following the disintegration of Mughal

Introduction

authority in the late seventeenth century.[20] But the picture which emerges from colonial 'histories' of the Punjab's instability, violence and long established tradition of communal animosity is only a partial and by no means 'innocent' portrayal. It consistently underestimates the shared cultural vales of the rural Punjabi communities.

Songs, proverbs and folklore provided one element of this. The tragic love tales of Hir Rajha, Sassi Punnu and Sohni Mahival were popular with all communities. The first was constantly retold until Waris Shah gave it a final form. Sufis also infused such folk tales with a spiritual message. From the time of Shaikh Ibrahim Farid Sani (c. 1440–1675) onwards a number of Sufis composed in Punjabi, thus establishing it as a language which transcended religious community. Indeed, the impact of such Sufi poets as Sultan Bahu and Bullhe Shah on the development of Punjabi literature has been seldom appreciated. Sufism acted as a focus of religious devotion which reached out far beyond the Muslim community. This is seen not only in the inclusion of Baba Farid's verses in the Granth, but in such celebrated episodes as the 16th century Qadiri Saint, Lal Husain's devotion to the Brahmin boy Madho. This attachment was so great that the latter's name became prefixed to his.[21]

Nineteenth century religious revivalists saw their main task as undercutting the rural population's shared cultural values and practices. Thus the urban **ulema** and the Chishti revivalists **pirs** led by Pir Muhammad Suleman of Taunsa sought to purge Sufism of 'un-Islamic' practices. Whilst the Tat Khalsa sought to rid the Gurdwaras of Hindu 'idols.' Revivalists from all communities peddled the myth of a golden age, when their faith was pristine and unsullied by 'syncretic' tendencies. 'Fuzzy' community identities were to be replaced by clearly defined boundaries. This process was vividly illustrated by the emergence of Punjabi as a focus of contention. Muslim and Hindu elites increasingly encouraged their co-religionists to deny that it was their mother tongue. Instead, they were to inform the decennial census enumerators that these were Urdu and Hindi respectively. At the least, the language was to be culturally appropriated by being written in the Persian and Devanagri scripts. Punjabi was in fact increasingly portrayed as a Sikh language.

Religious revivalists manipulated the past to meet the pressing challenges of the present. The modernising impulses of the colonial state however increasingly threatened not only religious outlooks, but the socio-economic stability of the rural areas from which the bulk of the Indian Army's recruits were drawn. The British, however successfully safeguarded the influence of the rural powerholders by privileging the 'tribe' as the focus of identity in the 1900 Alienation of Land Act. A significant divide thus opened up between the political culture of town and countryside. In the Punjabi villages politics revolved around the factionalism of tribal society. Conflict in the towns was structured around religious identity. The 'agriculturalist' identity and ideology continued to dominate, when Khizr made his first faltering steps on the political stage in the late 1930s.

iii

Khizr's overriding political characteristic was his loyalty to the Raj. He reviled nationalist politicians as demagogues who were out of touch with the 'real India'. British officials had been singing the same tune since the turn of the century. Khizr's outlook was rooted in his family history. By the end of his public career such loyalty was not to be reciprocated. Throughout 1945–6, he relied heavily on the advice of the British Governor Sir Bertrand Glancy. An honest and highly principled man himself, Khizr never considered that the British might abandon their Unionist allies. He was shocked by Wavell's' capitulation' to Jinnah at the time of the 1945 Simla Conference and later believed that Attlee had deliberately misled him concerning British intentions regarding the timing of the British withdrawal. It may have been wishful thinking, but he had hoped for the smack of firm Government, not abject surrender with the consequent turmoil of Partition. Khizr typically did not, however allow a sense of betrayal to spoil his friendships with former officials.

Khizr's loyalism, was not based on self-interest, but rather on the belief that the Imperial connection ensured the Punjab's prosperity. He would have both entered politics earlier and switched allegiance to the Muslim League if he had been motivated solely by power. Despite his feudal stereotype, he was a highly individual leader with his own distinctive style and aptitude for constructive statesmanship.

Khizr cut a dashing figure on the political stage. His immaculate dress and distinctive Tiwana turban added to his presence. Before Partition, he never abandoned **achkans** and **sherwanis** for the Cheap John Suits and tootal ties beloved of Muslim League student activists. The **turrah** which jutted out from the top of his turban added to his stature. The constant attendance of a retinue of retainers completed the aura of power and glamour.

Introduction

This stylishness was inherited from Umar who was a showy and vain man who loved to be the centre of attention. He had overawed Khizr as a child. Even when he had grown up, Khizr deferred to the family patriarch. Umar in fact almost bullied Khizr into politics. Ironically, it enabled him to at last step out from under his father's shadow. Khizr's outward display masked an insecurity bred of paternal dominance. The latter may also have prompted his numerous marriages. In later years, however, they in all probability represented compensation for a sense of growing failure and declining political and economic potency.

Khizr brought a consensual approach to politics. He built bridges across communal divides and ultimately between the rural and urban communities. After the 1946 provincial elections, he brought together the feuding Congress and Akali parties in a final futile attempt to shore up the Punjab's communal harmony. In short he was a pragmatic practitioner of consociational democracy.[22] Not that he would have understood the latter term. He was not well read and never possessed intellectual pretensions. His pleasure lay in field sports and in later years, records, never in books. Moreover, Khizr's political goals were vaguely if at all defined. But we must not underestimate the repercussions of his consensual statecraft. It was only after he was finally ousted from power in March 1947, that the Punjab plunged into the civil war which disfigured Indian independence. Khizr's ability to manage conflict in the dangerously divided Punjab of the early 1940s, merits his consideration as a serious political figure. Indeed, his style of political accommodation carries an important lesson for the contemporary Indian subcontinent which is riven with ethnic and religious violence.[23]

Khizr's role in 1946–7 raises a number of questions. What cultural and political imperatives lay behind his much vaunted cry of 'Punjab for the Punjabis?' Why did he not display the traditional Tiwana opportunism and accommodate himself to the Muslim League advance? Tiwana history and the culture of 'amoral familism'[24] should have convinced him to abandon the Unionist programme. The product of a family whose fortunes had risen because of the expediency it had displayed from the time of Ranjit Singh onwards, Khizr risked throwing all this away by refusing to endorse the Two Nation Theory. It beggars belief that he was too obtuse to respond to Muslim League blandishments or threats.

It will be part of this book's argument that Khizr's career can only be understood in terms of the interplay between his personal traits

7

Khizr Tiwana, the Punjab Unionist Party and the Partition of India

and the cultural and political environment of the British Punjab. The opening section traces the Tiwana history and assesses the impact of Khizr's education and relationship with his father. It then examines the political context provided by Punjabi Unionism.

Part two chronicles Khizr's rise to the Premiership from his beginnings as a fledgling Minister in Sikander's cabinet. It discusses the Unionist political inheritance. This is followed by Khizr's successful role as a war leader. The third section of the book concentrates on the conflict between Khizr's vision of the Punjab's future and that envisaged by the Two Nation Theory. Considerable attention is devoted to the Jinnah-Khizr talks in 1944 and their political fall-out. There is also an attempt to explain why Khizr continued with a power-sharing arrangement, despite the crushing electoral defeat in the rural constituencies in 1946.

The epilogue graphically reveals the violence which followed the Unionists' demise. It also provides a brief sketch of Khizr's later life. The study concludes by considering the relevance of the Unionist political approach for contemporary South Asia.

Notes

1 Over 17 million Muslims lived in the Punjab where they accounted for 53 per cent of the population. Only Bengal boasted a larger Muslim population in British India.

2 From the time of Alexander the Great onwards successive waves of invaders passed through the region en route from central Asia to Delhi.

3 See, for example, D.Gilmartin, *Empire and Islam Punjab and the Making of Pakistan* (Berkeley,1988).

4 See, for example, S.M. Ikram, *Modern Muslim India and the Birth of Pakistan* (Lahore, 3rd revised edition).

5 T. Ali, *Can Pakistan Survive?* (Harmondsworth, 1983) p. 29.

6 Imran Ali, *The Punjab Under Imperialism, 1885–1947* (Princeton, 1988) p. 237 & ff.

7 Satya M. Rai, *Legislative Politics and Freedom Struggle in Punjab 1897–1947* (New Delhi, 1984) pp. 234, 315.

8 'As you well know', Latifi wrote to Gandhi in June 1944, 'The Unionist Ministry is the last provincial stronghold of the British bureaucracy in India. The Punjab of Sir Bertrand Glancy . . . carries on the traditions of the Punjab of Sir Michael O'Dwyer. Now when the League, as representative of the Muslim majority in the Punjab is out in the battlefield storming this British stronghold no man or woman who loves freedom and democracy can sit idle with folded hands.' *Ibid.*, p. 302.

9 He was called Malik Muzaffar Khan and was of course the father of Sultan Bibi, Khizr's first wife.

Introduction

10 The subsequent marriage rather than the liaison may have been unusual. Sir Malcolm Darling who was a leading expert on rural Punjabi society recalled Khizr was hated in his home district because he was miserly and 'wenched' with his tenants' women. Quoted in, C. Dewey, *Anglo-Indian Attitudes. The Mind of the Indian Civil Service* (London 1993) p. 186.

11 Interview with Nazar Tiwana, New Delhi 10 December 1993.

12 For details see, Hafeezur Rehman Chaudhry, 'The Shrine and Langar of Golra Sharif' in A.S. Ahmed (ed), *Pakistan. The Social Sciences Perspective* (Karachi, 1990) pp. 190–205.

13 Maulana Faiz Ahmad Faiz, Mihr-i-Munir (Golra, 1973?) refers to Umar as being a *murid* of Pir Golra, but Nazar Tiwana in a personal communication to the author has denied this fact.

14 Omar Hayat Tiwana, 'Requiem for a provincialist. Sir Khizar Hayat Tiwana 1900–1975.' *The Friday Times* (Karachi) 19–25 January 1995 Special Supplement Page 11.

15 Private family communication to the author, November 1993.

16 For a remarkable insight into British attitudes see, C. Dewey, *Anglo-Indian Attitudes. The Mind of the Indian Civil Service* (London, 1993).

17 See, H.K. Trevaskis, *The Land of the Five Rivers* (Oxford, 1928).

18 For further details on the variations in the Punjab's agrarian structure see, Malcolm Darling's classic account in *The Punjab Peasantry in Prosperity and Debt* (London, 1928).

19 For further details see, I. Talbot, *Punjab and the Raj 1849–1947* (New Delhi, 1988).

20 See, J.S. Grewal, *The Sikhs of the Punjab* (Cambridge 1990).

21 L.R. Krishna, *Panjabi Sufi Poets A.D. 1460–1900* (Karachi, 1977) p. 16.

22 According to consociational theory, the maintenance of stable democracy in societies riven by primordial divisions depends on elite accommodation. This is institutionalised in such devices as grand coalition mutual veto, proportionality and segmental autonomy. The idea of consociationalism is especially associated with Arend Lijphart's studies. See, for example, A. Lijphart, *The Politics of Accommodation Pluralism and Democracy in the Netherlands* (Berkeley 1968) and A. Lijphart, 'Consociational Democracy' *World Politics* xxi (1969) pp. 207–25.

23 This idea is argued at greater length in I. Talbot, 'Back to the Future? The Unionist Model of Consociational Democracy for Contemporary India and Pakistan' Unpublished seminar paper.

24 See for example, C. Dewey, 'The rural roots of Pakistani militarism' in D.A. Low (ed) *The Political Inheritance of Pakistan* (London, 1991) p. 277.

Part One

Inheritance

Chapter One

The Tiwanas of Shahpur

The huge crowd spilled over the polo ground to the gate of the family cemetery. The flag draped coffin temporarily rested under an awning to shield it from the bright North Indian April sun, as the **janazah** was recited. The mourners arranged themselves in rows opposite the corpse framed by the backdrop of mango and banyan trees which grew alongside the canal bank at its rear.

This was no ordinary funeral. Sikh peasants their long hair wrapped in brightly coloured loose turbans, big bellied Muslim village elders stroking their thick up-twirled moustaches and **sahukars** in their crisp dhotis and white Gandhi caps had all come to pay their respects. Thousands of labourers and tenants had trekked in from the villages which surrounded the Kalra estate, whilst landlords and officials had been driven from the district headquarters at Shahpur. They had all come to honour the late Umar Hayat Khan Tiwana, or the 'General' as he was commonly called. His father, Malik Sahib Khan had constructed the canal and carved out the Kalra estate from a grant of waste land on the bank of the Punjab's Jhelum river. He had received this from the British in reward for his 'meritorious' services during the Great Revolt of 1857. Umar had succeeded to the estate as a minor just over twenty years later. His career had, however, taken him far beyond its bounds, to the provincial capital of Lahore, to the British summer capital at Simla and ultimately to London as a member of the Council of the Secretary of State for India. There he moved with ease in the highest social and political circles at the heart of the world's greatest Imperial power. This was a meteoric rise for a family whose forbears had wandered penniless in the barren wastes of the **thal** desert.

After the seated people had raised their hands in silent prayer on behalf of Umar's soul, the chief mourner as was the custom declared,

12

The Tiwanas of Shahpur

'I am pleased with the will of God', he then gave them permission to retire. Khizr then proceeded with his closest relatives to the family graveyard. Umar's corpse was placed on its back in the grave with his face turned towards Mecca and fatihah was offered in his name.

Khizr was the most powerful man in the British Punjab at the time of his father's death. Although still only forty four, he had held Government Office for seven years, and had been Premier for the last eighteen months. Even more unusual was the fact that he led a party which still in the 1940s stood outside the mainstream of either Indian nationalism or Muslim separatism. Indeed, Khizr had broken off highly publicised negotiations with Jinnah, the leader of the All-India Muslim League to attend the burial.

Khizr's elevation to the post of Punjab Premier climaxed the advancement of his family's fortunes which had commenced with the collapse of Mughal authority in the region. The Tiwanas' rise to prominence had been based on military prowess and the accompanying ownership of land. A degree of luck and considerable political acumen had comprised the other ingredients. Khizr stood four-square in this family tradition but ultimately to his cost abandoned its cherished principle of accommodation with the central authorities. In order to fully appreciate his career, it is essential to explore the Tiwanas' earlier history.

i

The Tiwanas were not originally Punjabis, or Muslims. According to bardic traditions, they were descended from the Parmaras Rajputs who ruled in the Dhar, Mandu and Ujjain areas of central India (present day Madhya Pradesh) in the ninth and tenth centuries A.D. Geneological sources are inevitably scanty, but oral traditions recount that the Tiwanas can trace their ancestry to Jagdev Parmar who was a great warrior and ruler of the late eleventh century A.D.[1]

By the end of the reign of Jagdev's nephew, Yasovarman (1133 A.D.) the Parmara dynasty was disintegrating. It received its **coup de grace** at the hands of Iltutmish (1211–36 A.D.) the former Turkish slave who established the Delhi Sultanate. In the wake of his capturing and plundering Bhilsa and Ujjain, Rai Shankar who was directly descended from Jagdeva and other members of the Parmaras migrated from Dharu (near Mandu) to Rajputana, from whence they later moved into the Punjab.

Rai Shankar according to tradition had three sons, Gheo who is depicted as the ancestor of the Ghebas, Teo or Tenu whose descendants are the Tiwanas and Seo, the forefather of the Sials. Teo's descendants founded the village of Mataur, near Narwana in the present day Jind district of Haryana. The village still possesses the largest Hindu population of Tiwanas in Punjab and Haryana. The Tiwanas fanned out from Mataur to other regions of the Punjab.

One branch of the family established themselves, at the end of the fifteenth century in what was then the uninhabited jungle countryside of Patiala. According to tradition, Baba Chand Tiwana was advised by a Jalf Gujjar seer to select a settlement near the **deras** of yogis at a place now called Chinarthal[2] which is situated about 13 miles from Patiala. The seer's promise that Baba Chand's clan would multiply and his writ would 'run over a large area' seemed to come true as Chinarthal became the centre of a cluster of eleven more villages. The famous Tiwana family of Indian judges (Sardar Sadhu Singh Tiwana, Sardar Iqbal Singh Tiwana and Sardar Charan Singh Tiwana) comes from the village of Ditturpur some 3 miles from Chinarthal.[3] Chinarthal village contained both Muslim and Sikh Tiwanas at the time of Partition. The former migrated to Pakistan, but the bulk of the Tiwanas in Patiala, had converted to Sikhism in the second part of the eighteenth century.

Increasing population pressure led Sikh Tiwanas from Chinarthal area to found new villages in the Ludhiana, Mansa, Jullundur and Bathinda districts. The village of Kot Lallu (Mansa district) was for example founded by migrants from Chinarthal Kurd. This is the natal village of Justice Kalwant Singh Tiwana. Ghudda (Bathinda district) is inhabited by Tiwana families who migrated a century ago from Tauhra village.[4] The eminent Punjabi[5] writers, Bibi Dalip Kaur Tiwana and Bibi Manjit Kaur Tiwana come from the small village of Nichi Rabon (Ludhiana district). Other important Tiwana villages include Jindalpur near Bhadson in Nabha **tehsil** of Patiala where Baba Chand first encamped, Lasoi (now in Sangrur district) which was founded by settlers from Chinarthal and Madhopur. The latter is a small village situated on the Grand Trunk Road about a mile and a quarter from Sirhind in the direction of Rajpura town. Despite its size it has produced a number of leading engineers among whom Sardar Narinder Singh Tiwana became Chairman of the Central Pollution Control Board of India.[6]

14

The Tiwanas of Shahpur

ii

The Muslim branch of the Tiwanas traces its descent from Rai Melo Tiwana. According to tradition he wandered together with his followers to the outskirts of Pakpattan (the ancient Ajodhan) sometime after 1195 A.D. This prosperous town was a principal crossing point of the Sutlej river and was thus a major nexus of trade between the Delhi region in the east and Multan in the west. It was also a prominent religious centre, indeed its name means 'holy ferry.' Shaikh Farid al-Din Ganj-i-Shakar(1173–1265) had established a **khanqah** at Pakpattan in the early thirteenth century. The **pir**'s shrine still attracts massive crowds of disciples. Baba Farid as he is known to his devotees is acknowledged as the leading Chishti Sufi Saint of the Punjab.[7] According to family tradition, Rai Melo Tiwana accepted Islam after Baba Farid had miraculously restored his large herd of cattle which had wandered off into the jungle.[8]

Sials, Khokkars, Gondals and Joiyas also claim conversion by Baba Farid. Mohammad Habib has however maintained that Baba Farid along with other early shaikhs of the Chishti order did not seek to convert non-Muslims.[9] Richard Eaton has reconciled the claims of the Rajputs and Jats with this problem by depicting conversion as a slow process in which ' tribes' were drawn into the ritual life of the shrine which grew up after Baba Farid's death.[10] This argument carries considerable weight for those ' tribes' which settled in the **dargarh**'s vicinity and established economic, kinship and political ties with it. But the Tiwanas were only transient visitors. Indeed according to their account, Baba Farid himself was instrumental in securing a grant of land for them from the Muslim Governor of Multan.[11]

The existence of Muslim, Hindu and Sikh branches of the same family is not unusual in the Punjab which throughout much of its history was a turbulent frontier region. There are for example, Muslim and Sikh Gills and Manns. There appears little evidence, however before the 1920s of sustained social interaction between the Muslim Tiwanas of the West Punjab and their Hindu and Sikh brethren in Jind and Patiala. The rise to prominence of Umar and later Khizr Tiwana did, however prompt an exchange of letters which have only recently come to light. They cover the period 1925–38 and mainly contain correspondence between Umar, Khizr and Sardar Sadhu Singh Tiwana.[12] The latter, for example, congratulated Khizr on his Ministerial appointment in a letter dated 11 March

15

Khizr Tiwana, the Punjab Unionist Party and the Partition of India

1937.[13] He corresponded again four months later, accompanying his missive with a consignment of mangoes. The sardar's cultivation of his Muslim relatives bore fruit in December 1937, when Umar wrote on his behalf to the Patiala Premier, Sir Liaqat Hyat Khan. It took another nine months and a further supporting letter from Umar, however, before Sardar Sadhu Singh Tiwana achieved his cherished ambition of promotion as a District and Sessions Judge.[14] He does not appear however to be merely an opportunist on the make from his distant relatives. There is a genuine warmth in his letters to Umar as can be seen in the following extract:

> I offer my heartiest congratulations on the appointment of your beloved son, Major Khizar Hayat Khan, as Prime Minister of the Punjab. It is a matter of great pride for the Tiwana community as a whole to see the illustrious young man of this family to occupy this post of responsibility and prestige at so young an age. We the members of this family living in this part of Punjab wish to pray to Almighty God to shower all his bounties upon him and grant him full success in his new career.[15]

Sardar Sadhu Singh Tiwana does not appear to be the only Patiala Tiwana who was in contact with the Shahpur branch. I am also informed by Justice Kulwant Singh Tiwana that his father who was a Deputy Superintendent of Police at Bhatinda met Umar on a number of occasions.[16] The intercourse between Sikh and Muslim Tiwanas in pre-Partition Punjab has been a well kept secret. Whilst not too much should be read into the scanty details which are available, such contacts could only have strengthened the cross-communal political stance of both Umar and Khizr, although as we shall see its roots lay more in their common educational and military experience.

iii

Rai Melo settled at a place called Darya Khan which was renamed Tatta Tiwana. This was the fringe of the **thal** area of the Sind Sagar Doab. Ten miles or so in the distance the precipices of the Salt range rose to a height of 4,000 feet. The land on the south side of the range descended in steep gulleys and ravines. Despite its inhospitable nature, this area provided a refuge from the attention of Imperial armies.

The area around Tatta Tiwana itself formed a narrow plain where cultivation was carried out in small patches on the substratum of

The Tiwanas of Shahpur

hard level soil. To the south and west of this plain the **thal** area itself began. This was a barren wasteland of sandy hillocks, stunted bushes and karil and jand scrub which provided small quantities of fuel. It was not until the introduction of large scale irrigation that the wastes of this area could be brought under cultivation. Before that time all it could sustain was a sparse population of herdsmen and cultivators eking out a precarious existence. Rai Melo required all the toughness he had inherited from the great warriors, Jagdev and Rai Shankar for every day was a battle for survival.

The region's best agricultural land lay in the flood plain of the Jhelum river. Embankments or bunds controlled the flood waters. The high summer temperature and aridity of much of the soil in the Shahpur region meant that control of water supplies was essential for survival. In most of the **thal** itself, water was only found some fifty or so feet below the surface.

The Tiwanas eventually migrated from their ancestral village in the **thal** waste to the more fertile areas along the banks of the Jhelum. Finally, Umar's father, Malik Sahib Khan established an estate at Kalra on the Lahore side of the Jhelum. Khizr grew up on this estate and eventually managed what had become the largest and most wealthy of all the Tiwana landholdings.

Social conditions were as forbidding as the climate and landscape which greeted Rai Melo Tiwana. During the thirteenth century the Mongols frequently disturbed the Punjab's peace. They remained only for short periods, but wreaked considerable havoc.[17] Their inroads meant that the Punjab's Governors during the remainder of the Delhi Sultanate maintained only a tenuous hold over such western areas as Shahpur. Control of land in this as other parts of the Punjab meant power. In the absence of a stable political structure, Rai Melo and his descendants were forced to fight to maintain the **jagirs** which they had inherited. They battled so well that they extended their properties. They also established a reputation as a martial 'caste' which had immense implications in the colonial era.

iv

Whilst Muhammad bin Tughlak was ruling in Delhi and dreaming of the conquest of China in 1325, the Tiwanas were fighting fierce local conflicts with Baluch tribesmen for control of the Mianwali bank of the Jhelum river. The position which Rai Awadr had achieved was confirmed by his sons' good relationship with Khizr Khan, the

Viceroy of Multan following Timur's invasion of the Punjab in 1398.[18] Tatta Tiwana was still, however little more than a village and even the leading Tiwanas lived a spartan existence. It should be recalled that Lahore itself at this time was so poor that Timur did not bother to plunder it. The collapse centuries later of Mughal authority following the death of Aurangzeb, however provided the disturbed conditions in which the Tiwanas tightened their grip on the local peasant cultivators and weaker Rajput 'tribes.'

Mir Ali Khan had moved from Tatta Tiwana to the village of Oukhli around the middle of the seventeenth century. He built forts and constructed a complex of wells. This investment paid dividends as it encouraged new settlements of peasant cultivators who grew vegetables and grain. The increase in economic activity not only added to his rental income, but provided a wider range of service castes and opportunities for taxing local markets. Here one can see in microsm evidence of the Punjab's growing seventeenth century prosperity as a result of Jat agricultural settlement and the emergence of new towns on and around the trade routes.[19] Mir Ali Khan controlled an ever increasing tract of land. By his death it stretched on the eastern side of the Jhelum as far as Kundian, and on the west to Jindwala.

His son Mir Ahmad Khan continued to push forward the clan frontier founding the settlement of Mitha Tiwana about the year 1680. This was an important power base, for as the name implies, it controlled springs of sweet water. This was a rare commodity in a region whose salt strata turned natural supplies so brackish that they were unfit for either human or animal consumption. Without water neither beast nor man could survive the scorching heat of May and June when the thermometer regularly rose to 115 degrees.

Mir Ahmad Khan's advance from the original Tiwana settlements brought him into conflict with adjoining Awan clans. This can again be seen as part of a wider dislocation of existing agrarian relationships as a result of socio-economic development in seventeenth century Punjab. The Awans were no match for his horsemen and suffered a heavy defeat in a fierce battle at Hadali five miles from Mitha Tiwana.[20] Hadali, along with Hamoka and Mitha Tiwana were later to form the three main settlements for the branches of the Tiwana family. Umar and Khizr were descendants of a junior branch or section of the Mitha Tiwana group. The Awans' defeat increased the resources at Mir Ahmad Khan's disposal. He continued a pattern of settlement in which the Tiwana lineage elites

The Tiwanas of Shahpur

occupied fortified central villages which controlled the cultivating population living in scattered hamlets.

Whilst the details are sketchy, it is possible to speculate in a manner similar to Richard Fox that this period also marked increased differentiation within the Tiwana clan. In Fox's view agricultural intensification and the need for war leadership were crucial factors in the emergence of Rajput 'tribal' leaders head and shoulders above their free kinsmen.[21] The availability of 'waste' land and of opportunity for military service, together with the small size of the 'tribe', however were to allow many Tiwanas to continue an ' independent' life style. None were peasant cultivators, for the Tiwanas like other Rajputs possessed deep rooted prejudice against taking to the plough. This was left to local low 'caste' cultivators such as Jats and Gujars. Where Tiwanas were tenants they shared a natural identity of interests with their 'tribal' landlords with whom they continued to attend social functions and form part of a close-knit community.

During the lifetime of Dadu Khan (Mir Ahmad Khan's son) Mitha Tiwana flourished from a fortified village into a small market town. The tenants of the Tiwanas marketed their grain brought by bullock or camel cart from the adjoining villages. Small scale merchants traded in cloth resting in the newly built **serais**. Artisan communities had also grown up to service the lineage aristocracy. There was also the beginnings of a trade in horses which were essential for maintaining the Tiwanas' military capacity. Trade was still, however very localised and Mitha Tiwana would have appeared a mean settlement to the visitor from Lahore or Multan. Moreover the Mughal authorities extracted much of the agricultural surplus from the Salt Range **pargana** to pay for their soldiers and officials in Kabul.[22] But the process of slow economic expansion was impressive and the Tiwanas' control of rural production gave them steadily growing income.

Dadu Khan's immediate family included six sons by his two wives. Squabbles over the succession ended in battle in which his eldest son Sher Khan triumphed, but at the cost of his brothers' death and fratricide. Sher Khan embarked on a life of warfare with the Awans which further increased his landholdings at their expense. He also founded a new fortified settlement of Nurpur Tiwana in 1745.[23] From this base he continued to extract revenue from the scattered hamlets of the local low 'caste' cultivators.

Sher Khan's career must be understood in the context of the

Khizr Tiwana, the Punjab Unionist Party and the Partition of India

disturbed conditions in early eighteenth century Punjab. There were revolts against Mughal authority not only of the Sikhs, but Muslim chiefs, such as the Ghakkars. These can be seen as part of a rural upsurge against the Mughal ruling class and their urban khatri allies.[24] The crippled local administration could no longer provide the salaries for the governor of Kabul with the result that it emerged as a strong centre of independent power. Nadir Shah's invasion and the plunders of Abdali in 1748 dealt a final blow to the region's tottering economy.

Sher Khan died a violent death, but unexpectedly not in battle but as a result of an accident at a powder magazine. Armed forces and conflict were rapidly increasing at this time, so Sher Khan needed as much war **materiel** as he could lay his hands on. The fact that he could invest in large quantities of gunpowder as well as the traditional Tiwana horses is a testament to the economic success of the clan. By the end of his life he had extended the Tiwana landholdings right up to the area of rock salt deposits at the base of the Salt Range escarpment.

The steady revenue from the salt mines supplemented the Tiwanas' rental income. The Warcha salt mine came into the Tiwana family's control through their marriage alliances with the Noons. These were originally rivals who had been defeated by Sher Khan. The first Noon bride for the Tiwanas was a prisoner of war, therby beginning a complex set of marriage alliances which were to continue for the next two centuries.[25] When Sher Khan died, he left two sons, Khan Muhammad Khan and Khan Beg Khan. The former's sister was married to Saipal Khan Noon who controlled the area in which the Warcha mine was situated.[26] The wealth which indirectly accrued to Khan Muhammad caused intense jealousy between him and Beg. The agreement by which they respectively controlled Nurpur and Mitha Tiwana was rapidly eroded.

The conflict was no less bloody than that of earlier sibling rivalries, but it took on a different significance because of the Tiwanas' increased power. This dragged other communities into the struggle and culminated in the decisive intervention of the Punjab's new Sikh ruler, Ranjit Singh.

v

The Sikhs' initial intrusion into Shahpur's local politics resulted from Jaffir Khan's call for their assistance against Khan Muhammad Khan

The Tiwanas of Shahpur

who was attacking his Baloch stronghold and strategic river crossing of Khushab.[27] The Tiwana chief with typical ruthlessness had broken all hospitality rules in imprisoning Jaffir Khan's father, Lal Khan the chief of Khushab.

Ranjit Singh himself was called on in 1803 to shore up Khan Muhammad Khan's position against Beg. The Sikh warrior had conquered Lahore just four years earlier thereby marking the beginning of a Sikh empire.[28] Ranjit Singh consented to trap Beg by asking him to go hunting. When Beg presented himself however, he was immediately arrested.[29] The family account is silent on this issue, but the one eyed Sikh 'lion of the Punjab' must have been paid blood money for his part in the trap.[30] Khan Beg was handed over to his brother and was murdered whilst in prison. The family version of events appears disingenious, when it maintains that this took place without Khan Muhammad Khan's approval.[31]

Khan Muhammad Khan's involvement of Ranjit Singh in his family disputes had been most unwise. The Sikh Chief was determined to extend his sway over the whole of the West Punjab as well as oust the Afghans from Kashmir and their strongholds east of the Indus. The Tiwana chiefs were still small fry in this greater scheme of things, but Ranjit Singh needed to mop up their territories and those of their Gakkhar, Baluch and Awan rivals to extend his empire westwards. Accordingly he sent a force to Nurpur in 1817 to exact tribute from its chief, Malik Muhammad Khan's second son, Ahmad Yar Khan. Ranjit Singh's general sank wells as he marched into the heart of the parched thal. Nothing could now check the Sikh advance. The Tiwana fort at Nurpur fell to the superior Sikh forces after a brief siege. Ahmad Yar Khan was forced in despair to flee south to the Mankera territory.

Ranjit Singh impartially annexed the fiefdoms of Sikh and Muslim chiefs alike. Unlike the Mughals who had allied with existing notables until the early eighteenth century when they no longer possessed the resources to coopt them, the Sikhs exerted a levelling influence, decapitating the former tall poppies.[32] This process left a permanent mark on the landholding structure of the Punjab's central and eastern districts. It also resulted in the eclipsing of the fortunes of such well established Rajput tribes as the Ghakkars and Janjuas of the Rawalpindi division. The parvenu Tiwanas because they resisted longer and displayed more political adroitness were, however to rise above the 'Rajput crisis' which saw former ruling families forced into exile, exterminated or reduced to the position of tenants.[33]

21

Administration of the Rajput territories was placed in the hands of kardars.[34] They were assisted in the localities by qanungos, muqaddams and patwaris. Ultimately Sikh troops were called upon to secure the revenue collections. Like his contemporary Napoleon, Ranjit Singh introduced a career open to talent. Common troopers could rise to wield considerable power at the expense of former ruling elites. One such new man, Hari Singh Nalwa was given the jagir of Mitha Tiwana.

Ranjit Singh not only rewarded army commanders like Hari Singh Nalwa with jagirs, but also nazims and kardars. The jagirs were intended to meet the costs of maintaining troopers. Ranjit Singh also, however alienated revenues to Muslim and Hindu as well as Sikh religious institutions. The shrine of Baba Farid at Pakpattan, for example was one such recipient.[35] Finally, greatly reduced jagirs were awarded to deposed chiefs, to provide them with a pension. Early British settlement reports paint a pathetic picture, however of the poverty to which the proud Hindu Rajputs of the north-eastern hills had been reduced by Sikh rule. The Muslim Rajputs of the north west Punjab fared better in that their communities were more unified and less easily decapitated. But such notable 'tribes' as the Ghakkars were never to recover the Sikh destruction of their power. The Tiwanas also found that the Sikhs were formidable foes who were determined to exert a lasting impact on the Sind Sagar Doab, unlike for example the earlier Durrani invaders. But they were able to turn the Sikh presence to their advantage by building up military connections with them.

The Tiwana chiefs quickly recognised that they could obtain jagirs and state offices if they cooperated with Sikh power at the centre. A later generation demonstrated similar realpolitik, when it hitched its fortunes to the British presence. The key to the Tiwanas' value to the Sikhs and British alike was their role as military 'collaborators.' Long years of fighting for survival in the Salt Range had trained them in weaponry and made them masters of horsemanship. This effectiveness was reinforced by their military ethos and social solidarity. Soldiering was a way of life for those members of the 'tribe' who made up the retinues of the Tiwana chiefs. It gave them independence, manliness and honour and kept them from the 'demeaning' lot of tenants and peasant cultivators.

Ranjit Singh's political strength rested on his army, so he sought support from the cavalry of chiefs who he had subordinated. He was especially eager to enlist the help of the Tiwana maliks who had put

The Tiwanas of Shahpur

up such a stiff resistance to the Sikh armies. Thus, in return for the service of 60 horsemen, Ahmad Yar Khan was awarded the jagir of Jhawarian. This military connection enabled two other Tiwana maliks, Sahib Khan and Alam Khan to hold the office of kardar of Nurpur Tiwana, and Mianwali under Ranjit Singh's successors.[36] Their control of this pivotal office ensured that the Tiwana chiefs, unlike other Muslim notables, were not brought down to an equality with the Jat and Gujar cultivators in the villages and hamlets which they had once dominated.

Ahmad Yar Khan supplied cavalry contingents for Ranjit Singh's campaign against the Nawab of Mankera.[37] The Sikh Maharajah was so impressed by their role in his victory that he ordered a detachment to be permanently quartered in Lahore. They joined the huge cantonment which according to an American visitor to the city in 1820 had been built on the site of the Mughal suburbs.[38] Whilst the Sikh and Muslim cavalry appear to have held great fascination for Ranjit Singh and his court,[39] the Punjab kingdom's real strength by this time lay in its modernised infantry and artillery under the command of such well known European officers as Allard, Ventura and Avitabile. Nevertheless with the presence of the Tiwana troop, the clan possessed direct access to the extra-local levels of power. Not that the leading Tiwana representative in Lahore, Allah Yar Khan's brother, Khuda cut a particularly impressive figure. His main task was to superintend Ranjit Singh's hunting expeditions, for an annual payment of Rs 2,500.[40]

Khuda's son Fateh Khan, however achieved greater prominence in the service of the Sikh Kingdom. On Hari Singh's death he resumed the jagir of the Tiwana's hereditary domain. His career was nevertheless chequered, as his fortunes rose and fell with those of his patrons in the snakepit of the Sikh court following the death of Ranjit Singh on 27 June 1839. The Tiwana chief's main patrons were Raja Dhian Singh, successively the wazir of Ranjit Singh and Kharak Singh his successor and eldest son and Jawahar Singh who was the brother of Maharani Jindan. From the former he received control of the salt mines at Warcha, whilst the latter made him nazim (Governor) of an extensive territory which included not only the traditional Tiwana lands in the Sind Sagar Doab, but parts of Jhelum and Rawalpindi and the whole of Dera Ismail Khan and Bannu.[41] The Tiwanas had progressed far since their initial wanderings to the foot of the Salt Range.

Involvement in the Sikh court's politics was, however highly dangerous. Sardar Attar Singh Sandhanwalia and Ajit Singh Sandhanwalia who had risen to prominence in Ranjit Singh's day, murdered Maharaj Sher Singh and Raja Dhian Singh on 15 September 1843. The death of Fateh Khan's friend and patron forced him to flee from Lahore. Fateh Khan captured the fort of Mitha Tiwana early in June 1844 and plundered the surrounding area. But he was driven away after a battle with the larger Sikh armies which left over 450 dead and wounded.[42] After a period of refuge in Bannu, he recrossed the Indus and raised a tribal revolt amongst the Waziris against the central Sikh power. Retribution was swift. Mangal Singh Siranwali's troops sacked Mitha Tiwana. Further twists in the palace politics, however transformed Fateh Khan's fortunes. The fall of Hira Singh from the office of **wazir** and the rise to prominence of Jawahar Singh gave the Tiwana chief the governorship which he had been seeking.

Fateh Khan was now deeply embroiled in the increasingly confused court politics. The British were meanwhile collecting men and weapons on the frontiers of the disintegrating Sikh kingdom. Jawahar Singh called on the Tiwanas to suppress the revolt of Prince Pashaura Singh against the Regency Council which was then ruling the Punjab. Pashaura Singh surrendered Attock Fort to Fateh Khan after receiving assurances concerning his safety. He was subsequently murdered, however on Jawahar Singh's instructions. This duplicity so enraged the increasingly powerful Sikh army that the minister paid for it with his own life. Fateh Khan proceeded to put as much distance as possible between himself and the contending factions in Lahore by travelling post haste to take charge of his Governorship in Dera Ismail Khan.

The Tiwana chief's power was short lived. It involved a further catalogue of treachery, bloodshed and murder of some of his Afghan enemies. He eventually fled in January 1846 when the Lahore authorities nominated a new Governor. The 'badlands' of the Salt Range once again provided the Tiwana chiefs with a sanctuary. Fateh Khan's flight coincided with the Sikh army's treacherous defeat at the hands of the British far to the east in the battles of Pherushahr and Sabraon. The East India Company was the rising power in the Punjab and the scene was set for another act in the Tiwanas' rise to prominence.

The Tiwanas of Shahpur

vi

The Punjabi chiefs' response to the East India Company's crises during the second Sikh War (1848–9) and the 1857 revolt significantly influenced their family's fortunes during the Raj. The Tiwanas passed these crucial tests with flying colours. The British rewarded them with cash, grants of land and titles. The Tiwanas also ensured that they were at the forefront of the Punjabisation of the Indian Army during the 1880s.[43] It was from this favourable background that Umar and Khizr rose to positions of prominence in national and provincial politics.

The first Sikh War had ended with the British occupation of Lahore on 22 February 1846. The Jullundur Doab became a possession of the East India Company. The British also exerted considerable influence through the office of Resident in the surviving Sikh kingdom of Lahore. The disaffection of Maharani Jindan Kaur who had been removed as Regent and of the economically embarrassed Sikh soldiery[44] encouraged further conflict with the British. The interventions of the Resident, John Lawrence, further increased its likelihood. The Governor-General Dalhousie[45] viewed with satisfaction the opportunity to tidy up the East India Company's possessions in north west India.

The second Sikh war commenced in April 1848 with the uprising of the forces of Diwan Mul Raj, the Governor of Multan. The British might have locally contained it, if their intention to annex the Lahore Kingdom had not been so bruited abroad. This encouraged Sardar Chattar Singh Atariwala, the governor of Hazara and his son Raja Sher Singh to join the rebellion. They fatally failed, however to coordinate military activities with Mul Raj.[46]

The Tiwanas did 'good service' during this crisis. Fateh Khan worked closely with Herbert Edwardes who had earlier in 1848 secured his release from imprisonment for debt in Govindgarh prison. Edwardes sent him to Bannu in June 1848 to relieve Lieutenant Reynell Taylor. When the four regiments of Sikh Infantry mutinied in September and killed the sole British officer Colonel John Holmes, Fateh Khan refused to surrender the inner fort of Dalipgarh. It could not resist a long seige, because of inadequate water supplies. The defenders desperately dug a well in the fort itself. Eventually, Fateh Khan and his retinue sallied out to obtain water. According to Edwardes' colourful account, Fateh Khan cried aloud to the besiegers, 'I am Mullick Fatteh Khan Tiwannah! Do not shoot me

25

Khizr Tiwana, the Punjab Unionist Party and the Partition of India

like a dog; but if there are any two of you who are equal to a man, come on!'[47] At the climax of a life of violence, he died in a hail of a hundred bullets at the gateway of the fort.[48] The Tiwana chief was posthumously revenged, however, as his son Fateh Sher Khan at the head of four hundred horsemen played a leading role in the Multan campaign against Mul Raj who surrendered on 22 January 1849.[49]

Fateh Khan had five nephews, the eldest of which Qadir Bakhsh had jointly inherited the Mitha Tiwana properties in 1837. Qadir's son, Sher Muhammad Khan Tiwana seized 12 forts from the Sikhs during the second Sikh war. They included, Mitha Tiwana which had briefly fallen and Khushab, Sahiwal and Shahpur. Umar's father, Malik Sahib Khan[50] also played a prominent role. He fought with his cavalry at the battles of Rajoa, Bhera and Chachran. The combat at the last battle was so intense that his sword had to be prised from his swollen and bloody hand.[51] Malik Sahib Khan's defeat of the Sikh army of Bhai Maharaja Singh marked a turning point in a war which had initially gone badly for the East India Company. After the battle of Gujrat on 22 February, Sardar Chattar Singh Atariwala and his son surrendered to the British at Rawalpindi in March 1849. Within a fortnight, Maharajah Dalip Singh had signed the document which legalised the British annexation of the Punjab.[52]

vii

John Lawrence, the first Chief Commissioner of the British Punjab favoured the interests of the cultivators rather than the landowners. He fell out with his brother Henry, a fellow member of the Punjab Board of Administration, over the treatment of the **jagirdars** left by Sikh rule.[53] The debate raged fiercely over the fate of the Sikh **jagirdars** of the central Punjab. But the British were keen to confirm the landed authority of the Tiwanas and other 'tribal' leaders who had supported them against the Sikhs in the conflicts of 1845–6 and 1848–9 in the West Punjab. Such families as the Noons, Tiwanas, and Hayats of Wah were to subsequently play central roles in the future colonial administration of the localities.

The British recognition of such 'tribal' leaders paid a rich dividend in 1857. Historians remain divided over the causes and nature of the uprising of that year,[54] but agree that this was the supreme moment of truth for the British in India. The crucial support of the Punjab's chiefs safeguarded the Raj. It ended any doubts concerning the desirability of maintaining the influence of the rural intermediaries.

The Tiwanas of Shahpur

On 10 May 1857, soldiers of the Bengal Army mutinied at Meerut. News of this event reached the Punjab at midnight two days later. The concentration of European troops in this key frontier region left towns in the Gangetic Plain open to attack. The fabric of Government collapsed in Oudh which had been recently annexed by the British and also in the North Western Provinces. Henry Lawrence was killed in the fighting in Oudh to which he had been recently transferred. John Lawrence organised irregular forces of Punjabi cavalry to snuff out disturbances in the region before mounting an attack to recapture Delhi.[55]

Groups of sepoys mutinied in their Punjabi cantonments of Ferozepore, Jullundur, Ambala and Jhelum. When a body of sepoys massed for an attack on the British district headquarters at Shahpur, Malik Sahib Khan rode over from Mitha Tiwana to parley with the anxious British deputy commissioner. Their meeting entered the Raj's folklore.

Malik Sahib stood before Mr. Ousley, salaamed and offered him the handle of his sword with the point directed to his own body and said, 'I have fifty horsemen and I can raise three hundred. I can clothe and feed them, and if no questions are asked, I can find them arms too. They and my life are yours.[56]

Malik Sahib Khan's dramatic gesture was the first offer of assistance to the beleaguered authorities in the West Punjab. Moreover, it was proffered at a time when the triumph of British arms was uncertain. The deputy commissioner was well aware that he could have mounted only token resistance, if the Tiwana chief had joined the 'rebels.' The British thereafter remembered that the Tiwanas' loyalty had stood firm when it had been put to the test.

Malik Sahib Khan's forces defeated the sepoys of the Bengal Army in battles at Jhelum and Ajnala during the course of July. In one episode they captured 200 'rebels' without firing a shot.[57] In August, the Tiwana troop joined the forces which John Nicholson was massing[58] in Amritsar to recapture Delhi. By this stage the Tiwana contingent had been swollen to a thousand **sowars** with the addition of the forces of his brothers, Malik Fateh Khan and Malik Jahan Khan, nephew Sher Muhammad Khan, and great nephew Fateh Sher Khan. They joined the British forces on the Ridge outside Delhi. The beseiged city finally fell on 14 September.The aged Mughal Bahadur Shah escaped with his life, but the British exacted a heavy retribution on its other Muslim citizens.

Following the seige of Delhi, Malik Sahib Khan with his brothers took part in several other actions including the battle of Kalpi which sealed the fate of the Rhani of Jhansi. Malik Sahib Khan then accompanied General Napier on his campaign in central India. The British were so impressed by the fighting capacity of the Tiwana irregulars that a detachment was incorporated in the regiment of the 2nd Mahratta Horse at Gwalior which was raised for duty in central India. In the military reorganisation at the end of the revolt, the unit became the 18th Bengal cavalry.

When the Prince of Wales (the future George V) visited India in 1906 he became Colonel in chief of the regiment which changed its title to the 18th (Prince of Wales' Own) Tiwana Lancers. Finally in 1921, the 19th Bengal Lancers amalgamated to form the 19th King George V's Own Lancers. Both Umar and Khizr displayed great pride in wearing the regiment's scarlet uniform and blue pagari in their capacity as Honorary-Colonel. Tiwanas held most of the regular Indian commissions in the regiment, as the British saw their 'natural leadership' as vital to discipline in a fighting force recruited entirely from the Salt range.

The creation of the Tiwana regiment climaxed the 'tribes's emergence as military sub-contractors of the state. Henceforth military service and their local power as landholders were closely enmeshed. Army pay and pensions enabled Tiwana chiefs to both increase agricultural productivity in their home villages, and invest in land elsewhere. No other Muslim Rajput 'tribes' formed their own regiments, but they were heavily recruited in the Indian Army from the late 1870s onwards. By the outbreak of the First World War they accounted for 1 in 5 of all recruits, whilst Punjabis as a whole represented 3 in 5 of its strength.[59] The economic multiplier effects of military service enabled the transition from 'tribal' chief to West Punjab landlord to be completed. A military-agricultural lobby also emerged. Provincial autonomy which was introduced by the 1935 Government of India Act gave it full expression. The Unionist Party became its mouth-piece and fittingly a Tiwana served as the last Unionist Premier.

viii

The British rewarded the Tiwanas[60] as indeed they did other Punjabi notables for their loyalty in 1857. The descendants of Malik Fateh Khan received a **jagir** and seat in the **darbar**. Malik Sahib Khan was

The Tiwanas of Shahpur

given the title Sardar Bahadur and rewarded with the Star of India. He also received a grant of over 8,000 acres of crown waste land on the Lahore side of the Jhelum river. It was from this that he carved out the Kalra estate.[61] At first, however he settled on land at Megha which was a small ferry point facing the Dhak railway on the other bank. The nearest bridge was twenty miles downstream at Khushab. Megha's position meant that it was subject to periodic flooding. Hence Malik Sahib Khan's move some ten miles or so inland to Kalra. The landholding at Megha, however, still remained in the family, in 1952 Khizr was to construct a two storey building on a plot of land there for his eldest son Nazar and his wife Sita.

Malik Sahib Khan began horse breeding in 1862 shortly after the end of his military service. He also bred cattle and sheep. The successful clearing out of a disused inundation canal by the British Deputy Commissioner Mcnabb in 1860 encouraged him to construct a series of private canals. Other landowners in the district such as Malik Hakim Khan Noon, and Malik Sultan Mahmud Khan of the Hamoka branch of the Tiwanas followed this pioneering example.[62] The piranwala canal ran 15 miles and irrigated 2,500 acres, the main Malik Sahibkhanwala canal irrigated over 13,348 acres in its 12 miles stretch.[63] All but one of the Shahpur district's eight private canals were in fact owned by members from various branches of the Noon and Tiwana families.[64] The canal irrigation sustained a commercialised system of farming in which tenants sharecropped such produce as wheat and cotton. It also, however, underpinned the semi-feudal authority of the Tiwanas by establishing them as powerful 'waterlords' with control over the sale of water to other cultivators as well as their own tenants. Such scholars as Imran Ali see the maintenance of the Tiwanas' special water rights in the 1920s and 1930s at the expense of the construction of a Shahpur branch of the Lower Jhelum Canal as irrefutable evidence that the Colonial State sacrificed development goals for the pursuance of stability by placating 'politically loyal and important groups.'[65]

Despite numerous marriages,[66] Malik Sahib Khan did not possess an heir to his burgeoning estate. He estimated this at 3 million rupees in 1864.[67] Like other Tiwana chiefs, he followed the rule of primogeniture so only a single male heir was required. Finally, at the age of 65 he abandoned the practice of minimal lineage endogamy and married a young woman from the Thabal 'tribe'.[68] This did the trick, for Umar was born at Megha on 5 October 1874. Even Government Officials were invited to the lavish birth celebrations, although these were somewhat marred by Malik Sahib Khan's poor health.[69] The British presence presaged Umar's remarkable career as a 'loyalist' and intimate of Governors, Viceroys and the King-Emperor.

Umar as was the traditional custom started the study of the Quran at four. His classes with Maulvi Fazaluddin a follower of Pir Sial had hardly commenced, however when his father died.[70] Shortly before, Malik Sahib Khan had attempted to get a court order from the district judge declaring Umar to be a ward, but he collapsed during the proceedings which had to be abandoned.[71] The Tiwanas' local importance ensured, however that Umar was made a ward and the Kalra estate was administered by the Court of Wards from March 1879 onwards.

Umar's minority was spent under close British supervision. Before his admission to Aitchison College in 1888, he was educated by private tutors and lived with the administrators of his estate, accompanying them each summer to the Salt Range hill station of Sakesar. Umar of course imbued far more than a knowledge of English during this period of intensive supervision.

The Kalra estate was administered by James Wilson and Malcolm Hailey. During the sixteen and a half years it was under British supervision, Kalra's resources were greatly developed. New stables, granaries and wells were constructed at the cost of Rs 56,000. The stud was increased from 35 to 183 horses and mares. Nearly 4,000 extra acres of land were also purchased for the estate. Other additions included a half share in the Miani canal which was acquired for Rs 30,000 and brought in a return of around Rs 3000 per annum. In line with the policy regarding all Court of Wards' estates, loans were negotiated to purchase land in the newly created Canal Colonies.[72] Kalra's annual income alone at the time of its release stood at Rs 105,000.[73] This was a very substantial sum of money in those days.

ix

British rule immeasurably enriched all branches of the Tiwana family. Malik Sahib Khan's nephews also extended their lands and constructed private canals. The Hadali Tiwanas for example, whose leading representative, Mubariz Khan ended his army career as a risalder-major in the 18th Bengal lancers, owned a private canal which irrigated 8,000 acres.[74] The Hamoka Tiwanas, for their part

The Tiwanas of Shahpur

created a thriving stud farm to provide remounts for the Indian Army.

It would be wrong, however, to depict the Tiwanas as **parvenus** who owed everything to the British and thereby repaid them with unquestioning loyalty. This chapter has revealed how they accrued power as a result of their military prowess over a number of centuries. Well before the advent of the British, their control of land and scarce water supplies had given them a leading position in the Salt Range region. Like other West Punjab chiefs and **pirs**, colonial rule transformed them into 'landed gentry' with opportunities to extend landholding into the fertile Canal Colony districts as well as to carve out estates from wasteland grants. Umar was, however to exploit the new economic and political opportunities better than most. He developed exceptionally close ties with the colonial administration. This not only cemented the Mitha Tiwanas' local predominance, but also allowed him to transcend the limited political world of the Shahpur district.

Notes

1 I am indebted for this and all the information in this section to, D.S. Tiwana, 'A Brief History of Tiwanas' (privately produced pamphlet 1992) p. 6 & ff. There is an interesting background to this publication by Darbar Singh Tiwana who is a member of the Faculty of Punjab Agricultural University, Ludhiana.In January 1990 late Justice Iqbal Singh Tiwana, Mr Nazar Hayat Tiwana (Khizr's son) S. Teja Singh Tiwana, S. Narinder Singh Tiwana and Justice Kulwant Singh Tiwana met in Delhi and decided to organise a Tiwana brotherhood. Its first meeting was held in Chandigarh at the residence of Justice Kulwant Singh Tiwana on 19 January 1992. The fraternity sought to establish contacts between Tiwanas living in India, Pakistan, United States and Canada. A scholarship scheme for Tiwana students was created. The brotherhood also aimed to encourage historical study into the family history.Darbara Singh Tiwana presented the above pamphlet to the Annual General Meeting held at his house in Patiala on 3 December 1992.
2 This is a corruption of 'Chand thal' meaning a place of Baba Chand. The village now boasts a population of around 10,000 and is situated on the left bank of the Bhakra main line canal. *Ibid.*, pp. 19 & ff.
3 Sardar Sadhu Singh Tiwana became a judge in Patiala State, his two sons were judges of the Punjab and Haryana High Court.
4 Tauhra village with a population of around 4,000 is adjacent to Chinarthal. It is said to have been founded by Saho who came from Chinarthal. *Ibid.*, p. 23.
5 The former has received a prestigious Sahitya Akademi award for her Punjabi fiction, the latter was a recipient for her Punjabi poetry.

Khizr Tiwana, the Punjab Unionist Party and the Partition of India

6 *Ibid.*, p. 25.
7 For further details consult, K.A. Nizami, *The Life and Times of Shaikh Farid-ud-Din Ganj-i-Shakar* (Delhi 1973).
8 G.R. Mehr (ed), *General Sir Umar Hayat Khan Tiwana Sawaneh Hayat awr un ki Khandani Tarikh ka Pas-e-Manzar* (Lahore 1965) p.20 & ff.
9 M. Habib, 'Shaikh Nasiruddin Mahmud Chiragh-i-Delhi as a great historical personality', *Islamic Culture* (April 1946) p. 140.
10 R. Eaton, 'The Political and Religious Authority of the Shrine of Baba Farid in Pakpattan, Punjab' Unpublished Paper, University of California, Berkeley, 7 June 1979.
11 Mehr *op.cit.*, p. 24.
12 There is also a letter dated 7 January 1935 from Sardar Sadhu Singh Tiwana congratulating Allah Bakhsh on being awarded the title of Nawab. Even more fascinating is a reply to a letter from Malik Ghulam Mohammad Khan Wadhal Tiwana of 5 September 1938 in which the Sardar writes, 'As regards certain queries made by you regarding the descent of our clan, I am making further enquiries and shall let you know very soon.' Sardar Sadhu Singh Tiwana to Malik Ghulam Mohammad Khan Wadhal Tiwana, 5 September 1938.
13 This letter along with the others was given to me by Justice Kulwant Singh Tiwana. The letters have been subsequently donated to the University of Southampton and are kept with the Unionist Party Papers in the Hartley Library. Sardar Sadhu Singh Tiwana to Khizr, 11 March 1937.
14 'I am very thankful', Sardar Sadhu Singh Tiwana wrote to Umar on 5 September 1938, 'to your honour for again recommending my case to Nawab Sir Liaqat Hyat Khan, Prime Minister of Patiala, who has been very kind to promote me.'
15 Sardar Sadhu Singh Tiwana to Umar 1 January 1943.
16 Interview with Justice Kulwant Singh Tiwana Chandigarh, 10 December 1993.
17 The Mongols invaded the Punjab five times during the thirteenth century. Lahore was briefly occupied in 1241.
18 Khizr Khan was later to become the ruler of Delhi and establish the Syed dynasty in 1414.
19 For a broader perspective on these changes see, M. Alam, *The Crisis of Empire in Mughal North India Awadh and the Punjab 1707–1748* (Delhi, 1986).
20 Mehr *op.cit* p. 42.
21 R.G. Fox, Kin, Clan, Raja and Rule (Berkeley 1969).
22 Alam *op.cit.*, p. 84.
23 Mehr op.cit., p. 55 & ff.
24 Alam op.cit., p. 201.
25 The Tiwanas were strengthening their position at this time by strategic marriage alliances with other surrounding tribes as well such as the Mudials, Mestals and Chal.
26 For further details see Chapter 8 of Mehr op.cit p.62 and ff.
27 This was second only in importance to the crossing upstream at Jhelum over which passed the Grand Trunk Road on its journey from Peshawar to Lahore.

The Tiwanas of Shahpur

28 For details of Ranjit Singh's conquests see, I. Banga, *Agrarian System of the Sikhs: Late Eighteenth Century and Early Nineteenth Century* (New Delhi 1978).

29 Mehr *op.cit.*, p. 71.

30 Lady Wilson quotes a sum of £7000 being paid to Ranjit Singh. Lady Wilson, *Letters from India* (London 1911) p. 124.

31 Mehr *op.cit.*, p.72.

32 Aside from its religious inspiration, the Sikh uprising against the Mughals acquired an egalitarian character because of its socio-economic composition of 'dispossessed zamindars, impoverished peasants and pauperized lower urban classes.' Alam *op.cit.*, p. 317.

33 The eclipse of the once powerful Ghakkars was so complete that they were later 'forced even to work as coolies on the railways for their chiefs could no longer provide for themselves let alone their tribal retainers.' D. Brief, 'The Punjab and Recruitment to the Indian Army 1846–1918.' Unpublished M.Litt thesis, Oxford University 1984 p. 76.

34 For details consult, J.S. Grewal, *The Sikhs of the Punjab* (Cambridge 1990).

35 *Ibid.*, p. 108.

36 Whilst Hari Singh Nalwa held the jagir of Mitha Tiwana he delegated local authority to Fateh Khan son of Khuda Yar Khan.

37 I.A. Malik, *The History of the Punjab 1799–1947* (Delhi 1983) p. 120 &ff.

38 Quoted in C.A. Bayly, *Rulers, Townsmen and Bazaars. North Indian Society in the Age of British Expansion 1770–1870* (Cambridge 1983). p. 203.

39 Grewal *op.cit.* m, p. 103.

40 Beli Ram the Treasurer was receiving about 60,000 rupees a year in cash, a General like Hari Singh was paid over 8 lakhs. Payment was usually in the form of jagirs rather than cash. Grewal op.cit p. 107.

41 Malik *op.cit.*, p. 122.

42 For details of this period see, H.R. Gupta (ed), *Punjab on the eve of the First Sikh War 1844* (Hoshiarpur, 1956) pp. 208 219, 221, 245 & 291.

43 This proceeded apace during the period of Lord Roberts command of the Indian Army (1885–1893). It was rationalised by the development of the 'martial castes' theory.

44 For further details of the impact of the Treaty of Bhyrowal of December 1846 see, S.K. Sohni, 'Aspects of the Administration of the Punjab. Judicial, Revenue, Political 1849–1858' Unpublished PhD Thesis Durham 1965. pp. –30.

45 Grewal *op.cit.*, p. 125.

46 Grewal *op.cit.*, pp. 126–7.

47 H. Edwardes, *A Year on the Punjab Frontier in 1848–9* Vol. 2 (London, 1851) p. 640.

48 For another account of Fateh Khan's final days see Mehr *op.cit.*, p. 123 & ff.

49 For details see, L.H. Griffin & C.F. Massey, *Chiefs and Families of Note in the Punjab* (revised edition) vol. 2 (Lahore, 1910) p. 178 & ff.

50 He was Qadir Bakhsh's younger brother.

33

Khizr Tiwana, the Punjab Unionist Party and the Partition of India

51 Mehr *op.cit.*, p. 153.

52 The boundaries of the new province stretched from Delhi to the Afghan frontier. It was not until 1901 that the five frontier districts were separated to form the North West Frontier Province.

53 Sohni *op.cit.*, p. 78 & ff.

54 See, for example, A.T. Embree, *1857 In India. Mutiny or War of Independence?* (Boston 1963).

55 The Bengal sepoys had installed the octogenarian Bahadur Shah as leader of their revolt in Delhi as a renactment of former Mughal glory. Their action in reality was little more than a parody of the past.

56 Quoted in Wilson *op.cit.*, p. 129.

57 Mehr *op.cit.*, p. 164.

58 This included not only Muslim forces from the West Punjab, but also Sikh contingents. These numbered the spiritually influential Bedis, the important Ramgarhia, Sindhanwalia and Ahulwalia landowning families and even the Majithas who had taken up arms against the British as recently as the second Sikh War.

59 C. Dewey, 'The rise of the "Martial Castes." Changes in the Composition of the Indian Army, 1876–1914.' Unpublished Paper, Table 2 p.50.

60 For details see, L.H. Griffin & C.F. Massey, *Chiefs and Families of Note in the Punjab* (revised edition) Vol. 2 (Lahore 1910) p. 174 & ff.

61 J. Wilson, *Shahpur District Gazetteer* (Lahore, 1897) p. 119.

62 A private canal irrigated the 2,000 acre Kot Hakim Khan estate which Malik Hakim Khan Noon purchased from the Government. A private canal also watered the valuable Nurpur estate, west of Bhera. The Sultan Mahmudwala canal in the Shahpur tehsil irrigated the 4,000 acres of land owned by the Hamoka Tiwanas.*Gazetteer of the Shahpur District* 1917 (Lahore 1918) pp. 111, 113.

63 *District Gazetteer of the Shahpur District 1883–4* (Lahore 1885) pp. 8–9.

64 Imran Ali, *The Punjab Under Imperialism 1885–1947* (Princeton, 1988) p. 82.

65 This of course is the main thesis of his work. He cites the Tiwanas as just one example of the way in which the Colonial State strengthened the position of dominant classes at the expense of economic efficiency. This retarded nationalist development and ensured that 'agricultural expansion did not produce a social base conducive to rapid change.' *Ibid.*, pp. 81 & ff; 237 & ff.

66 Mehr *op.cit.*, p. 186.

67 Mehr *op.cit.*, p. 190.

68 She outlived her husband and only died in 1935. Both Umar and Khizr were in London at the time for the Jubilee celebrations.

69 Mehr *op.cit.*, p. 201.

70 Mehr *op.cit.*, p. 209.

71 Mehr op,cit p. 186 & ff.

72 For a classic account of the development of the Canal Colonies and their social and agrarian impact see, M. Darling, *The Punjab Peasant in Prosperity and Debt* (Columbia reprint 1978) p. 111 & ff.

73 'Report on the Administration of Estates Under the Charge of the Court

The Tiwanas of Shahpur

of Wards for the Year ending 30 September 1896.' (Lahore 1897) pp. 5, 18–19. Punjab Departmental Annual Reports L 5 VI (3) IOR.

74 *Shahpur District Gazeteer* (Lahore 1917) p. 111.

Chapter Two

Father and Son

The Mall or **thandi sarak** as it was popularly known ran through the heart of the Punjab's capital Lahore. Proceeding south westwards from the famous landmark of Queen Victoria's statue at Charing Cross, one passed further symbols of the British ruling presence. Facing each other across the road were the immaculate English style gardens named after Sir John Lawrence and the imposing entrance to Government House. Just a few minutes walk away another impressive building came into view with its extravagant domes. This was the main building of Aitchison College. It had been founded in 1886 to educate the sons of Punjab Chiefs and landlords.

Aitchison or Chief's College was set in 150 acres of grounds. It boasted three boarding houses, a mosque, mandir and gurdwara, playing fields, parade ground, riding school, gymnasium, dairy farm and a hospital. The Principal's residence was set back from the main building and shaded by trees. Umar and Khizr stayed here during their years at the College.[1] Umar had been one of its earliest pupils, in the days before a regular academic session was established. Indeed, if he had been just three years older, he would have attended the Ambala Court of Wards' School out of which Aitchison grew. The third boarding house was only completed during Umar's days at the college, as was the gymnasium which was endowed by his estate.[2]

During both Umar and Khizr's day, those College students who were not living with English members of staff, were allocated large suites of rooms. They employed servants who could be seen each morning carrying their masters' boxes of books from the boarding houses to the main school building.[3] Classes had been preceded by an hour of riding. The day finished with prayers and homework preparation. The College's strict neutrality in matters of faith meant that religious education was at first optional. It could only be given

36

Father and Son

out of school hours and had to be separately paid for. By the time that Khizr became a pupil in 1908, religious teachers had been appointed. A further twenty years was to pass, however before attendance at worship was compulsory and religion was introduced into the curriculum. Such changes did not affect the friendly atmosphere in which Hindu, Muslim and Sikh boys mixed freely together.[4] Indeed, when C.H. Barry became Principal in the early 1930s, he successfully integrated the boarding houses which had been previously divided on communal lines.[5]

Barry introduced a number of other reforms. He gradually abolished the practice of private rooms and cooks, valets and grooms. Along with dormitories, he increasingly added other features of the English Public School system. Blazers and grey trousers replaced **achkans** and **shalwars**, team games were emphasised and a friendly rivalry was encouraged between Aitchison and its counterparts, Mayo College at Ajmer and Rajkumar College at Rajkot. He also exercised a rather more generous interpretation of the eligibility rules so that sons of high government officials and professional men rubbed shoulders with the scions of Princely houses and Punjab Chiefs. When Barry became Principal he remarked that there were more cows in the dairy than boys in the school.[6]

Khizr who had succeeded his father as a member of the School's Management Committee[7] strongly supported Barry's reforms. The young Principal inevitably encountered opposition. The Maharajah of Patiala was a particularly vocal opponent. Khizr's backing as committee chairman was therefore especially welcome. Even when he was a Minister, Khizr attended to Aitchison's affairs. If there was urgent management business, he would come alone to Barry's residence or ask the Principal to call on him at home.[8] Khizr demonstrated the same determination in pursuing what he believed was the right course of action in the College's life as he was to reveal in the wider affairs of the province.

Khizr and Umar were active members of the Aitchison Chiefs' College Old Boys' Association (Accoba). Indeed, Umar had played a leading role in launching it and establishing the annual dinner. This sustained college cross-communal friendships throughout adult years. They even survived the 'great divide' of 1947[9] amongst many of the students.

Roop Chand and Mohan Singh were two of Khizr's closest non-Muslim friends at Aitchison. The former was the son of Rai Bahadur Ram Saran Das whose Lahore based family had made their money in cotton ginning. They owned a well known house 'Lal Koti' near the shrine of Hazrat Data Ganj Baksh. Roop Chand possessed one of the first private airplanes in Lahore and on a number of occasions in the early 1930s took a reluctant Khizr up for a ride above the city. He later joined the Indian Airforce ending this career as a Wing Commander.[10] Mohan Singh was a rich Sikh Jat from Rawalpindi. Khizr was to seek Mohan's assistance when a temporary rift emerged between Umar and himself early in 1936.

Aitchison College's cosmopolitan atmosphere and emphasis on the value of the British connection formed part of a wider Imperial ideology and administrative policy. This succeeded in creating the conditions for the establishment of a political hierarchy which transcended religious identity and was wedded to the Colonial State.

i

In addition to Aitchison, Khizr and his father shared the experience of close ties with the 'family' regiment. They attached great importance to their honorary commissions in the regiment which bore their name. Indeed, one of Khizr's last public engagements was to attend a gathering in London of the former British officers of the 19th Lancers. Umar both served the regiment in overseas engagements and actively encouraged Tiwanas, Awans and other 'martial castes' to enlist. In his capacity as Shahpur recruiting officer he personally enrolled 1500 Rajputs into the army during the First World War. The Tiwanas of Mitha Tiwana alone provided eight commissioned officers. In the Khushab tehsil 1 in every 7 Tiwana males had enlisted.[11]

Umar had first seen active service in 1903 during the British Somaliland expedition against Sheikh Sayed Muhammad Abdille Hassan (styled by the British as the 'Mad Mullah'). He helped raise recruits for the camel corps before serving as an assistant commandant. His role as a transport officer in the 54th camel corps frequently placed him in the advance party.[12]

Soon after returning from this arduous expedition, Umar volunteered as a transport officer in an Indian Army force which was sent to Tibet. His veterinary skills were once again useful. The award of the C.I.E. amply compensated his temporary affliction with snow blindness. Other rewards soon followed including promotion to Captain and despatch to London as the Punjab representative at the Coronation of King George V. At the subsequent 1911

Father and Son

coronation darbar held amidst magnificent pageantry in Delhi, Umar served as a deputy herald and led the All-India procession which paid their homage at the Jharoka ceremony.[13]

Umar served the opening fifteen months of the First World War, with the Indian Expeditionary Force in France.[14] He then joined the Mesopotamian campaign paying the costs of the retinue of fourteen retainers which accompanied him.[15] Umar first entered the firing line in October 1914 during the retreat from Mons. At this time he was attached to the staff of the Ferozepore brigade which was in the vanguard of the remainder of the Lahore Division. He was mentioned in despatches for his actions at Luccatenre where he personally supervised the leading of the horses to safety, whilst under enemy fire. One shell landed in a cart of hay close to where he was standing.[16]

Umar twice visited England, during this period. On the first occasion, he was hospitalised following frost-bite. During the second he acted as the only Muslim representative at Lord Robert's funeral. Earlier he had been chosen for an audience with George V during his visit to France. Everyone else who waited on the King-Emperor at this time were rulers of Princely States.

Umar's most valued war service was in Mesopotamia where the British feared that Pan-Islamic sentiment would undermine the loyalty of Muslim troops fighting the Ottoman forces. Moreover, the Mesopotamian campaign involved not only conflict with the Turkish forces, but posed a threat to Muslim holy places.[17]

Umar was attached to the headquarters staff where he subsequently served as a one man troubleshooter, visiting the Indian soldiers in their various regiments to put their minds at ease. He penned a number of pamphlets to combat the ' menace' of Pan-Islamic ideals. In these he demonstrated that the Sherif of Mecca rather than the Caliph was the proper spiritual head of the Muslims. He also argued that the British had always revered Muslim Holy Places and would protect them. The extract below encapsulates his argument. This is taken from his pamphlet on jihad which was written to dispel 'vain attempts' 'emanating from a German source' that Turkey was fighting a holy war.

No case has ever occurred where the British have hindered Muhammadans in any way as regards their religion or compelled them in any way to do anything which is forbidden to them.. The British Empire controls a far greater number of Muhammadans than any other world power. All the residents

Khizr Tiwana, the Punjab Unionist Party and the Partition of India

of India will readily admit that the English have never interfered with their respective religions.. Up to now there is no instance in Iraq-i-Arab of the English damaging any mosque, nor is there any possibility of such an occurrence.. They would never attempt to convert a Muhammadan to another religion, for have they not always helped the Muslim pilgrims, whom robbers frequently molest when on their pilgrimage to Arabia. The present war cannot therefore be termed a religious war.[18]

Umar was also given the task of hearing soldiers' grievances connected with property or matrimonial disputes at home. He removed one major cause of unrest by ensuring that a proper funeral service (**Janazah**) was arranged for Muslims.[19] Cremation grounds were at the same time set aside for the Hindus. Umar kept abreast of grievances through the reports he received from a network of regimental committees. This 'intelligence' also enabled him to uncover corruption in the supply and transport depots and detect the methods by which soldiers maimed themselves and poisoned camels in order to be invalided home.[20]

Umar's constant travelling to the various regiments undermined his health. He was hospitalised first in Basra and then in Bombay, when his knees became so swollen that he was unable to walk or ride. These efforts did not, however go unrewarded, for he was promoted to the rank of Major and awarded a Knighthood. The Tiwana estates were also further extended by the award of fifteen squares of land in the Canal Colonies.

Khizr's military career inevitably appears undistinguished in comparison. But he too saw action in the cause of the King-Emperor. Khizr volunteered for service at the time of the 1919 Punjab disturbances. He was attached to the 17th Lancers which guarded Government House and other public buildings in Lahore. Khizr accompanied the regiment to the front at the time of the third Afghan War. Although still only a teenager, he earned a mention in despatches and was rewarded with an O.B.E. in 1921.

The military connection coloured Umar's and Khizr's political outlooks. It strengthened both their loyalism and non-communal stance. Brigadier John Woodroffe who served in the 19th Lancers has recalled how the British officers were always welcome visitors in the Shahpur district. 'When I paid the first of many visits to Tiwana country', he has written, 'I stayed with Umar Hyat who was living in

Father and Son

retirement in a very fine house near the villages of Hadali and Mitha Tiwana. It was a wonderful experience and after 4 days I felt I was fully accepted as a member of the Tiwana tribe. I met all the families at various informal gatherings all of which had members who had served or were serving with the regiment.'[21]

The 19th Lancers consisted of three squadrons: 'A' was drawn from the Sikhs of the Amritsar district. 'B' from the Hindu Jats and 'C' from the Muslims of the Salt Range. This did not however result in communal polarisation partly because the headquarters squadron consisted of 'mixed classes'. But in main because of the strong loyalty to the regiment which arose not only from the common experience of active service, but from the number of sons who followed long established family traditions of enlistment.

Umar in his address to the regimental reunion of November 1935 highlighted the importance of military service for the 'Punjab tradition.' 'There then followed a stirring address from our recently appointed Honorary Colonel, Sir Umar Hayat Khan', the regimental history relates, 'who stressed the staunch loyalty of the Army to the Crown, the fine reputation of the Regiment and the bond of comradeship between all classes and creeds when united by the Regimental spirit.' Umar concluded that 'it may well be that the creation of this unity (is) the greatest achievement of the Indian Army and its British officers.'[22]

Umar throughout his life strongly upheld the 'martial castes' theory of military recruitment. 'Everybody could not become a soldier', he declared in a speech to the Council of State in March 1922, 'If a cart horse is put in a race it will not do and similarly if a race horse is put onto a cart, it cannot pull cart. People in India are like that, especially in the North. If a person is weak he is unable to stand the cold and dies; the theory of the "survival" of the fittest is correct. There are some places where there are people with limbs like our fingers. How on earth can they fight.'[23]

These social darwinist sentiments echoed the British view of recruitment which had developed in the 1880s. It is uncertain whether Umar merely internalised the colonial discourse or cleverly upheld the interests of his community in a way calculated to evoke sympathy. He continually reiterated these arguments to official commissions. His intervention undoubtedly influenced the Skeen Commission in favour of the 'martial castes'. Umar's greatest success was to ensure that ex-servicemen were enfranchised at the time of the 1919 Montagu-Chelmsford Reforms.[24] This enabled the martial lobby to dominate the restricted electorate in many key West Punjab constituencies.[25] Sir Michael O'Dwyer, the Punjab Governor who responded so favourably to the martial lobby's representations had more than coincidentally developed a close friendship with Umar in his days as a junior assistant commissioner.[26] Sir Michael O'Dwyer's 'skewing' of the electorate undoubtedly paved the way for both the Unionist predominance and Khizr's Premiership.

Khizr shared his father's conservatism and support for the 'martial castes.''The clear signs of approaching Allied victory have lead to a quickening of political activity in India', he wrote to Sir James Grigg, the Secretary of state for war in September 1944, 'many political parties are seeking to strengthen their position in order to gather the fruits of victory to which they have contributed nothing.. These non-cooperation bargainers now hope, to secure, first, the solution in their favour of the present political deadlock, and later the framing of India's constitution in a manner which will give them all that they want.. There is a growing fear among those Indians who have loyally supported the war effort.. that when the fate of their country is being decided their voices will go unheard in the clamour raised by the more vocal groups who have stood apart from the Allies and who claim to be the sole representatives of India.'[27]

Khizr later in the same letter restated the official view of O'Dwyer and others that the professional politicians did not represent the interests of the 'real' India.

As a clinching argument, he sought to link the loyalist endeavours of 1939–45 with those of 1857. This thesis came naturally to him, given the Tiwanas' family history, but it might not have so felicitously flowed from the pen of other politicians.

A great wave of loyalty has swept the Province similar to that which swept it in 1857.. of the wave of loyalty in the Punjab no further proof is needed than this fact that we have furnished more than twice the number of recruits we furnished in the last war and the fine response of certain other parts of India indicates that there also is a wave of loyalty. The force of this loyalist movement must not be wasted. It should be conserved and exploited for the common advantage of India and of Britain.. I ask that (the loyalist classes) should be given an effective voice in any discussions on the solution of the present deadlock and of India's future constitution.[28]

Khizr vainly stood out for this belief at the 1945 Simla Conference. It

Father and Son

was, however, anachronistic even in the Punjab context by this juncture and was positively antediluvian in All-India terms. Wavell, whose own military background made him sympathetic to the 'martial castes', nevertheless noted concerning Khizr's appeal that, ' as long as the Congress and Muslim League can sweep the polls at any general Election it is impossible for HMG to say they do not represent the people.. We obviously cannot at this stage go back on our promises on the excuse that we must fulfil an obligation to "our friends".'[29] Khizr became increasingly disillusioned with the British response to his views. It troubled him that they did not reciprocate the landowning and military classes' loyalty and devotion.

iii

Despite this common educational and military background, father and son differed dramatically in character. Umar was a much more forceful and ambitious person. He in fact set himself the goal of a Princely lifestyle and status. Where Umar was generous and self-indulgent, Khizr was parsimonious and modest.

Umar's ambitions were fostered by his mixing with members of ruling households both at Aitchison and in subsequent years.[30] He was on especially good terms with the Hindu ruler of Jammu and Kasmir, Maharaja Sir Hari Singh. He served the British not only out of concern for his community, but out of a craving for personal recognition. This was rewarded with the titles which the British showered upon him and by his audiences with the King-Emperor. His ego was further boosted in 1912 when Lord Hardinge visited the stud farm at Kalra. A Viceroy's visit was a privilege generally enjoyed only by the Princes.

The burgeoning Kalra estate enabled him to play at being a Prince. It possessed its own militia. Umar also designed an estate flag. It was a red, green and saffron tricolour on which were set a crescent and star. Umar also aspired to the liberality and patronage expected of a member of a ruling house. He maintained various charitable institutions in his **ilaqa** (locality) including a free school, a dispensary, and a veterinary hospital. These were made available not only for his tenants, but for the surrounding villages. He built a mosque and a temple on his own estate and provided subsistence allowances for orphans and widows. Further afield Umar's patronage of Shahpur's Government College ensured that it survived despite its small enrolment.[31]

Khizr Tiwana, the Punjab Unionist Party and the Partition of India

Landowners and local officials were provided with opportunities for shikar on the Kalra estate. The game consisted principally of duck, quail and jackals. Umar was especially fond of falconry and was also proud of his greyhounds. He organised a monthly greyhound racing event in Sargodha. Mr K. Morton (Shahpur District Commissioner 1937–9) in an interview in 1990 provided a vivid recollection of Umar on one of these occasions, 'sitting on a string charpoy resplendent in lavender achkan and shalwar and Tiwana pagri sipping from his brandy flask.' Morton added that Umar's greyhounds always won.[32]

Umar also patronised the pastimes of wrestling, tent-pegging and pirkoudi. He not only presented cups and gold bracelets as prizes for the players, but paid for the establishment of an inter-district tournament. He took his polo, tent-pegging and pirkoudi teams around the various military cantonments.[33] Umar always organised various sports and entertainments for visiting British dignataries. This was not just a form of self-advertisement. It also displayed the Rajputs' physique which Umar was quick to point out equipped them so well for military service.

The annual horse show at Sargodha was another recipient of his munificence. This was the greatest fair in the district and drew people from a wide area, not only because of its livestock on display, but also because of its hucksters and fairground entertainments. The huge gate built in Umar's memory can still be seen at the fairgrounds today.

Umar engaged in the conspicuous consumption expected of a Nawab. In addition to the Kalra house, he owned properties in Simla, New Delhi, Sargodha and Lahore. The Simla properties, 'Loriston' and 'Garden View' overlooked the precipitous race-course at Annandale with its forested backdrop. One of his Sargodha houses boasted a banqueting hall which could accommodate a hundred people. In Lahore he owned two houses, his favourite was at 21 Beadon Road, a property which stood opposite Dayal Singh College. When he was living in London in the early 1930s, he rented a property in the exclusive Regent's Park locality where he held open house every weekend. Chaudhri Rahmat Ali was one of the regular visitors. It is ironic given Khizr's later political stand, that the Cambridge undergraduate penned part of the famous, *Now or Never* pamphlet calling for a fully independent Muslim State on one of these occasions.[34]

Other trappings of Umar's status were the retinue of servants

44

Father and Son

which accompanied him on his travels abroad and his cars. He was the first Indian to possess a motor vehicle in the Shahpur district and owned three or four automobiles in the 1920s. His favourite vehicle was a seven seater Fiat. Later in the mid 1930s he also purchased a Buick.[35] Abdul Ghani the main driver was a larger than life character, noted for his humour and sense of mischief. A favourite local family drive used to be to the Salt range. This involved a twenty or so mile drive to the prosperous market town of Khushab to cross the Jhelum via the steel Thal bridge, before ascending to the peak of the range. A metalled road wound its way up to the grassy hill of Sakesar resplendent with its wild oak and olive trees. Sakesar because of its equable climate some five thousand feet above sea-level was the Shahpur district headquarters in the summer months.

In addition to patronising his tenants, Umar helped Tiwanas and other notables escape from the clutches of the moneylenders. The 1930s witnessed a growing problem of rural indebtedness, brought on mainly by falling agricultural prices, but also partly by the kind of conspicuous consumption we have noted above. The Batra money-lenders of Sahiwal and Girot, like their counterparts elsewhere in the province, grew fat on the financial indiscretions of the landowning class. By 1937 rural indebtedness amounted to around Rs 200 **crores** (a **crore** is ten million) and the Punjab's farmers annually paid back in interest on their loans 4 to 5 times the aggregate amount of land revenue and the water rate. Umar lent about 5 **lakhs** of rupees to Sher Muhammad Khan Tiwana, the Syeds of Jahanian Shah and the Baloches of Saiwal and Girot to enable them to escape from the clutches of the moneylenders.[36]

Umar's lavish lifestyle in London which included the patronage of his famous chess players, Sultan Khan and Fatima, threatened to plunge his own family into similar financial straits. Whilst Kalra was a prosperous and productive estate, it could not maintain him in the style of a Prince. Khizr who managed the properties in his father's absence was all too aware of this fact. Unlike Umar he kept a tight rein on the purse strings. It was Khizr's reluctance in releasing funds which thwarted Umar's plans to purchase his rented Regent's Park house.[37] Matters came to a head, after they had both attended the 1935 Silver Jubilee Celebrations in London of King George V and Queen Mary.

Khizr claimed that Umar's personal assistant Malik Ghulam Muhammad had embezzled funds during the seven years that his father had lived in London. He wanted a law suit to be filed against

45

Khizr Tiwana, the Punjab Unionist Party and the Partition of India

him. Umar stuck by 'B.A.' as he was known to the family. Khizr called in his Aitchison schoolfriend Mohan Singh to audit the accounts. He found a number of discrepancies. Umar however refused to take any action against a loyal retainer who had served him since the First World War. Before the row was finally patched up, Khizr, his mother and his eldest son Nazar left Kalra to stay for a month as Mohan Singh's guests in Rawalpindi. Mohan Singh brought them Rs 50,000 in cash to tide them over at this time.[38]

Khizr would not normally have crossed his father who he held in awe. But their different attitudes to money always caused problems. Khizr indulged in few luxuries save the occasional good polo pony or racehorse imported from Britain for breeding. He did not share his father's interest in cars, chess or greyhounds on which he expended large sums. Nor was he as willing to lavish funds on the more impecunious members of the 'tribe.' With the passing of the years, Khizr became increasingly frugal.

Umar remained the family patriarch even when Khizr was a Minister. Khizr thus used his relative Allah Bakhsh Tiwana as an intermediary when he openly admitted his marriage to his' servant' Fateh Bibi. He knew that Umar would disapprove of this liason with a woman who was formerly married to a tenant. The marriage was in fact only admitted because of the need to enrol his son by it, Fateh Hayat, at Aitchison.[39] The boy had been called Sher Mohammad at birth. When Khizr was a Minister he still did not live openly with Fateh Bibi. She stayed in a rented apartment where he visited her at night. When he moved into a new residence at 47 Wellington Mall in 1942, still out of deference to Umar, Fateh Bibi was housed in an annex. Umar continued to meet with local revenue officials and make recommendations concerning appointments even when Khizr became Premier. Again son dared not approach father directly over this potentially embarrassing situation. Khizr once more used Allah Bakhsh as an intermediary.

iv

Khizr lacked both his father's willpower and ambition. He possessed no aspirations for pursuing a political career beyond the level of the local district board. Many of the happiest years of his life were spent overseeing the Kalra estate during the 1920s and 1930s. He was never to recapture the stability and security of these years. Indeed in his final days he became increasingly restless. He had nevertheless,

46

Father and Son

been able to successfully use some of the influences from this period, during his decade of political prominence. The Kalra estate formed both a haven and a model for his vision of the Punjab's future.

Kalra had undergone considerable development since the days of Malik Sahib Khan. From a modest beginning with just 35 mares, the Kalra stud had become the largest in the Punjab. By the turn of the century there were 200 horses in the stables and the estate covered nearly 30,000 acres.[40] The main crops were wheat, maize, cotton and some sugar cane.

The cash crops were taken the twenty odd miles by road to Sargodha. Nowhere symbolised more clearly the changes which British rule had brought to the district. Although it had only been built at the turn of the century, it had outstripped Shahpur as the most important town in the district with the development of the Jhelum Canal Colony and the construction of the new Rech Doab branch of the North-Western Railway. By the eve of partition Sargodha possessed a population of around 55,000, three-quarters of whom were non-Muslims. Agricultural products were both processed in its factories and shipped by rail to Karachi.

The heart of the Kalra estate was the family dwelling which Malik Sahib Khan had constructed in the 1880s. It was modelled on a circuit house with its single storey, porch verandah and large living room with its high airy ceiling. The house was reached by a drive off the bazaar road, this linked the estate with the Sargodha to Jhawarian road. The polo ground ran between the house and the intersection of the canal and bazaar road. The family graveyard and mosque faced across the road to the polo ground. Behind this was the vegetable garden and orchard with its oranges and mangoes. The outbuildings included a guest house, the female quarters, stables, granaries and estate office. The guest house which contained fourteen bedrooms had been occasionally occupied by James Wilson and Malcolm Hailey during the time of the Court of Wards' administration of the estate.

Most of its staff including the head accountant and deputy manager were Hindus, although the general manager who reported directly to Khizr was a Muslim. The stud and cattle farm was also run by Muslims. The head groom was a Tiwana. Employment for more lowly members of the 'tribe' was also provided in the estate militia. The 'kardars' in the outlying villages were invariably Sikhs.

Kalra village adjoined the house. It was surrounded by an embankment which guarded both it and the house from the Jhelum's

Khizr Tiwana, the Punjab Unionist Party and the Partition of India

flood waters. By the 1930s, Kalra's population of family servants, tenants and traders had swollen to around five thousand. The small bazaar of around twenty shops was entirely owned by Hindus. But most of its inhabitants were Awans, Sials and Gondals. There was in fact a far greater Hindu population some five miles away in Jhawarian. The dimly lit village contrasted with the house and outbuildings at night time, when the latter was brightly illuminated by electricity. But Umar and Khizr had furnished it with other facilities such as a primary school where free lessons were provided, a dispensary and post office. The nearest telegram office was in Jhawarian[41] and even the house itself did not boast a telephone until the 1960s.

Khizr liked to start his day with a ride, before commencing his duties around 9.00 am as honorary magistrate of the **ilaqa**. Later in the morning he would receive tenants, relatives and local officials. After lunch he would either ride out to the outlying farms accompanied by his estate managers or visit relatives. His daily routine also included an afternoon walk in the winter months. He always dined early and had retired to bed by 10 or 11 o'clock having given the domestic staff their orders for the following day.

This regular rhythm of life was to be severely shaken by Umar's insistence that Khizr enter the 1937 Punjab elections. These were the first to be held under the terms of the 1935 Government of India Act. Khizr was drawn outwards from the local world of Kalra to the wider spheres of provincial and All-India politics. But he continued not only to hanker after the former, but to bring its values to the Centre.

Kalra's local communal harmony validated the beliefs which Khizr had acquired in the more rarefied atmosphere of Aitchison. Its *langar* open to all symbolised this as much as the **mandir** which Umar had constructed for his Hindu workers. Each winter all communities in a hectic three or four days dammed the Jhelum with sandbags to ensure the water supply to the private canal system. The well being of the local economy depended on such cooperation. This background encouraged Khizr's belief that any partition of the Punjab was economically nonsensical and would result in disaster. Urban politicians who were unaware of the cross-communal cooperation which was necessary for agricultural operations were unreceptive to such arguments.

Kalra also influenced Khizr's approach to office. As first a Minister, then Premier he kept in close touch with the activities of

Father and Son

every department and was free to be seen by officials at every level. He continued to act in public administration as he had done at Kalra, talking to managers, tenants and workers alike. In a real sense he viewed his growing public responsibilities as merely an extension of those he had undertaken as a big landlord in Shahpur.

Notes

1 Umar was at Aitchison from 1888–1893. During this period, Mr. J.C. Godley was the Principal. Khizr attended between 1908–1916 when Mr. F.A. Leslie-Jones was the Principal.
2 F.S. Aijazuddin, *Aitchison College Lahore: 1886–1986 The First Hundred years* (Lahore 1986) p. 25.
3 Ibid., p. 40.
4 When the College first opened, it had twelve pupils, five Muslims, six Sikhs and one Hindu. In 1932, its enrollment consisted of twenty Muslims, forty three Sikhs and fourteen Hindus. Aijazuddin *op.cit.*, p.94.
5 Aijazuddin *op.cit.*, p. 59.
6 Interview with C.H. Barry 9 August 1991.
7 This included the Maharajah of Patiala, the Nawab of Bahawalapur, Sir Sunder Singh Majitha, Khizr as Chairman, ex-officio members included the Commissioner of the Lahore Division, Deputy Commissioner Lahore, Director of Public Instruction Lahore and General Officer controlling Lahore District.
8 Barry interview *op.cit.*
9 Personal communication to the author of Nazar Tiwana who followed in the footsteeps of his father and grandfather in becoming a College pupil.
10 Interview with Nazar Tiwana, New Delhi, 11 December1993.
11 *War Services of the Shahpur District* n.d., IOR Pos 5545 p. 18.
12 For further details consult, *A Brief Account of the Career of Colonel Nawab Malik Sir Umar Hayat Khan Tiwana* (Simla 1927) p. 23 & ff.
13 *Ibid.*, p. 20.
14 A history of its activities is contained in, Sir James Willcocks, *With the Indians in France* (London, 1920).
15 In this he was of course carrying on a family tradition. When Malik Muhammad Mubariz Khan of the Hadali Tiwanas entered the 9th Hodson's Horse in 1885, he supplied an entire troop of retainers at his own expense.
16 *A Brief Account op.cit.*, p. 40.
17 These included the Dome of the Rock, the third Holiest place in Islam in Jerusalem and the Shia shrines of Karbala and Najf.
18 *Nawab Sir Umar Hayat Khan Tiwana. The Man and His Word* (Lahore 1929) p. 284 & ff.
19 *A Brief Account op.cit.*, p. 48.
20 *A Brief Account op.cit.*, p. 50 & ff.
21 J.H.P. Woodroffe Unpublished manuscript p. 60.

Khizr Tiwana, the Punjab Unionist Party and the Partition of India

22 J.G. Pocock, The Spirit of a Regiment. Being the History of the 19th King George V's Own Lancers 192–47 (Aldershot 1962) p. 29.

23 Nawab Sir Umar *op.cit.*, p. 105.

24 A Brief Account *op.cit.*, p. 69.

25 Under the system of dyarchy introduced by the Montagu-Chelmsford Reforms only 745,000 Punjabis had the right to vote (3.1% of the total population. *Indian Franchise Committee* (London 1932) Vol 1, p.64.

26 C. Dewey, *Anglo-Indian Attitudes. The Mind of the Indian Civil Service* (London 1993) p. 218.

27 Khizr to Sir James Grigg 18 September 1944, T.P., V, p. 221 & ff.

28 *Ibid.*, pp. 223–4.

29 Wavell to Amery 20 September 1944, *T.P.*, V, p.44.

30 There were always a number of sons of Princely Rulers at Aitchison. A third of the 96 pupils enrolled in 1934–5, for example came from the Native States. Aitchison College Lahore Annual Report 1934–35 p. 4. V/ 24/944 IOR.

31 P. Singh (ed), *Chhotu Ram in the eyes of his Contemporaries* (New Delhi 1992) p. 130.

32 Mr. K. Morton interview, Great Wilbraham Cambridge 13 December 1990.

33 *A Brief Account op.cit.*, p. 6.

34 The Text of *Now or Never* is reprinted in: Syed Sharifuddin Pirzada, *Evolution of Pakistan* (Lahore 1963), pp. 263–9.

35 This car was lent to Sir Sikander for the joint marriage celebrations of his two sons and daughter in December 1942. Sikander suffered a fatal heart attack after the festivities, opening the way for Khizr to assume the Premiership.

36 *A Brief Account op.cit.* p. 60.

37 Personal communication to the author of Nazar Tiwana.

38 *Ibid.*

39 Fateh Hayat was born in 1934 whilst Umar was abroad.

40 'Report on the administration of estates under the Charge of the Court of Wards for the year ending 30 September 1896' (Lahore, 1896) p. 18. Punjab Departmental Annual Reports L5 VI(3) IOR.

41 Jhawarian also possessed the nearest sub-hospital and senior school.

Chapter Three

The Unionist Party

Khizr inherited the paternalistic outlook and trappings of power associated with a feudal chief. His army service strengthened devotion to the Crown. For two decades he lived the conventional existence of a large Punjabi landowner. In 1937, however he received instantaneous promotion to Ministerial rank in the Unionist Government of Sikander Hayat Khan. Within five years he had assumed leadership of the Unionist Party and Government. What kind of party did he inherit? How did its values and outlook fit with those which he had acquired at Aitchison and Kalra?

The Unionist Party[1] emerged as a formal grouping in the Punjab Legislative Council in 1923. Landlord parties existed in a number of provinces by this time. But the Unionist Party differed in that it cut across 'class' and 'community' interests. It drew support from large landowners and peasant proprietors and appealed to the Hindu Jats of the Ambala division as well as the Muslim 'tribes' of the West Punjab. Indeed the Jat leader Chaudhri Chhotu Ram played a leading role in the party's development. From a rather uncertain beginning, the Unionist Party emerged as the predominant force in the region. The Punjab's political landscape thus acquired a unique character. Men committed to the Imperial connection dominated the era of Provincial Autonomy. The Unionists' continued attachment to the British was symbolised by the fact that a nominated non-official, Owen Roberts representing Europeans and Anglo-Indians played a role in its politics and indeed served as a parliamentary private secretary in the Khizr Ministry.

The Unionist Party of Khizr's day thus bore the imprint of British attitudes towards political representation and identity. The colonial state had quite deliberately linked its authority with the structure of rural Punjabi society. The traditions which had emerged during the

51

leadership of Fazl-i-Husain and Chhotu Ram also of course shaped the Party. Before turning to an examination of Khizr's Unionist inheritance, however, we should briefly remind ourselves that not all Punjabis fitted easily into the British mould for the region's political development. A new type of 'communal consciousness' had grown up in the region's cities as a result of the modernising impulses of colonial rule and the accompanying elite economic and political competition. The British sought to isolate the rural population from this 'communal contagion.'

The 'communal' threat alone was, however insufficient to explain the British economic and political engineering in the Punjab which as Imran Ali has argued, retarded the 'national movement' and 'capitalist revolution' in the region. The cooperation between the large landholders and the Colonial State was primarily motivated by the Punjab's emergence as the sword arm of India. This development was itself partly rooted in the rural elites' response to the 1857 Revolt.

i

The loyalty of the Muslim and Sikh landowners of the newly annexed Punjab region in 1857 confirmed the school of thought associated with Henry Lawrence. This sought to govern with the assistance of rural intermediaries. The British richly rewarded those who had stood by them in their darkest hour.[2] The Tiwanas were the most successful but by no means the only rural family which embarked at this time on what were to prove lengthy and lucrative 'loyalist' careers. The Noons and Hayats shared a similar history.

Officials recognised the need for securing the support of the rural elites, however, not only because they were local peacekeepers,[3] but because they were military contractors. The Tiwanas, as we have noted, exemplified this role, although it was played by many other Rajput 'tribes' following the Punjabisation of the Indian Army. This resulted from the thorough overhaul of military organisation after 1857.

By the eve of the First World War, the Punjab so dominated the Indian Army that three-fifths of its recruits were drawn from the region. Moreover, they hailed from a narrow range of Hindu Dogra, Sikh Jat and Muslim Rajput 'martial castes' which represented less than 1 per cent of the subcontinent's total population.[4] Punjabis saw action in the mud of Flanders, in the deserts of Arabia and in the bush

The Unionist Party

of East Africa, winning over 2,000 decorations, including three Victoria Crosses.[5] The Punjabi' martial castes' continued to dominate the Indian Army throughout the inter-war years. At no time did the Punjabi contingent drop below three-fifths of the total strength. The imperative to secure the loyalty of the' martial castes' understandably exerted a profound impact on the Punjab's political economy.

ii

The British adopted a number of policies to secure rural stability in the sword arm of India. Overriding all other considerations, until it was fatally dislocated by the Second World War, was the imperative to defend the rural power structure. This was achieved by the following methods: first by associating the 'natural leaders' of the' agriculturalist tribes' with their executive authority; second, by ensuring that the rural leaders politically controlled the economic forces set in train by the colonial encouragement of a market-oriented agriculture; third by using the resources which this provided to reward the agriculturalist population rather than stimulate industrial development; fourth by establishing a framework of political representation which institutionalised the division between the 'agriculturalist' and' non-agriculturalist' population.

The British identification of the 'tribe' as the focus of rural identity underpinned all of these policy initiatives. Indeed, the maintenance of the tribal structure of rural society became the legitimising principle of British rule, thereby obscuring realpolitik imperatives. However, as David Gilmartin has revealed,[6] the definition of the 'tribe' was vague and 'workable principles for tribal grouping were extremely elusive'.[7] The British therefore created their own around the artificial construct of the 'agriculturalist tribe.' Although this built on pre-existing social structures, it was a political definition enshrined in the 1900 Alienation of Land Act. This measure not only 'crystallized the assumptions underlying the British Imperial administration' but 'translated' them into popular politics. Henceforth, both the justification of British rule and the programme of the leading men of the 'tribes' and clans who banded together eventually in the Unionist Party was the 'uplift' and 'protection' of the 'backward' agriculturalist tribes.

The British co-opted the 'natural leaders' of rural society into their administrative system by means of the semi-official post of the zaildar. This was unique to the Punjab's local administration. The zaildar was responsible for a circle of villages, on the one hand supervising their headmen and aiding the implementation of government policy, on the other representing their interests to the colonial administration. This mediatory role was highly prized. It was endowed both as a reward for loyalty and as a recognition of local power. In the central and eastern districts where agrarian society was 'flatter', the possession of a zaildarship created rather than reflected local influence. Subordinate to it but serving a similar purpose was the post of sufedposh. 'Tribal' chiefs and landowners were also tied to the administrative system by being made honorary magistrates and members of the darbar. Khizr loyally performed these roles in the Kalra ilaqa throughout most of the inter-war period, during Umar's absences in New Delhi and London.

Posts were also reserved for agriculturalists in the official ranks of the local administration. Sir Michael O'Dwyer's governorship witnessed an especially sharp increase in the agriculturalist tribes' representation in the public services. In the Irrigation Branch of the Public Works Department this rocketed from 29 to 66 per cent of the officials.[8] Such reservation strengthened 'tribal' as against 'communal' identity.

The Pax Britannica encouraged the commercialisation of agriculture. The British also vastly extended irrigation facilities and slashed transport costs. The West Punjab underwent an agricultural revolution as arid subsistence production was replaced by the commercialised production of huge amounts of wheat, cotton and sugar.

The Shahpur district stood at the forefront of this transformation. The Lower Jhelum Canal converted the waste of the Kirana bar into first class irrigated land. This was parcelled out into 337 colony villages or 'chaks'. New market towns came into existence where the agriculturalists brought their commercial crops. These were linked by rail to Sargodha from where 500,000 tonnes of wheat were being annually despatched to Karachi[9] by the 1920s. At this date the Punjab produced a tenth of British India's total cotton crop and a third of its wheat. The region had thus emerged as the pace-setter of the subcontinent's agricultural development well before independence. At the most conservative estimate, per capita output of all crops had increased by nearly 45 per cent between 1891 and 1921.[10]

The Lower Jhelum was just one of the Punjab's nine Canal Colony areas. These transformed the endless waste and scrub of the Jhang,

The Unionist Party

Lyallpur and Shahpur districts into flourishing agricultural regions. The Lyallpur district which had been only sparsely populated by nomadic herdsmen possessed a million inhabitants within thirty years of the opening of the Chenab Canal in the 1880s. Three and a half million rupees worth of crops were annually produced from its Lower Chenab Canal Colony. The whole area was neatly laid out into plots of land known as squares, with market places, towns and villages spaced along the roads and railways which criss-crossed the Colony. By thus 'creating villages of a type superior in civilisation to anything which the region had previously experienced'[11] the British hoped to establish a model for the Punjab's development.

The Canal Colonies were also intended to mop up surplus population from the crowded districts of the central Punjab. Large numbers of Sikh Jats migrated to the Lower Chenab Canal Colony where they eventually owned a third of the land. In all, a million Punjabis moved to the nine Canal Colonies. They not only relieved congestion but formed a market for the produce of other regions, as the colonists specialised in cultivating a narrow range of cash crops. Furthermore, they remitted much of their income to their home villages.

The Canal Colonies' creation coincided with the Punjab's emergence as the sword arm of India. Indeed enlistment was encouraged by the British policy of rewarding ex-servicemen with lucrative grants of land in the Canal Colonies. Much land in the Lower Bari Doab Canal Colony was set aside for this purpose.[12] The vast increase in productive land also enabled the British to earmark large areas for breeding horses and cattle for the Indian Army. During the First World War, the Lyallpur Canal Colony provided huge amounts of wheat and flour for the troops and gifts of horses and mules were made to the Army.[13] The Shahpur District was, however the main area for Army horse breeding. In all 200,000 acres within it were leased for this purpose.[14]

The Tiwanas were heavily engaged in this activity. We have already noted the famed Kalra stud[15] which was visited by Lord Hardinge when he was Viceroy, as well as by Lord Arthur Cecil and General Lock Elliot during the deliberations of the Royal Horse Breeding Commission. Umar also established a stud farm for army remounts in the Jhelum Canal Colony where he took up 80 squares of land on horse-breeding terms.[16] Some of the best specimens of horse flesh in the whole of the Punjab were bred there. Broodmares were frequently imported from as far afield as England and Australia for bloodstock purposes. For in addition to converting to dairying, the Khizrabad farm concentrated on race horse breeding, when tanks replaced horses in the cavalry regiments of the Indian Army.

Although the bulk of the land in the Canal Colonies was sold to peasant proprietors, the Punjab Government reserved areas to reward both the' martial castes' and the 'landed gentry.' At the end of the First World War over 420,000 acres of Colony land were distributed to just 6,000 Commissioned and Non-Commissioned Army Officers.[17] Under the terms of the 'landed gentry status' seven and a half per cent of the Lower Bari Doab Canal Colony alone was earmarked for the landowning elite.[18] It is important to note that such land was amongst the best in the whole of the subcontinent and was highly valued. As late as 1925 the demand for, admittedly inferior, land in the Lower Bari Doab Canal Colony was so great that the only place large enough to accommodate the hordes of bidders at auction time was the Montgomery Race Course.

The Tiwanas like other Punjab chiefs shared in this bonanza. When Umar was a minor, about 90 squares of land in the Chenab Colony was purchased on his behalf at an action. The main village was called Umarpur. The Government also gave him 43 squares on **nazrana** terms during his minority.[19]

British rule, however, also swept away the barriers which had previously prevented moneylenders from acquiring land in the countryside. As land prices rose – the result of the Pax Britannica, as well as improved communications and irrigation – it became increasingly tempting for landowners to pledge land in return for easy credit. Moneylenders supported by a westernised legal system foreclosed mortgages on the lands of agriculturalist debtors. In other parts of India, most notably Bengal, following the Permanent Settlement of 1793, land had changed hands dramatically in this way. A similar process in the Punjab, however, would threaten political stability in a region of immense importance to wider Imperial interests. Furthermore, it would strike at the heart of its administration's strongly held assumptions and beliefs.

S.S. Thorburn in his book, *Mussulmans and Moneylenders in the Punjab* sounded the tocsin. Thorburn, a Deputy Commissioner in the Dera Ghazi Khan district highlighted the alarming rate at which land was being alienated to moneylenders.

The large Muslim landlords of the trans-Indus districts were not, however the moneylenders' only victims. The Hindu Rajputs of the submontane districts of Ambala Division also suffered at the hands

The Unionist Party

of powerful moneylenders who, 'exact free services and free fuel, fodder and ghi and (take their) dues as much in grain as in cash.'[20] The Hindu Jat cultivators of the agriculturally poor Rohtak district also suffered from the moneylenders' exploitation. Their subservience was vividly illustrated in village meetings where the moneylender sat in place of honour at the head of the **charpoy** with his peasant clients at his feet.

The British first attempted to solve this problem with piecemeal measures. They took a large number of encumbered estates under the wing of the Court of Wards Administration. It soon became apparent, however, that more sweeping action was required. After a sharp internal debate concerning the virtues of intervention against sticking to laissez-faire principles, the Punjab Government implemented the 1900 Alienation of Land Act. It barred the transfer of land from agriculturalist to non-agriculturalist tribes. The former were designated by name in each district. They included not only the Rajput martial caste landowners and Jat, Arain and Gujar cultivators, but the Muslim religious elites – the Syeds, Sheikhs and Qureshis. The measure not only halted their expropriation by the non-agriculturalist commercial castes of Khatris and Banias, but also provided the framework for the structuring of politics around the idiom of the' tribe', rather than of religious community. The Unionist Party's agriculturalist ideology was directly rooted in this legislation.

The maintenance of the safeguards provided by the Alienation of Land Act became a shibboleth with the rural elite. 'I am emphatically of the opinion that no act has done or is calculated to do more good to the agricultural community of the Punjab than the Land Alienation Act', Umar, for example declared in February 1907 during the course of a speech to the Punjab Legislative Council. 'It was at the outset feared by a few that the act would not work successfully and that it would end in nothing but the inconvenient contraction of the zemindar's credit. But time has shown that they were imaginery fears only. The object of the act was to avert the seriously large transfers of land from the classes who were hereditary owners to the moneylenders. And that object has been splendidly attained.'[21]

By the beginning of the 1930s, however, the 'Magna Carta' of the agriculturalist tribes was shot through with loopholes. Moneylenders used such devices as the **benami**[22] transaction to acquire land, to a background of mounting indebtedness brought on by the dramatic falls in the price of cash crops. This was grist to the mill of Mian Fazl-i-Husain and Chhotu Ram who were engaged in the tricky task of welding the loose Unionist grouping into a modern party. The growing animosity towards the moneylenders in all rural communities provided them with an obvious political platform. The extension of the safeguards provided by the original 1900 Legislation became their 'big idea.'

The British had in fact earlier prepared the ground for a rural domination of Punjab politics. They introduced a 'tribal' idiom in representative politics by ensuring that zails constituted the constituencies for election to the district boards. Zails or circles of up to 50 villages were administrative units which had been carved out to coincide as far as possible with the prevailing tribal settlement patterns.[23] When from 1919 onwards wider constituencies were established, it was of course impossible to obtain a perfect fit between them and tribal blocks of land. Nevertheless, the British ensured that during the period of dyarchy, political power in the countryside remained the prerogative of the leading landowners. Only members of the agriculturalist tribes, as defined by the 1900 Alienation of Land Act were allowed to stand as candidates for the rural constituencies of the new Legislative Council created by the Montagu-Chelmsford Reforms.[24] The institutionalisation of the political divisions between the rural and urban populations was thus completed.

The 1935 Government of India Act increased the franchise, but at the same time it introduced a greater number of rural constituencies which were geographically narrower than under the system of dyarchy. Their boundaries were drawn to coincide with tehsils which contained consolidated 'tribal' groupings. British administrative decisions had thus created a favourable environment for the predominance of rural interests which were committed to 'tribal' rather than religious identification in politics.

iii

The Unionist Government which Khizr entered in 1937 also bore the imprint of the party's founders Chhotu Ram and Mian Fazl-i-Husain. Whilst both men had been firm political allies, they represented two distinctive strands of Unionism. Chhotu Ram stood for a ruralist populism which unified agriculturalists around hostility to the moneylender 'other.' Fazl-i-Husain represented a more 'communalist' outlook which saw the Unionist Party as a vehicle for measures which primarily benefitted the Muslims. The Chhotu

The Unionist Party

Ram' strand' ultimately foundered because it failed to institutionalise populist urges. Whilst the Fazl-i-Husain 'strand' increasingly contradicted the Unionist Party's cross-communal support base. Khizr's Premiership was engrossed in attempts to reconcile these Unionist traditions. It is therefore important to examine them in some depth.

Chhotu Ram unlike his Muslim Unionist colleagues came from a peasant background. His father, Chaudhri Sukhi Ram was a poor proprietor from the obscure village of Garhi Sampla. His education depended on scholarships and the support from a wealthy benefactor, Seth Sir Chhaju Ram of Alakhpura. By the time Chhotu Ram had finished his studies at Lahore, Delhi and Allahabad, he headed the new generation of educated Jat leaders which had emerged during the early years of the twentieth century. They shared the commitment to secure the 'uplift' of their people.

The Hindu Jats of the Ambala division suffered under the twin burdens of indebtedness and famine. They, in fact inhabited some of the poorest agricultural tracts in the Punjab including the notorious famine area of Hissar. The Jats' fortunes improved in their Rohtak heartland when the British introduced irrigation and the cooperative movement into the region. It was here that Chhotu Ram commenced legal practice in 1912. The following year he organised the opening of an Anglo-Sanskrit Jat High School. He also encouraged Jat enlistment in the Indian Army during the First World War because he realised the benefits this would bring. An immediate spin-off was Michael O'Dwyer's decision in 1915 to recommend the heads of all Government departments to increase the number of Jats in their employment.[25] In the longer term this involvement with military recruitment forged a bond between him and Khizr. Despite their vastly different backgrounds and personalities they were to become close political friends.

Chhotu Ram stood head and shoulders above the Muslim Unionists as a public speaker. He addressed crowds of peasants for hours on end without the use of a microphone. His slow delivery captured the directness and simplicity of the Punjabi language. His violent and sometimes lewd diatribes against the moneylenders was also quintessentially Punjabi. He dubbed the moneylenders black banias and termed them blood-suckers. A popular song at his meetings was:

Zamindar ziada jan de aik baat mann lai, Aik bolana lai seekh, aik dushman pehchan lai.[26]

59

Zamindar forget about other things but accept my one advice,
Learn to express yourself and recognise your enemy.

As a result of his friendship with Ahmad Yar Khan Daultana he also cultivated an interest in Iqbal's poetry and would quote such couplets as, 'Khuda ke bande to hain hazaroon, banno mein phirte marre marre, Main uska banda banoonga jisko khuda, ke bandoon se pyar hoga.' (Thousands of God's worshippers wander in the jungles. I shall worship him who loves God's children.)[27] Chhotu Ram's oratory provided a populist appeal for the Unionist Party.

Mian Fazl-i-Husain was a Lahore-based politician whose became prominence rested on a successful legal practice begun in Sialkot in 1901 and involvement in the **Anjuman-i-Himayat-i-Islam**. He belonged to the Bhatti Rajput family of Batala in the Gurdaspur district. He had first entered the Legislative Council as a member for the Punjab University constituency -not the background from which one would imagine the successful leader of a rural political party would emerge. But his political acumen and influence[28] were so great that the Muslim landowners turned to him for guidance.

Mian Fazl-i-Husain possessed no personal communal bias. But he realised that Muslim interests could be better served through the Unionist Party than by adopting a purely Muslim political platform. Iqbal, who was a member of the Punjab Legislative Council from 1927 to 1930, along with other urbanite Muslim members of the Unionist Party shared this view.[29] It was possible at this time for such Punjabi Unionists as Iqbal and Sir Abdul Qadir to simultaneously play leading roles in the Muslim League organisation.[30]

Mian Fazl-i-Husain was as alert as Chhotu Ram to the benefits of securing government patronage to improve the position of the landowners, especially as the Muslims constituted the overwhelming majority of the rural population. His introduction of communal quotas for admission to Government College Lahore and Lahore Medical College (40% Muslim 40% Hindu 20% Sikh) created a storm. This reached its peak when Raja Narendra Nath, the Hindu Mahasabha leader, introduced a censure motion in the Council in which he dubbed the Muslim Minister the 'Aurangzeb' of the Punjab.

Mian Fazl-i-Husain moreover, was well aware that the Punjab's political arithmetic necessitated cross-communal co-operation as no single community could command an absolute majority.[31] The reformed Punjab Legislative Council comprised 23 official and nominated members and 71 elected, of whom 35 were Muslims, 15

The Unionist Party

Sikhs and 21 Hindus and others.[32] Furthermore, he recognised that the Unionist platform in the Punjab could form a useful base from which to speak for the Muslim provinces of India in All-India politics.

In 1930, Mian Fazl-i-Husain left the Punjab to join the Viceroy's executive council. His absence weakened the cohesion of the Unionist grouping. This short term loss, however, was far outweighed by Fazl-i-Husain's ability to argue the case of the Unionist dominated All-India Muslim Conference in constitutional discussions. The 1935 Government of India Act, and the Communal Award which had preceded it, reflected Fazl-i-Husain's powerful influence.

Landowners accounted for over 60 per cent of the Punjab's restricted electorate. This stood at just over of two and a quarter million voters, just 1 in ten Punjabis.[33] Moreover, non-agriculturalists were still disallowed from contesting rural constituencies. This resulted in men committed to the imperial connection dominating every government which was elected in the new era of provincial autonomy.

iv

Mian Fazl-i-Husain, however faced a number of difficulties when he returned to Punjabi politics at the end of March 1935. Rumours circulated that Sikander Hayat Khan was about to challenge his leadership. Sikander was a member of the Khattar landlord family of Wah in the Attock district. He had first entered the Punjab Council in 1921. Despite factional rivalry with the Noons and Tiwanas, Sikander shared far more in common with them than Mian Fazl-i-Husain. Like them he was personally close to the British because of a family tradition of loyalty that dated back to 1857. Indeed he had earlier come into conflict with Fazl-i-Husain because he had agreed that a British Official should take his place as Revenue Minister, while he briefly officiated as Governor in 1932 and 1934.[34] Sikander received support not only from the Khattar faction, but other landowners who did not want the urbanite tail to wag the Unionist dog. Chhotu Ram, however, stuck with Fazl-i-Husain out of loyalty.

Fazl-i-Husain won the opening round of their tussle, when in 1935 he adroitly manouvred Sikander into the post of Deputy Governor of the Reserve bank of India, an appointment which would keep him well out of harm's way. Factional tensions within the Unionist Party, however continued unabated. Indeed, early in 1936 Sikander's allies,

Ahmad Yar Khan Daultana[35] and Mir Maqbool Mahmood[36] issued a statement proposing the formation of a new cross-communal party in the Punjab.

Fazl-i-Husain responded by issuing a call for the reorganisation of the Unionist party in February 1936 so that it would be in good shape to contest the forthcoming provincial elections. He rather inauspiciously relaunched the Party on 1 April 1936. The defence of the 1900 Alienation of Land Act again formed a major plank of the Party programme. Raja Narendra Nath in an address to a Non-agriculturalist conference in 1936 scathingly declared that the Land Alienation Act was to the Unionists, 'what the Vedas and the Holy Quran are to the Hindus and the Musalmans.'[37]

Mian Fazl-i-Husain also chalked out a scheme to form Unionist Party branches in the villages. Factional rivalries, however, hindered this task. The Unionist Party owed its eventual success in the 1937 Provincial Assembly elections once again to the local influence of its candidates, not to grassroots organisation. Fazl-i-Husain did, however, ensure that an open split was averted. Maqbool Mahmood, for example was given the important office of propaganda secretary.[38]

This show of unity was important, as Jinnah was beginning to fish in the Punjab's troubled waters. He journeyed to Lahore at the end of April and took tea at Mian Fazl-i-Husain's residence.[39] Jinnah failed to persuade his host to abandon the Unionist approach to politics and allow all the Muslim candidates to contest under the Muslim League banner. Fazl-i-Husain died before a second meeting could take place. But Sikander, who succeeded him as Unionist leader, continued to warn off the Muslim League. Jinnah's Punjab Parliamentary Board was thus limited to Iqbal and a few other urbanites and a faction of the Ittehad-i-Millat Party.[40] Mian Fazl-i-Husain's and later Sikander's reading of the situation proved correct. The Unionists' tried and trusted approach won them a resounding victory in the 1937 provincial elections. The Muslim League humiliatingly secured just a single seat.

Whilst Jinnah unsuccessfully attempted to call a new world into being to redress the balance of the old, Umar along with other landowners looked to provincial autonomy to consolidate their local power. Their sentiments were summed up by the Unionist Party manifesto which stated, 'For the first time under the British Rule, the Government of the Punjab is coming in the hands of Punjabees. Its success or failure will primarily rest with us.'[41] Umar could not spurn such a call to duty. He also realised that the Tiwana **maliks'**

The Unionist Party

traditional role as intermediaries between their tenants and Government demanded that they take up seats in the Provincial Assembly. It was inconceivable now that constituencies so closely mirrored 'tribal' blocks of land to allow 'outsiders' to represent the Tiwana villages. Umar thus prevailed upon his reluctant son to stand for office. Neither man could guess at the future repercussions of this decision for their family, or their province.

Notes

1 Its original title in 1923 was the Punjab National Unionist party.
2 For details see, I. Talbot, *Punjab and the Raj 1849–1947* (Delhi 1988) p. 50–3.
3 During the 1919 Rowlatt satyegraha both the Noons and Tiwanas provided contingents of horsemen to patrol the railway lines in their Shahpur district. Umar himself took charge of a long section of line. *Shahpur District War Effort* (Lahore n.d.,) p. 61.
4 C. Dewey, 'The Rural Roots of Pakistani Militarism' in D.A. Low (ed) *The Political Inheritance of Pakistan* (Basingstoke 1991) p. 264.
5 Talbot *op.cit.* p. 45.
6 D. Gilmartin, *op.cit.* p.18 & ff.
7 *Ibid.*, p. 29.
8 Punjab Legislative Council Debates, 12 March 1925 p. 408 & ff, V/9/3424 IOR.
9 *War Services of the Shahpur District* n.d. IOR Pos. 5545 p. 8.
10 N. Charlesworth, *British Rule and the Indian Economy 1800–1914* (London 1982) p. 26.
11 M.L. Darling, *The Punjab Peasantry in Prosperity and Debt* (New Delhi, 1977) p. 116.
12 Talbot *op.cit.*, p. 40.
13 G.F.D. Montmorency, *History of the War in the Lyallpur District* (Lahore, n.d.) p. 36 IOR Pos 5545.
14 Imran Ali forcibly argues that this represented a 'major division of economic resources towards an activity that could be of little benefit to agricultural development.'Imran Ali, *The Punjab Under Imperialism 1885–1947* (Princeton, 1988) p. 239.
15 At the time of the outbreak of the South African War in 1899, Umar offered all his Kalra stud of around 400 horses to the Imperial cause, although this was graciously declined.
16 *Nawab Sir Umar Hayat Khan Tiwana. The Man and His Word* (Lahore 1929) p. 560.
17 B. Josh, *Communist Movement in the Punjab 192–1947* (Delhi 1979) p. 25. This was of course in addition to their generous pensions. By 1928, over Rs. 140 lakhs were being annually paid out in pensions. There were 16,000 military pensioners in the Rawalpindi district alone.
18 F.C. Bourne, *Final Settlement Report of the Lower Bari Doab Canal Colony* (Lahore, 1935) p. 3.

Khizr Tiwana, the Punjab Unionist Party and the Partition of India

19 Nawab Sir Umar Hayat Khan *op.cit.* p. 560.
20 M. Darling, *Rusticus Loqitor* (Lahore, 1929) p. 74 & ff.
21 Nawab Sir Umar Hayat Khan *op.cit.*, p. 815.
22 Urban moneylenders acquired land in the countryside by a process which became known as the benami transaction. They appointed agents in the villages who were members of agriculturalist tribes and asked their debtors to transfer land in the name of the agent so that it never officially passed out of agriculturalist hands. The Unionist Ministry of Sikander introduced legislation in 1937 to close this loophole.
23 D. Gilmartin *op.cit.*, p. 20 & ff.
24 The Reforms' most notable feature was the introduction of dyarchy in which popularly elected Ministers were put in charge of the 'Transferred Departments'.
25 *War History of the Rohtak District* (Lahore n.d) IOR Pos 5547, p. 8.
26 Cited in P. Singh (ed) *Chhotu Ram in the eyes of his Contemporaries* (New Delhi 1992) p. 60.
27 *Ibid.*, p. 72.
28 During the years 1917–20 he was simultaneously General Secretary of the Punjab Muslim League and President of the Punjab Congress. He was also President of the High Court Bar Association and influential within the Punjab University.
29 The Unionist Party's founding charter had not excluded urban members although it included a pledge to uphold the Alienation of Land Act as a protection for the 'backward' classes.
30 Sir Abdul Qadir, for example, Presided over the 1926 Delhi Session of the All-Indian Muslim League, Iqbal was of course Secretary of the Muslim League, whilst serving as a Unionist member in the Punjab Council.
31 Under the terms of the 1916 Lucknow Pact the Muslims had sacrificed their majority position in the Punjab Legislature to secure weightage for the Muslim minority areas. Muslims formed 55 per cent of the Punjab's population.
32 The situation of no one community commanding an absolute majority continued under the terms of the 1935 Government of India Act which gave the Muslims 86 out of the 175 seats in the Provincial Assembly.
33 For further details see, Talbot *op.cit.*, p. 96.
34 Iftikhar Malik, *Sikander Hayat Khan A Political Biography* (Islamabad, 1985) p. 30.
35 He was a Rajput from the Mailsi area of the Multan district. He had been first elected to the Punjab Council in 1921.
36 Maqbool Mahmood was an urbanite who had entered the Punjab Council in 1923. He was a close relative of Sikander by marriage.
37 Gilmartin *op.cit.* p. 115.
38 Malik *op.cit.*, p. 40.
39 See, Syed Nur Ahmad, (C. Baxter ed.) *From Martial Law to Martial Law. Politics in the Punjab 1919–1958* (Boulder 1985) p. 140.
40 This group had sprung to prominence at the time of the 1935 Shahidgunj Mosque agitation. It had been organised by Maulana Zafar Ali Khan, but he resigned from the Muslim League Parliamentary Board in June.
41 Gilmartin *op.cit.*, p. 109.

Part Two

The Pinnacle of Power

Chapter Four

Apprentice to Power

Khizr stood for the Khushab constituency in the provincial elections held early in 1937. Umar did most of what passed for electioneering, calling on the landed families of Tiwanas and Noons for their support. Together, they owned 85,000 acres of land in the Khushab **tehsil**. Awans, however, formed the majority of the 20,000 voters. Their opportunity to flex their electoral muscle was scuppered when Khizr paid their leading representative Rs 10,000 to withdraw too late in the day for a substitute to file his nomination papers[1] by the 23 November deadline. By this means he was thus elected unopposed to the Assembly.

The other Shahpur seats were closely fought. In the Bahwal **tehsil**, Malik Sardar Khan Noon defeated the uneasy coalition of the Ranjha and Gondal[2] 'tribes' to secure election.[3] The fiercest struggle of all, however, raged in the Shahpur **tehsil** between Allah Bakhsh Khan Tiwana[4] and Nawab Muhammad Hyat Qureshi. Allah Bakhsh narrowly triumphed by 408 votes in a memorable contest.[5] His victory procession in Shahpur town was headed by an effigy of his opponent riding backwards on a donkey.[6]

The elections in the Tiwana heartland like those in other rural constituencies revolved around traditional factional rivalries, rather than modern party appeals and programmes. The Shahpur contest demonstrated this most clearly. The opposing candidates were in fact both affiliated to the Unionist Party. Indeed, Nawab Muhammad Hyat Qureshi had not only served as a Unionist in the Legislative Council from 1926–36, but had issued a pamphlet attacking opponents of the Alienation of Land Act.[7] It was 'tribal' rivalry not hostility to Unionism which had led him to enter the lists. Allah Bakhsh Tiwana triumphed because the Noon-Tiwana[8] faction rallied to his support rather than because of the efforts of local party workers. In the Shahpur district as elsewhere, Unionists swept the board. But the results masked how thin the veneer of Unionism was spread across the surface of rural political alliances which were articulated in terms of 'tribal' solidarity. Unionism at best legitimised local power, nowhere was it its fountain-head.

The Unionist Party's electioneering clearly revealed this reality. Whilst the Muslim League and Congress held mass rallies which were addressed by political heavy-weights such as Maulana Shaukat Ali, Vallabhbhai Patel, Sarat Chandra Bose and Nehru,[9] the Unionist Party adopted a low key approach. Jinnah smelt a rat. 'Why', he asked a rally in Lahore, 'do the Unionist leaders not come out to the people to seek their suffrage? Why do they not address public meetings?' The answer he gave was that, 'the Unionists believe that the officials of the Government (are) working for them in the districts and villages.'[10] It was, however, not the bureaucracy, but the 'natural' leadership of the rural elite which was working quietly in the Unionist Party's favour. 'Tribal' solidarity, decided the outcome in many rural constituencies.

The Unionist leadership had also approached the **pirs** for support.[11] They controlled many votes through their networks of devoted **murids**. **Pirs** from the older established shrines were tied into the rural hierarchy through the large landholdings attached to their shrines and intermarriage with their Rajput disciples. Their alliances with the 'tribal' chiefs were also strengthened by the 1900 Alienation of Land Act. The **pirs**' support provided a religious legitimisation which countered the identification with Islam of the urban 'communal' parties.'Villagers, you know, follow these "Pirs" blindly', the Gurdaspur Unionist organiser observed in May 1936, 'Take care of the "Pirs". Ask them only to keep silent on the matter of the elections. We don't require their help but they should not oppose us.'[12] In the event, Pir Fazl Shah of Jalalpur was the only leading **pir** to oppose the Unionists. He used his immense religious influence in the Jhelum district to support his uncle, Raja Ghazanfar Ali Khan who stood on the Muslim League ticket. He subsequently switched allegiance when Sikander offered him a parliamentary secretaryship.

Many independent candidates also joined the Unionist Party after the results were declared. At the final count, the Unionist Party claimed the allegiance of 99 out of the 175 Assembly members. Its greatest strength lay in the rural Muslim constituencies in which it commanded 73 out of the 75 seats. In the towns, however, where

Apprentice to Power

social and economic influence was less crucial, it had won just 1 of the 9 Muslim seats. The Unionist Party demonstrated its Hindu Jat support by capturing all but one of the general rural (ie. Hindu) seats in the Ambala division.

The leading landowners thus still retained the levers of power in the new era of provincial autonomy. The Congress and Muslim League between them had managed just 19 seats. The Punjab appeared immune from the Congress tide which had swept away landlord parties elsewhere in India, whilst the Muslim League had suffered a humiliating setback in a major centre of Muslim population. Sikander and Chhotu Ram were, however, both well aware that the Unionist Party's success had depended largely on the standing of its local 'candidates'[13] and that only a third of those enfranchised had actually voted. They therefore sought to widen the Unionists' support by both establishing a local Zamindara League organisation and introducing a programme of agrarian reform. The most pressing task, however, was ministry formation.

i

The new ministry which was sworn in on 1 April 1937 bore many of the hallmarks of what theorists of consociational democracy would call a 'grand coalition.'[14] Sikander accommodated all communities within his cabinet. Its non-Muslim members were drawn both from the Unionist ranks (Chhotu Ram) and from its coalition partners, the Khalsa Party (Sunder Singh Majithia[15]) and the National Progressive Party (Manohar Lal). Moreover, the Premier only appointed Hindus and Sikhs after sounding out their respective communities. This approach contrasted dramatically with the Congress' behaviour in the seven provinces which it controlled.[16] The Government accounted for 120 out of the 175 Assembly members drawn from all of the region's communities.[17]

Sikander not only carefully balanced the communal composition of his Cabinet, but its Muslim factional representation. He thus needed to include a member from the Noon-Tiwana group from Shahpur. Khizr on paper hardly appeared the favourite as he was its most junior and politically inexperienced member. Umar, however, lent his considerable influence to his son's advancement.

Umar had been friendly with Sikander's father, Nawab Muhammad Hayat Khan who had died in 1901. In fact he had exchanged turbans with him.[18] Sikander thus could not easily ignore his advice, especially after Umar persuaded Allah Bakhsh Tiwana to step aside. Allah Bakhsh would have been a good catch for Sikander with his administrative experience as an Extra-Assistant Commissioner and service on the Imperial Council in New Delhi from 1931 onwards. Sardar Khan Noon's poor command of English ruled him out as a serious contender. Khizr was accordingly elevated into the Cabinet, as Minister of Public Works and Local Self Government. Sikander's and Khizr's paths had scarcely crossed until this time. Khizr lacked the Premier's administrative experience and social sophistication, but they were to draw closer in office.

Khizr was a political novice. He lacked public speaking skills and administrative experience. Not that the former was too great a handicap in an Assembly which Malcolm Darling likened to 'the babel of coolies at the station when the mail train arrives.'[19] Khizr became a Minister not through his own abilities, but because of Umar's reputation and the family's social and political importance in the Shahpur district. But despite this unpromising background, he became a valued member of the government who not only ran his own department well, but took on wider tasks. Sikander, for example gave him in the strictest confidence, charge of the home portfolio dealing with the police and law and order. He thus handled the relationship between the Unionists and the Khaksar movement of Allama Mashriqi early in 1940.[20] Khizr was also responsible for the security arrangements for the historic Muslim League Session which took place amidst considerable tension in Lahore, shortly afterwards. With the outbreak of the Second World War, Khizr had also taken charge of the Manpower Committee of the Punjab War Board and the Civil Defence Departments.

Chhotu Ram in a private letter written shortly after Khizr became Premier looked back favourably on his earlier career. 'Khizr as Minister', he declared to Mian Fazl-i-Husain's son Azim, 'displayed unmistakable signs of courage, strength and independence.'[21] Sir Bertrand Glancy also confidentially praised Khizr's Ministerial performance. 'Khizr Hayat Khan Tiwana has considerable capacity and much determination and forcefulness', the Punjab Governor noted on 8 July 1941. 'He takes a keen and effective interest in the Departments entrusted to his charge. Coming as he does from a great landholding family he has little sympathy for townsmen and traders. His outlook on life is largely baronial, and he is apt to be intolerant and to indulge at times in sabre-rattling. Still he pulls his weight in the team and is a distinctly valuable member of the Cabinet. His value

Apprentice to Power

should increase with age and experience.'[22] Glancy was scathing in his assessment of some of Khizr's colleagues. He once described Mian Abdul Haye as scarcely a 'very satisfactory member of the team', while Sardar Dasaundha Singh[23] was dismissed as of 'negligible assistance'. 'His intentions are good, but his mental calibre is regrettably low.'[24]

ii

Sikander sought to establish a network of Unionist branches which would create a locus of power independent of the rural notables. The trick was to work through them to found an organisation which might later be used to thwack them into line. The task proved beyond him, although a beginning was made in October 1937. The invitation to hold a Zemindara League meeting at Mamdot Villa, Lahore was in fact issued over the signature of Allah Bakhsh Tiwana. About two hundred leading landowners attended. Umar was voted unanimously to the Chair. Khizr also attended in his capacity as a Minister and was voted on to the sub-committee which was empowered to give effect to the resolution calling for the establishment of a Zemindara League 'with branches throughout the province for the protection of the rights and interests of all owners of land, peasant, proprietors and tenants in the province'.[25]

A patchy organisation was established during 1937–8. This was significantly strongest in the East Punjab where Chhotu Ram's populist style won support from the Jat peasant proprietors. The lack of progress elsewhere was a costly failure. A great opportunity had been lost to institutionalise the popular support aroused by the Ministry's agrarian programme.

Early in 1937, Sikander launched a six year programme of rural improvement which set aside money for the establishment of schools, medical centres, model farms and improved drainage and sanitation. The Ministry also passed a number of measures to fulfil its promise of 'lightening the burden of the peasantry.. and uplifting the backward classes'. Debt Conciliation Boards were established in all the districts which scaled down agriculturalists' debts from Rs. 4 crores to Rs 1.5 crores. The Ministry also issued a notification under Section 61 of the Civil Procedure Code which exempted the whole of the fodder crop of an agriculturalist debtor and a proportion of the yield of his grain crop from attachment in the execution of civil decrees.[26]

Khizr Tiwana, the Punjab Unionist Party and the Partition of India

The agrarian programme's centrepiece was provided by the laws introduced during the 1938 summer session of the Punjab Assembly. As land reform was unpalatable to the Unionist Party's elite supporters, Chhotu Ram was again given his head in pursuing the moneylenders and traders.[27]

The Registration of Moneylenders Act provided that a moneylender would not be assisted by the Law Courts to recover his loans unless he was licensed. His licence could be suspended if he was suspected of malpractice during which time he would be unable to sue for the recovery of his loans without the express permission of the Deputy Commissioner of his District. The Punjab Alienation of Land Second Amendment Act closed the loophole created by the **benami** transaction. Under this the moneylenders had appointed agents in the villages who were the members of statutory agriculturalist tribes, and required their debtors to transfer their land in the name of the agent, so that it never legally passed out of agriculturalist hands. The Amendment not only closed the loophole in the 1900 Legislation, but rendered void all previous **benami** transactions. The Restitution of Mortgaged Lands Act was another retrospective piece of Unionist legislation. Sunder Singh Majithia introduced the measure in the Assembly in June 1938. It enabled farmers to recover all the land which they had mortgaged before the passage of the 1900 Alienation of Land Act. The Hindu and Sikh moneylenders claimed that it was merely a cover for the expropriation of their land. They wanted it to cover transactions involving the agriculturalist moneylending class which had grown up after 1900. This demand was of course rejected. The upshot was that over 200,000 Hindus and Sikhs had to return an estimated 700,000 acres to its original owners.[28]

Chhotu Ram held a conference at Lyallpur early in September 1938 in which more than 150,000 agriculturalists demonstrated their support for these 'Golden Acts.[29]' Khizr arrived with Sikander and the other Ministers by train from Lahore on the evening of 3 September. The crowded station was decorated with Union Jacks and bunting.[30] The conference opened shortly afterwards in a huge **pandal** which had been erected on the Dusehra grounds. Khizr took his seat on the platform, but this was very much Chhotu Ram's and Sikander's show. They launched into a spirited defence of the 'Golden Acts' before an audience of Hindu, Muslim and Sikh Jats which was nearly suffocating with the heat, despite the constant whirring of 200 electric fans.[31]

Chhotu Ram addressed such gatherings clad in the attire of a

72

Apprentice to Power

village elder, carrying a knobbed stick and wearing a turban in his favourite white or parrot green colours. He insisted that only simple fare was provided for the guests and always preferred milk to be served rather than tea as this was the' real food' of the Jat.[32] He berated a speaker at a rally in Sonepat when he began to speak of religion before a mixed audience, declaring that this was no place to do so, thus reemphasising the Unionionist Party's secular outlook.[33]

In the Muslim minority district of Amritsar alone over 100 meetings were held at this time.[34] The Government had no need to bus in the throngs of farmers which attended these meetings for they came out of genuine enthusiasm.

The 'Golden Acts' smashed the Congress's hope of winning mass support in the villages, as they raised again the dilemma which had dogged its Punjab branch ever since the passage of the 1900 Alienation of Land Act, namely how to gain influence in the coutryside without alienating its wealthy moneylender benefactors. The Congress's evasions regarding the 'Golden Acts' further undermined its support in the towns, whilst in the villages it alienated the Hindu and Sikh cultivators.[35] At the Assembly level, the issue intensified the Congress's factional rivalry, whilst support for the reforms had, in the words of the Governor, 'the effect of pulling the Unionist Party together.'[36] The Congress song's attack on the Zamindari Ministers appeared increasingly forlorn:

> Utho naujawano zamana badal do Chhotu, Sikander, Tiwana badal do.Badal do Majithia, Joginder badal do Manohar, Haye, Daultana badal do.

> Arise youngmen! Change the world remove Chhotu, Sikander, Tiwana,remove also Majithia, Joginder,Manohar, Haye, Daultana.[37]

The Muslim League was similarly powerless. Malik Barkat Ali soldiered along as its sole Assembly member. Efforts to launch a vigorous propaganda campaign in the rural areas were blown off course both by the popularity of the 'Golden Acts' and its national organisation's dependency on the Unionists. This lasted until the outbreak of the Second World War strengthened Jinnah's position. From October 1937 onwards, Sikander had exacted a high price for his propping up Jinnah at the Centre. This was nothing less than the complete subordination of the Muslim League within the Punjab.

A Pact had been concluded between Sikander and Jinnah at the historic Lucknow Session of the All-India Muslim League. Its conflicting interpretations later caused much trouble between Khizr and Jinnah. In the late 1930s the Unionists, however held all the cards. Jinnah, therefore did not challenge their view that whilst Muslim Unionists could join the Muslim League, this was not to affect the continuation of the existing coalition Ministry in the Punjab. This would still be called the Unionist Party. In return for the Punjabi Muslims much needed support in All-India politics, Jinnah acquiesced in a virtual take-over of the province's Muslim League by Sikander and his supporters.

The 'old' Punjab League was tendentiously dissolved on the grounds that its constitution was irregular. Less than a month before Iqbal's death, an Organising Committee was formed under Sikander's Chairmanship with the task of creating a new Punjab League. After much procrastination and protest from League loyalists a new organisation was established in November 1939. Three more months passed before its first meeting was held under Sikander's chairmanship at his Lahore residence. The outcome predictably resulted in its domination by his supporters. A number of district officials resigned in disgust. A sufficient head of steam was built up to force a reluctant Jinnah to launch an enquiry. After an almost embarrassingly short stay in the province, the investigating committee gave Sikander's brainchild its imprimatur. This decision was a tremendous triumph for the Punjab Premier. It marked the zenith of the Unionist Party's power within the Punjab. Its two main rivals, the Congress and the Muslim League were now both impotent. Sikander's greatest influence in All-India Muslim politics came some five months later when he presided over the Sholapur Session of the Muslim League. The outbreak of the Second World War, however transformed the political scene. Sikander's hard won ascendancy was increasingly undermined.

iii

Khizr's department modestly contributed to the Sikander Cabinet's agrarian programme. Khizr oversaw a reform of the panchayat system. Panchayats were first established under British aegis in 1912. Further legislation in 1921 gave them a range of compulsory and optional functions. Restrictions on their powers and lengthy notification procedures, however resulted in the fact that by 1939 there were still only 1,142 panchayats for a total number of 36,000

Apprentice to Power

villages in the Punjab.[38] Khizr's task was to address this situation. He saw it in terms of the need of the peasant to have an 'increasing share in the political life of the country.' 'There is no better method of educating him', Khizr wrote in November 1941, 'and making him familiar with democratic institutions than through the Panchayat. The whole aim of the recent legislation ... has been to achieve this.'[39]

Abdul Haque who was on deputation from the Provincial Civil Service drafted the panchayat legislation. Khizr invited Chhotu Ram to attend the final discussion on the draft rules. The Jat leader's intervention ensured that the powers of Deputy Commissioners in relation to the Act were cut back.[40] Khizr next successfully guided the Punjab Village Panchayat Bill through the Assembly. On 28 October 1939, he finally presented to the House the Select Committee's report on the Bill. The ensuing Act streamlined the procedure for the establishment of panchayats. It also extended their administrative, fiscal and judicial powers. Optional functions under the 1921 Legislation were made compulsory. Magistrates were, moreover, prohibited from taking cognisance of offences triable by panchayats. They could now try civil suits to the value of Rs 200 and enjoyed enhanced powers for compelling both the attendance of witnesses and the production of relevant documents.[41]

The working of the new Act fulfilled Khizr's hopes. Within three years, the number of panchayats had increased from 1,142 to 6,978. During 1941 alone, they tried just under 50,000 criminal suits and civil cases, saving a vast sum of money which would ordinairly have been expended on litigation. Local panchayat officers provided village level education and organised games and tournaments. By the time Khizr had become Premier a start had been made in the provision of rural libraries. Twenty nine had in fact been opened in selected areas. Apart from providing education, in keeping with his own and the Cabinet's outlook, the libraries acted as centres for promoting communal harmony.[42]

Azim Husain, Mian Fazl-i-Husain's son served as Director of Panchayats, a department within the Ministry of Local Self-Government from 194–2.[43] He was thus well placed to comment on Khizr's performance as a Minister at this time. His outstanding characteristics were recalled as being his 'total confidence' and 'great sense of responsibility in running his departments' and his 'total personal integrity in financial matters.' This arose from the fact that like his father, Khizr saw public service as an opportunity to do good

75

Khizr Tiwana, the Punjab Unionist Party and the Partition of India

to people, not for personal financial gain. Indeed according to Azim Husain, he spent more on life style as a Minister/Premier and on entertainment than he received as a Government salary.[44]

Khizr valued Azim Husain's professional expertise. When he became Premier, he wanted him to return to Lahore from his job in New Delhi as an Under Secretary in the Ministry of Defence. Khizr's mounting problems with the Muslim League increased this desire. Chhotu Ram wrote on his behalf to New Delhi on a number of occasions.[45] Azim Husain was, however, reluctant to abandon a promising career at the Centre in order to return to Lahore. He had by this juncture risen to the post of Deputy Secretary in the Ministry of Information and Broadcasting. He nevertheless, provided informal advice on political issues and drafted public statements throughout Khizr's Premiership. Indeed, Azim Husain was present in Lahore on the day Khizr finally tendered his resignation.[46]

Khizr's Ministership coincided with the Public Works Department's completion of the Assembly Chamber in Lahore with its adjoining civic centre. The Fazl-i-Husain Library of Government College was also added at this time. The essential but less prestigious Lahore Sewage Scheme, the first of its kind in the province was also commenced during this period.[47] Khizr in addition saw through further improvements to the Punjab's infrastructure and irrigation networks. By the end of March 1942, the length of metalled roads had risen to 4,200 miles. It was during Khizr's period as Minister that modern surfaced roads were laid in the Salt range.

Khizr also pressed for improved irrigation facilities in his home region. The Thal project was commenced in May 1939 to provide perennial irrigation for 10 **lakhs** of acres in the Mianwali, Muzaffaragarh and Shahpur districts. War shortages led to a suspension of the project. But the Khushab branch work went ahead in connection with the Government of India's 'Grow More Food campaign' which Khizr vigorously supported as part of the Punjab's war effort.[48] Whilst careful to avoid the politics of personal favours, Khizr thus clearly used his patronage as a Minister to advance the interests of his region and its communities. He also more slowly mastered the skill of public speaking. His early performances in the Assembly were halting and diffident. With time he was to become a competent, although by no means compelling contributor to debate.

Khizr steadfastly supported the Ministry's wider pro-agriculturalist policies. He knew all too well of the problems of indebtedness in his native Shahpur region. Indeed looking back over the years when

76

Apprentice to Power

he wrote a fragment of his memoirs in the 1960s, he still spoke warmly of the Alienation of Land Act. It saved' the Muslim landholder', he wrote, 'and peasant proprietor who formed the backbone of the Muslim community in the Punjab, from becoming hewers of wood and drawers of water under the Hindu money-lenders.'[49]

Khizr also warmly sympathesised with the endeavours to promote communal harmony. Sikander had convened a 'Unity Conference' of the leaders of the different communities in Simla in July 1937. A special fund had later been instituted along with a Board of official and non-official representatives. The first of March was declared Communal Harmony day and was marked by an annual public holiday. During Khizr's Premiership, a Communal Harmony Committee was established in Lahore. Its President was Raja Narendra Nath and its Secretary Maulvi Mahomed Ilyas, the agent of the Bahawalpur State.[50] Khizr himself served as President of the Provincial Communal harmony Movement. On one occasion he reputedly retorted to Jinnah, 'There are Hindu and Sikh Tiwanas who are my relatives. I go to their weddings and other ceremonies. How can I possibly regard them as coming from another nation.'[51]

iv

Political importance if not greatness had been thrust upon him, yet Khizr remained largely unaltered by it. Whilst he eventually grew to like the trappings of power, politics still occupied only part of his life. He remained the dutiful son and returned to Kalra whenever he could. To compensate for the loss of its reassuring surroundings, he so to speak projected Kalra outwards, so that some at least of its patterns and practices of life were taken up in the provincial capital of Lahore.

Khizr initially lived at 'Al-Shams' 22, Queens Road. This property belonged to Nawab Allah Bakhsh Tiwana. The family residence at 21 Beadon Road which Umar had built prior to the outbreak of the First World War was occupied by his first wife, Sultan Bibi, her mother and Khizr's eldest son Nazar. Umar was living at Kalra throughout this period, although he met with Khizr around once a month either there or in Lahore. Khizr bought and renovated an old Lahore Cantonment House at 47 Wellington Mall and resided there for a time in 1942, but his official home remained 22 Queen's Road. The building teemed with servants, especially after he became

77

Premier. For in addition to his official staff, he brought around twenty family retainers from Kalra, including chowkidars from the so-called 'Kalra sepoy' force. Muhammad Ali, Khizr's valet who had left Kalra in the early 1930s also returned to service after he had become a Minister. He henceforth accompanied his master on trips abroad, when he also stood in as a cook. Muhammad Ali acted as an 'unofficial' Indian representative to the Paris Peace Conference of July 1946.[52]

Allah Bakhsh was a constant advisor and confidant. He smoothed relations between Khizr and the Unionist MLAs and later played a central role in the Premier's talks with Jinnah in 1944 and with the Congress and Akali leaders two years later. Allah Bakhsh's importance was openly acknowledged at the time, indeed he was jokingly called the 'Dr. Jekyl and Mr. Hyde'of Khizr. Perhaps for reasons of personal vanity, he encouraged the impression that he was the power behind the throne. His advice along with that of Zafrullah Khan was very influential when Khizr eventually quit as Premier. During his period of office in Lahore, Khizr strolled virtually every evening with Allah Bakhsh. Politics were invariably their most frequent topic of conversation. During the summer months, Khizr would drive down each weekend some thirty miles from his Simla home to see Allah Bakhsh. He had built his residence in the less glamorous surroundings of the hill cantonment at Solon, reputedly because he found the height restrictions on dwellings in Simla irksome.[53]

Khizr's non-political interests in Lahore centred around Aitchison College and the race course. The latter was less than a mile from the College on the opposite side of the Mall connected by the aptly named Race Course Road. Meetings were held at Lahore every Saturday from December to April. Leading socialites thronged the grandstand as at race meetings the world over, especially for the Boxing Day meeting of the Punjab Governor's Cup Race. But Khizr attended for the horseflesh not the fashion parades. He acted as a steward at the Lahore racecourse throughout his time as a Minister. Health problems restricted his own riding activities and he was now forced to spectate rather than compete in polo tournaments. He also entered his own horses for the Lahore meetings, although the thoroughbreds were sold off to trainers who competed in the more prestigious Bombay and Calcutta races. Khizr nevertheless had the pleasure to see one of his horses 'Barmaid' capture the Governor's Cup, whilst he held Ministerial Office.

Apprentice to Power

Khizr continued his association with Aitchison through the Management Committee and Old Boys' Association, although after the 1935 Jubilee celebrations which he largely masterminded, there was a lull in these activities. While Khizr was a Minister he would frequently go for a Sunday evening stroll in the grounds with his son Nazar who was an Aitchison student from 1934–44. After Khizr became Premier such activities were restricted, but he would still endeavour to visit the College each week.[54]

Nazar accompanied his family to Simla each summer in the annual migration of the Punjab Government to the cool of the hill station perched on a 7,000 feet spur of the lower Himalayas. He still remembers the golden summers of over half a century ago when his father opened his house to a stream of visitors. Although Khizr owned properties in West Simla at Annandale, he preferred to rent Victoria Place at Ellersby at the east end of the hill station. For this was nearer to the Punjab Secretariat and the Governor's half-timbered reproduction of an English country house at Barnes Court. It was also a large property with its own garage, tennis court, annex where the Tiwana ladies stayed and guest house. Another feature of the single storeyed dwelling which recommended it to Khizr was the spacious living room with its billiard table. He thus happily rented the property each summer from May to September from its wealthy owner Rai Bahadur Jodha Mall.

The real appeal of political life for Khizr lay not in the sense of power or excitement it brought. But precisely in the increased opportunities for the socialising which he enjoyed each year at Simla. This is not intended to demean his strong sense of duty or the application which he displayed as a Minister. By 1942, he had grown both in political maturity and administrative competence. But politics were still more a hobby than an overwhelming preoccupation. Indeed, Khizr largely saw the role of a Minister as that of a glorified landowner. This attitude proved a major weakness in the long run, but served him well until the Muslim League mounted its challenge. He did not view politics as a profession. Nor unlike some of his younger opponents was he attracted by the romance of a freedom struggle.

Khizr lacked the personal ambition to climb higher up the greasy pole of office. In the carefree days of the final months of peace, there was no inkling that the burden of guiding the province through the trauma of a second major conflict would ultimately rest on his shoulders. When he became Premier in 1942, it was thus a result of

79

circumstances, rather than the culmination of a lifetime's striving. Whilst the 'accident' of Sikander's premature death brought Khizr to power, it is nonetheless true that he rose to the challenge of his new destiny, bringing both courage and grace to the office.

Notes

1 C. Dewey, *Anglo-Indian Attitudes. The Mind of the Indian Civil Service* (London, 1993) p. 186.

2 The Gondals were originally pastoralists. They claimed Rajput descent but were enumerated by the British as Jats. They were heavily recruited into the Indian Army.

3 D. Gilmartin, *Empire and Islam. Punjab And The Making of Pakistan* (Berkeley 1988) p. 135.

4 His branch of the family owned around 4,000 acres in the Shahpur tehsil, the main landholding was at Hamoka.

5 For details see, K.C. Yadav, *Elections in Punjab 1920–47* (New Delhi, 1987) p. 91.

6 Interview with Mr. K. Morton Great Wilbraham Cambridge, 13 December 1990.

7 Gilmartin *op.cit.*, p. 134.

8 The Noons and Tiwanas had frequently intermarried. The main Noon estates in the Shahpur district were at Nurpur and Kot Hakim Khan.

9 In the last few days before polling, Nehru flew the length and breadth of the Punjab to address meetings Punjab FR for the first half of January 1937, 18/1/37–Poll., NAI.

10 *Civil and Military Gazette* (Lahore) 14 October 1936.

11 I. Talbot, *Punjab and the Raj 1849–1947*(New Delhi, 1988) p. 109.

12 Gilmartin *op.cit.*, p. 113.

13 The Unionist Party never published a list of official candidates before polling began. In most constituencies it adopted the policy of allowing the local faction leaders to fight it out amongst themselves. The winner was then declared the official Unionist candidate. In the Batala seat, for example, the victorious independent candidate, Mian Badr Mohyuddin was claimed as a Unionist despite the fact that he had defeated two 'official' Unionist candidates. Mahomed Hassan who was elected at Ludhiana was variously described in the electoral returns as an Independent, Congressman and Unionist. See. *The Times of India* (Bombay), 13 January 1937 & 8 February 1937; *Civil and Military Gazette* (Lahore) 3 February 1937.

14 For an elaboration of this element of consociation, see, A. Lijphart, 'Consociational democracy.' *World Politics* xxi, (1969), pp. 207–25.

15 Sunder Singh Majithia was an Aitchisonian who was Revenue Member in the Punjab Legislative Council from 1920–26. He was active also in the affairs of Khalsa College, Amritsar and the Chief Khalsa Diwan.

16 I.H. Malik, *Sikander Hayat Khan. A Political Biography* (Islamabad 1985) p. 49.

Apprentice to Power

17 United Kingdom: House of Commons, *Parliamentary Papers 1937–38 XX1* Cmd. 5589, 'Returns Showing the Results of elections in India, 1937' pp. 80–93. Cited in S. Oren, 'The Sikhs, Congress and the Unionists in British Punjab, 1937–1945', *Modern Asian Studies* 8, 3 (1974) p. 398.

18 Interview with Sirdar Izzat Hayat Khan, London 8 November 1993.

19 Darling Tour Paper 23 April 1939 Darling Papers Cambridge cited in Dewey *op.cit.*, p. 186.

20 For the background see I.H. Malik, *Sikander Hayat Khan. A Political Biography* (Islamabad, 1985) pp. 64–74.

21 Chhotu Ram to Azim Husain 4 January 1943. (Courtesy of Azim Husain).

22 Glancy Enclosure to Laithwaite 8 July 1941 Punjab FR first half of July 1941 L/P&J/5/244 IOR.

23 He took the place of Sunder Singh Majithia who died on 2 April 1941.

24 Punjab FR 11 January 1942. L/P&J/5/245 IOR.

25 Minutes of the Proceedings of the Provincial Punjab Zemindara League, Lahore Meeting Held at the Residence of the Nawab of Mamdot on Sunday the 24th of October 1937. Unionist Party Papers. Tiwana Collection, University of Southampton.

26 Director Information Bureau Lahore, *Five Years of Provincial Autonomy in the Punjab 1937–42* (Lahore 1942) pp. 15–16.

27 The story was told of how Chhotu Ram accompanied his father when he went to a **bania** to seek advice concerning his son's future. The moneylender threw the **pankha** cord to Chaudhri Sukhi ram and ordered him to pull it, while he was thinking over the issue. Chhotu Ram could not stand this humiliation and questioned the **bania** about the propriety of such conduct. This incident is said to have acted as a catalyst in Chhotu Ram's decision to dedicate his career to improving the peasants' social and economic status and to destroying the moneylenders' influence. H.L. Agnithori and S.N. Malik, *A Profile in Courage: A Biography of Chaudhri Chhotu Ram* (New Delhi, 1978), p. 2 &ff.

28 R. Narendranath, 'The Punjab Agrarian Laws and their Economic and Constitutional bearings' *Modern Review* 65, (1939), p. 30.

29 Punjab FR 6 September 1938 L/P&J/5/241 IOR.

30 *Civil and Military Gazette* (Lahore)4 September 1938.

31 *Civil and Military Gazette* (Lahore)6 September 1938.

32 P. Singh (ed) *Chhotu Ram in the eyes of his Contemporaries* (New Delhi 1992) p. 78.

33 *Ibid.*, p. 42.

34 *Tribune* (Ambala) 31 August 1938.

35 The damage which its vacillating attitude had done to its prestige was brought home in the Gurgaon District Board elections. Gurgaon was a district in which the Congress usually did well, but in the elections held there in October 1938 it captured only one of the thirty seats. Punjab FR 26 October 1938, L/P&J/5/241 IOR.

36 Punjab FR 8 July 1938, L/P&J/5/241 IOR.

37 Singh *op.cit.*, p. 74.

38 Azim Husain, *Panchayats in the Punjab* (Lahore 1941) p. 36.

Khizr Tiwana, the Punjab Unionist Party and the Partition of India

39 Foreword by the Honourable Major Malik Khizar Hayat Khan Tiwana in A. Husain, *Panchayats in the Punjab* (Lahore, 1941) p. iii.

40 Singh *op.cit.*, pp. 162–3.

41 *Ibid.*, pp. 43–4.

42 *Provincial Autonomy in the Punjab op.cit.*, pp. 62–4.

43 Azim Husain had begun his career as an Assistant Commissioner in the Punjab in 1937. Two years later he served as an Under Secretary in the Political Department of the Punjab Government. From 1939–41 he was Sub-Divisional officer in the Punjab Government.

44 Azim Husain Private communication to the author.

45 Early in April 1944, Chhotu Ram wrote to Azim Husain offering him the 'designation of Deputy Secretary' to the Premier. Chhotu Ram to Azim Husain 1 April 1944. (Courtesy of Azim Husain).

46 Azim Husain Personal communication to the author.

47 *Provincial Autonomy in the Punjab op.cit.*, p. 58.

48 *Provincial Autonomy in the Punjab op.cit.*, p. 52.

49 The document was written by Khizr probably with the assistance of Syed Nur Ahmad in the 1960s. Khizr gave a copy to Craig Baxter in 1968. It is cited here with his kind permission.

50 The other members were, S. Sampuran Singh MLA, Seth Lachman Dass Mehra, Mr.K.L. Rallia Ram headmaster Mission High School Lahore, Dr. Barkat Ali Qureshi a Professor of Oriental College and Maulvi Mahomed Shafi a former Principal of Oriental College. *Civil and Military Gazette* (Lahore) 2 April 1943.

51 Personal communication to the author from Arthur Lall, 23 May 1991.

52 Interview with Nazar Tiwana, New Delhi, 11 December 1993.

53 Interview with Nazar Tiwana, New Delhi, 10 December 1993.

54 *Ibid.*

Chapter Five

Inheriting the Crown

Sikander's sudden death at the age of fifty rocked the Punjab. He had been attending the triple wedding celebrations of his two eldest sons and daughter.[1] The Premier had first complained of stomach pains at around 9.30 pm on the evening of 26 December. Less than two hours later his wife discovered him unconscious on his bed. Sikander was dead by the time Colonel Mirajkar his physician had arrived.[2] Khizr summed up the feelings of his colleagues when he described Sikander's death as 'the greatest tragedy in these critical times. The loss would be mourned alike by all communities.'[3]

Sikander was buried with full military and police honours at the foot of the Badshahi mosque near the tomb of Iqbal. The massive funeral procession had stopped for a few moments at the shrine of Hazrat Data Ganj Baksh on its way to the burial place. Khizr had joined the large number of dignatories which included the Governor at the graveside. With tears running down his face he declared, 'The Punjab has been widowed. Sir Sikander was a unique individual, a just Premier a loving and affectionate friend and a deeply religious-minded man. His death at this critical time is an irreperable loss to the Punjab to India and to the Muslim community.'[4]

i

The 'critical times' to which Khizr repeatedly referred resulted from the state of the War in the Far East and the general political situation in India. The year which was about to close had been a tumultuous one. Japanese troops crossing from the mainland of Malaya had overwhelmed the supposedly impregnable island fortress of Singapore. Its surrender on 15 February 1942 had been in Churchill's words, 'the worst disaster and largest capitulation in British history.'

Khizr Tiwana, the Punjab Unionist Party and the Partition of India

A combination of the fall of Singapore and the pressure from Roosevelt prevailed upon Churchill to despatch Sir Stafford Cripps to India in March 1942. The reasons for the failure of the Cripps Mission remain controversial.[5] The Congress's response was to launch the 'Quit India' movement in August. The British had to deploy 57 batallions of troops to quell the greatest threat to their rule since the revolt of 1857.[6] The Cripps Mission itself despite its failure had moved the constitutional process forward by the offer of Dominion Status at the end of the War. It had also increased the standing of Jinnah and the All-India Muslim League by its encouragement of Pakistan through the principle of provincial option. This was to greatly strengthen Jinnah's hand in his dealings with the Punjab Unionists.

Sikander's steadfast support for the War effort during the troubled months of 1942 had proved priceless for the British. Sikander exhorted Punjabis to live up to their reputation as 'martial castes'and to once again act as the sword-arm of India. Like Khizr who was to succeed him, he held a commission and had seen active service. His family's commitment to the War effort was demonstrated by Shaukat's and Azmat's answering of the call to the colours.

Sikander's unconditional support for the war effort increasingly led to conflict with a revitalised All-India Muslim League organisation. The first clash occurred in July 1940. Jinnah directed that the Muslim Unionist members of the Punjab Provincial War Board should resign in accordance with Muslim League policy. Only the Punjab Muslim League President, the Nawab of Mamdot[7] heeded this demand. Even his resignation was a token effort, for shortly beforehand he had led a Unionist deputation to Bombay to argue for a special exemption from the ban.[8] If Jinnah had not reconsidered and lifted the ban less than a month after its introduction, he would have sailed into rough waters.

Although the Quaid-e-Azam lost the first battle, he won the war. He successfully persuaded a reluctant Sikander to resign from the Viceroy's National Defence Council in September 1941. The reasons for the Punjab Premier's capitulation are uncertain.[9] The consequences were, however alarmingly apparent. 'The Premier has, I am afraid become more vulnerable since he yielded to Jinnah at Bombay, the Punjab Governor wrote anxiously to the Viceroy in October 1941, 'the more intelligent amongst the Muslims are obviously doubtful as to whether the Unionist Party can remain indefinitely in the ascendant if it is tied to the wheels of the Muslim League.'[10]

Inheriting the Crown

The All-India Muslim League had basked in the 'sunshine' of official favour since the resignation of the Congress Provincial Governments in October 1939. Jinnah adroitly exploited these fortuitous cicumstances. The power relationship which had tilted so much in favour of the Unionists at the time of the 1937 Lucknow Pact now swung increasingly in the opposite direction. Sikander cut an ever more forlorn and isolated figure within the Muslim League Council and Working Committee. Jinnah made no attempt to still the growing criticism directed towards the Punjab Premier. This so upset Sikander that he threatened to resign first in August 1940 and then again in March 1941.[11] He finally quit a year later.

Jinnah increasingly challenged the Unionists in their own backyard, indeed at one juncture he even contemplated leaving his palatial surroundings in Bombay to settle in Lahore. Sikander studiously avoided a meeting with the Muslim League leader when he visited the Punjab in March 1941. During a second visit some eight months later, the Premier's new vulnerability was clearly visible. Sikander squirming with embarrassment attended the Muslim League conference over which Jinnah presided at Lyallpur. He effusively described the Quaid-e-Azam as India's greatest Muslim leader. He also publicly declared that he 'fully subscribed to the Lahore Resolution of the League which provided for territorial readjustment.'[12] This was intended to shore up the Unionist position. Instead it had the opposite effect. The Muslim League thereafter redoubled its efforts in the 'cornerstone' of Pakistan. While Sikander's earlier assurances to the Hindus and Sikhs now sounded hollow.

Sikander believed that communal stability was vital for the war effort. The Sikhs had traditionally supplied a large proportion of the Punjab's army recruits, while there were many Hindu contractors to the Army and Government. Sikh army recuitment in fact remained disappointingly low throughout the early years of the War. Such Akali leaders as Sampuran Singh had linked support for the war effort with the Congress demand for independence.[13] Sikander attempted to remedy the situation by publicly stressing that enlistment was in the wider political interests of the Sikh community. This logic was not lost on Master Tara Singh who distanced himself from the Congress opposition to the War effort. He finally quit the Congress in September 1940.[14] Relations between the Akalis and the Congress were dealt a further blow by the Rajagopalachari proposal's recognition of the 'principle' of Pakistan.[15] This breach opened the way for a coalition between the Akalis and the Unionists.

In June 1942, Sikander entered into a precarious pact with Baldev Singh who owed his seat in the Unionist Coalition to the backing he received from the Akali Dal.[16]

The Sikander-Baldev Singh Pact was mainly concerned with such social and religious questions as giving **jartka** meat the same status as halal meat. But it possessed one important political clause. This called for an increase in Sikh representation in those departments in which it fell below the fixed communal proportion of 20 per cent.[17] It was grist to the Muslim League's propaganda mill. Its daily newspaper *Dawn* was soon filled with reports of newly appointed Sikh officials discriminating against Muslims. Unfortunately from Sikander's point of view there was no smoke without fire. The Unionists' willingness to serve British wartime interests in this as in other areas undoubtedly weakened their position. It seemed to many Muslims that they were now willing even to sup with the devil. Muslim disquiet concerning the Sikhs' intentions was of course greatly increased by the Akali Dal's raising of the Azad Punjab scheme early in March 1943. The redrawing of the Punjab's boundaries so as to exclude the Rawalpindi division and part of the Multan division would give the Sikhs the balance of power in the remaining Azad Punjab area.[18]

The increasing prominence of the industrialist Baldev Singh also seemed to confirm that it was the Hindu and Sikh commercial classes who were reaping profits from the war, whilst the Unionists' traditional supporters suffered. Non-Muslim businessmen certainly grew fat on the lucrative government civil supply contracts for such items as hardware, textiles, leathergoods, tents and machinery. From 1939 onwards the Purchase department of the Punjab Government dealt in contracts to the tune of Rs 50 lakhs a year.[19]

There were growing complaints that revenue officials were coercing rural army 'volunteers'. The increase in desertions adds credence to this charge.[20] Inflation caused by the shortages of consumer goods was also wiping out the farmers' profits. These pressures cracked the impressive unity Sikander had instilled into the Unionist Party. During a debate in March 1942, the Government was criticised by its supporters over the policy of the export of wheat.[21] The Ministry was unable to respond, because its hands were tied by the central authorities.

Khizr thus inherited an increasingly unpopular Government. A despondent Chhotu Ram privately acknowledged early in January 1943 that the 'party has been living on its past prestige.'[22] Historians

Inheriting the Crown

have, however seldom recognised this reality. H. V. Hodson's comment that Sikander died in the 'full flight of power' is typical of this myopia.[23] The corollary is that a stronger man than Khizr would have been able to pull the Unionists' irons out of the fire. Craig Baxter, for example has speculated that the experience of Nawab Muzaffar Khan, Sikander's cousin and brother-in-law, 'might have enhanced the possibility of the Unionists staying together.'[24] Like Ayesha Jalal,[25] he depicts Jinnah as intervening more forcefully in the Punjab after Sikander's death because the Quaid-e-Azam sensed he had a 'weaker person with whom to contend.'[26]

The reality is rather different. Sikander's ambivalent attitude to Pakistan and attempts to limit the Punjab Muslim League's influence had irritated Jinnah for some time. They represented a serious slight to his growing power. Although Sikander had drafted the 1940 Lahore Resolution, in an address to the Punjab Assembly a year later he had seriously questioned the Pakistan scheme and called for 'hands off the Punjab'.[27] Khizr's Premiership should in this respect therefore not be seen as marking a major break. Nevertheless, Jinnah saw Sikander's demise as an opportunity to rein in the Unionists. It was vital to the All-India Muslim League's credibility to establish itself as the sole repository of political power in the Punjab. It needed to secure a position analagous to that of the Congress in the provinces which it ruled between 1937–9. It was thus not Khizr's 'weakness' which brought Jinnah hurrying to Lahore. He would have pressurised whoever had succeeded Sikander.

It is, moreover, far too simplistic to attribute the disintegration of the Unionist Party to the substitution of a 'weak' Khizr for a 'strong' Sikander.[28] The Unionists' demise stemmed from the wartime changes in both local and All-India politics. When viewed in this wider context, Khizr's ability to cling onto power, until just six months before Partition, appears far more remarkable than his defeat.

ii

Chhotu Ram who had acted as de facto deputy Premier ruled himself out as a leadership candidate in a speech at Rohtak on 28 December. Khizr was faced with just three rivals, Nawab Muzaffar Khan, Liaqat Hayat Khan and Feroz Khan Noon, but they were all older and more experienced than himself.

Nawab Muzaffar Khan, Sikander's brother-in-law was Umar's

contemporary. After a distinguished government service career including a stint as the reforms commissioner in the Frontier, he had been appointed revenue member in the Punjab council. He entered the Punjab Assembly in 1937 for the Attock North constituency. Almost as soon, however as his name was touted, he ruled himself out of any contest for the Premiership on the plea that he had already accepted a seat on the Punjab-North West Frontier Province Public Service Commission.[29] The main standard bearer for the Khattar faction of the Unionist Party now became Liaqat Hayat Khan. Liaqat was Sikander's elder brother. After a career in the Indian Police Service, in 1930 he had become the Premier of Patiala State.[30] Feroz Khan Noon was the final 'contender.' He was the leading member of the Noon 'tribe'. He had served as a Minister of Education in the Punjab Council from 193–6, before being appointed as the first Indian High Commissioner in London. He went from there in 1941 to become a member of the Executive Council of the Viceroy. He again achieved another Indian first when he held the defence portfolio in 1942.

Feroz's career in some respects resembled a later version of Umar's. Like his distant Tiwana relative, years spent out of the Punjab gave Feroz a certain aloofness from the factionalised politics of the Unionists. It was for this reason that *Dawn* favoured him to succeed Sikander. Feroz, however turned down an offer from the Governor and instead supported Khizr as Premier.[31] Khizr also possessed the recommendation of Umar's reputation and his own Ministerial record. Glancy worried whether Khizr could maintain the factional unity of the Unionist Party. He also, however looked for a leader who would work unreservedly for the war effort. Khizr's credentials as a member of the 'martial castes' with a family history of loyalty stretching beyond 1857 were of course impeccable in this respect.

Khizr breakfasted with Bertrand Glancy on the morning of 31st December. The talk turned not to politics, however but rather to polo, horses and shikar. The Governor broke with all protocol as Khizr was leaving. He strode after his guest and placing his hand on his shoulder remarked that 'You shall need to take yourself more seriously in future.'[32]

Later that evening, Khizr was once more driven along the stretch of the Mall which he knew so well. This time, however instead of continuing to Aitchison College, he turned off a mile or so earlier and entered the imposing gate of Government House. He left an hour

Inheriting the Crown

later, at the age of forty two, the youngest Prime Minister of an Indian province. No one could anticipate that he was to be the final leader of an undivided Punjab.

Khizr confirmed his four colleagues from Sikander's Cabinet in their posts. The remaining appointment was to be made later. His only other pronouncement was to declare that he would do all in his power, 'to serve the best interests of the province.'[33] Khizr's first public appearance as Premier was also low key, when he attended a meeting of the Punjab Literary League on Sunday 3 January. The gathering which was presided over by Raja Narendra Nath devoted itself entirely to Sikander's memory. Khizr used this opportunity to introduce what were to become the two common themes of his early years in office. 'The best way in which they could perpetuate the memory of the departed leader', he declared to the audience which included his colleague Chhotu Ram, 'was to continue the work which was dear to his heart, namely protection of communal harmony and unconditional support for the prosecution of the war.'[34]

The following day, Khizr had the satisfaction of being unanimously welcomed as Premier by a meeting of the Punjab Muslim League. After this acclamation he joined Chhotu Ram as a member of the bridegroom's party at the wedding of Syed Iqbal Ahmad, the son of Syed Nur Ahmad the Director of the Punjab's Information Bureau.[35] The process of 'anointing' Khizr as Sikander's successor was completed at a packed meeting of the Punjab Unionist Party held on 23 January. The accession of four scheduled caste MLAs[36] was also announced to this gathering. This raised the Unionist Party's strength to 104 and the Ministerialist Coalition to 120 in a House of 175 members. Khizr appeared to have inherited an unassailable position.

He now completed his Cabinet with the appointment of Shaukat Hayat Khan, Sikander's eldest son to his old post. This step was well received by the Khattar faction and the party as a whole. Khizr soon, however bitterly regretted[37] it, as Shaukat sniped at his lukewarm support for the Pakistan demand. Such 'disloyalty' undermined the long established unity amongst the 'martial castes' and was potentially disastrous for the Unionist Party.

iii

Khizr's honeymoon period in office lasted less than three months. Then further cracks in the Unionist ranks in the Assembly coincided

Khizr Tiwana, the Punjab Unionist Party and the Partition of India

with the beginnnings of a tussle with the All-India Muslim League. This culminated in the Punjabi Premier's expulsion and public vilification as a 'traitor to Islam.' Before these more serious threats materialised, however, he had to fend off an attack from the 'nationalist' opposition in the Assembly. Khizr's poise in this skirmish clearly illustrated the rapid strides which he had made since his diffident appearance in the Legislature in 1937.

Dr. Sir Gokul Chand Narang, the Hindu Mahasabhite and official leader of the opposition, in a forceful speech on 8 March condemned the Unionists for their 'inhuman, callous and scandalous' treatment of Congress prisoners. He questioned whether the Government's approach to law and order was based on its own free will, or whether the Ministers were no more than 'boobies' of the Central Government.[38] Khizr established his reputation as an eloquent parliamentary debator in his reply. In a 'loud and ringing voice which was certainly a great gain to the press gallery' he effectively refuted the charge of ill-treatment. He also argued that 'the Punjab Government being responsible for the maintenance of law and order applied locally the broad principles laid down by the Central government for meeting threats to public peace.'[39] The Punjab Premier later added that a solemn assurance by the detainees not to thwart the war effort was the 'minimum' condition for their release. The civil disobedience movement with its slogan of 'do or die' had been an open rebellion designed to cripple the war effort. He concluded with the familiar sentiment that 'communal harmony was indispensable for the success of the war effort.'[40]

Khizr received a more hostile hearing[41] at the Delhi Council meeting of the All-India Muslim League which coincided with the opening of the Punjab Assembly Budget Session. He travelled to Delhi on the evening of 5 March along with his cabinet colleague Mian Abdul Haye, and also the Nawab of Mamdot, Raja Ghazanfar Ali, Syed Amjad Ali and Bashir Ahmad.[42] He was immediately faced with a resolution moved by Maulana Abdul Hamid Baudami calling on the Muslim members of the Punjab Assembly to form a separate Muslim League Party as soon as possible and to act in accordance with League policy.

Khizr spiritedly replied that the resolution was unnecessary as a Muslim League party already existed in the Punjab Assembly under the terms of the Jinnah-Sikander Pact. He assured his hearers that he would endeavour to put life into it, so that it would be worthy 'of the great organisation of the Muslim League and the Muslims of the

Khizr Hayat Tiwana, 12 years old, dressed in
Kimkhab, snapped at a studio in Simla.

Tiwana polo team pictured at Kalra in the 1930s.

Sir Khizr and his son Nazar Hayat in 1935 at his farm in Khizarabad.

Khizr at the 1938 Muslim League Working Committee meeting. His predecessor as Punjab Prime Minister, Sir Sikander Hayat Khan, is seated between him and Jinnah.

General Umar Hayat with his entourage at his London home during his service on the Secretary of State's Council. On the far left of the back row is his chess protégé, the Grand Master Sultan Khan.

Three generations of Tiwanas. Sir Khizr (on the right) with his father General Sir Umar Hayat Khan and his son Nazar Hayat at Aitchison College, Lahore (circa 1943).

Sir Khizr and Lord Wavell, the Viceroy at Simla in 1945.

Sir Khizr with the Indian delegation at the 1946 Paris Peace Conference. The British Premier, Clement Attlee, is in the foreground.

Sir Khizr with the Indian Prime Minister, Nehru, during a brief visit in the early 1950s.

Khizr's funeral at Kalra, January 1975.

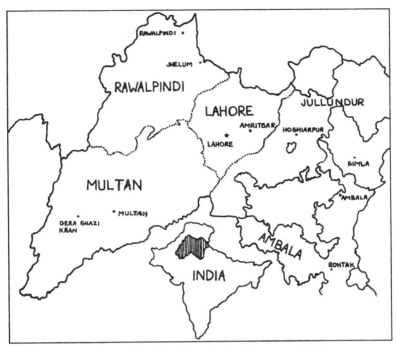

Divisions of the Punjab and principle towns 1921.

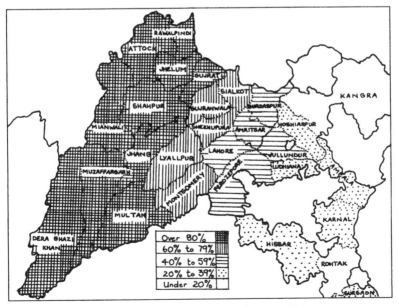

Distribution of Muslims by district 1921.
Source: PJB 1921 Census Part 1, 173

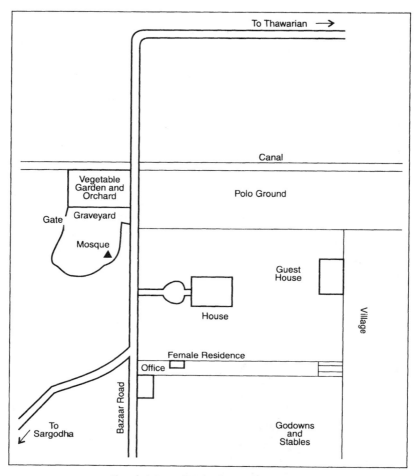

Sketch Map of Kalra by Nazar Tiwana.

Inheriting the Crown

Punjab.'[43] Jinnah ruled that the resolution should be withdrawn in the light of this explanation. He planted, however, a time bomb under the Unionist Government, when he added that 'Perhaps we may see the result before the next session of the All-India Muslim League.'[44] Jinnah simultaneously restated his interpretation of the Pact with Sikander. Even after this **tour de force** by Jinnah, Maulana Abdul Hamid Baudami withdraw his resolution with a certain amount of bad grace. Nor could he resist a final dig at Khizr by regretting that he had accepted the Governor's invitation as Premier without having consulted the Quaid-e-Azam. After this wigging, Khizr hurried back to the Punjab fearing that in future he would face a more serious summons to the headmaster's study.

If Jinnah had been a less cautious politician, he could in fact have inflicted further punishment on Khizr at this juncture. Local activists were already working up a head of steam over the delay in revitalising the Punjab Muslim League organisation. Jinnah chose for the moment to disown their 'unauthorised' actions.

Nawabzada Rashid Ali Khan, the President of the Lahore Muslim League had organised a Muslim League Workers' Conference in the Punjab capital shortly after Khizr had taken up office. It was attended by activists from as far afield as Mianwali, Campbellpur, Hissar and Rawalpindi. They decided after four hours heated discussion to establish a provincial Muslim League Workers Board, 'In view of the fact that the enemies of the League both inside and outside our ranks are asserting that there is no Muslim League in the real sense either in the province or the Legislature.'[45]

The Muslim League Workers Board aimed to establish new district and primary Leagues and to revitalize those which already existed so that half a million two **annas** League members would be enrolled in the Punjab. It also sought to raise at least Rs. 200,000 for the Central Muslim League Fund.[46] Finally the Conference elected a seven man secretariat.[47]

Jinnah had for some time patronised efforts at rural propaganda by student activists.[48] But this was a different matter. The latter had always worked through their separate Punjab Muslim Students Federation. The activities of the Workers Board threatened to establish a parallel Muslim League in the Punjab. The Quaid-e-Azam was unprepared to see the League's control pass from the Unionists into any hands except his own. He accordingly telegrammed Rashid Ali Khan on 13 February ordering him to suspend the Workers Board's activities.[49] The Nawabzada dragged his feet for a month before complying. This did not of course halt public criticism of the moribund state of the Punjab Muslim[50] League. Rabb Nawaz Khan, for example, complained to Jinnah in March that Nawab Iftikhar Hussain Khan was an obstacle to the Punjab League's advancement. How could it grow he asked Jinnah when its provincial President refused to allow Primary League branches to be established on his Ferozepore estate.[51] The Muslim League Workers Board episode itself did not threaten Khizr's position. But it revealed how the thunder of debate over Pakistan at the All-India level no longer so frequently passed by the Punjab.

Khizr walked straight into a row in the Punjab Assembly, when he returned from Delhi. Mian Muhammad Nurullah, the Arain representative for the Toba Tek Singh constituency[52] launched an unprecedented attack on the Unionist Government during a debate on irrigation. He termed it a 'symbol of die-hardism and conservatism'. Worse was to come. Mian Nurullah could be dismissed as a maverick who had already walked out of the Unionist Party.[53] But others chimed in who were still safely embraced in its bosom. Most damaging of all was the comment by Tikka Jagjit Singh Bedi that Chottu Ram paid no attention to the interests of the West Punjab zemindars, because of his strong 'pro-Ambala division bias.' Any rift between the Hindu Jat and West Punjab wings of the party would of course spell certain diaster. Allah Bakhsh Tiwana viewed this onslaught so seriously that he uttered his first words in the Assembly since taking up his seat in 1937. 'The Revenue Minister (Chhotu Ram) should be congratulated', he declared, 'for reconstructing inundation canals in the Pindadan Khan tehsil where people were doing so much for the war effort.'[54] His intervention did the trick in calming tempers, but the episode had dramatised the growing strains in the Unionist coalition.

Khizr sailed through the remaining debates. Minor legislation was enacted and there was some tidying up of earlier Acts. The Punjab Local Authorities War Services Act, for example allowed individuals to hold elective office at the same time as serving in an official capacity with respect to the war effort. The Punjab Restoration of Mortgaged Land (Amendment Act) enabled the Financial Commissioner to issue ordinances relating to case decisions or pending decisions. One of the most interesting and forward looking bills in the batch which was considered before the Assembly's adjournment on 26 March was the Punjab Maternity Benefit Bill. This was aimed at women working in munitions factories and was referred to a select committee.[55]

Inheriting the Crown

Sir Bertrand Glancy penned a perceptive end of term report on the new Premier. The Governor acknowledged that Khizr had 'an extremely difficult row to hoe'. He also identified his chief difficulty as being the absence of 'any convincing battle-cry with which to rally his followers.' Glancy declared, 'Khizr "has no inclination' to imitate Congress tactics and clamour for the independence of India, nor to abase himself to Jinnah and cry aloud for Pakistan. The pro-Zamindar campaign of the Unionist Party with its concomitant agrarian legislation has for the present more or less exhausted itself.. whatever cohesive effect it has exercised on the majority of the party has been gradually evaporating. The war effort and the interests of Punjabi soldiers still help to provide the machine with a certain amount of fuel, but as danger from the enemy has receded, this factor has become less potent than before.'

This sombre but realistic assessment in no way diminished Glancy's personal regard for Khizr. 'There is no denying that Khizr lacks the experience and political agility of his predecessor' Glancy noted, 'but he is in many respects a firmer character. He has a most attractive personality and he is very pleasant to work with. He is shrewd, even-tempered and blessed with a sense of humour. Though he is at heart an aristocrat and something of a reactionary, he keeps his prejudices in the background and is in my opinion essentially fair-minded. He has shown no signs of communal bias.'[56] The genuine respect which Khizr and Glancy held for each other repeated Umar's relationship with Michael O'Dwyer, or in much earlier times that of Herbert Edwardes and Fateh Khan Tiwana.

Glancy backed as far as he could, Khizr's non-communal, loyalist approach to politics. Khizr if anything listened too closely to his strictures against the 'disruptive' Muslim Leaguers. It was only later that he realised that Glancy's views were shaped by wartime British interests and that his superiors without compunction could jettison their alliance with the Unionists when it served the interests of an All-India political settlement. At the time, however, Khizr lamented when Glancy left India in April 1946. 'I can never adequately thank you for all your many kindnesses', he declared 'and for the patronage shown to me and my family during your term of office. I never deserved all I got.'[57]

The problems which faced Khizr if he tried to oppose 'communalism' with a 'convincing battle cry' of' tribal' solidarity were laid bear by the furore which arose concerning the activities of the Jats. The day after the Punjab Assembly adjourned, the All-India

Jat Mahasabha took place in Lahore. Christian, Muslim, Hindu and Sikh Jats shared the platform. They included such prestigious figures as Chaudhury Sir Shahabuddin, the speaker of the Punjab Assembly,[58] Chaudhry Sir Muhammad Zafrullah Khan[59] who was a judge of the Federal Court of India, in addition to Chhotu Ram himself. The meeting's atmosphere was summed up by Sir Shahabuddin who declared that, 'Jats no matter what religion they professed, should not forget that the same blood coursed through the veins of all of them. If they forgot it, they would perish.'[60] The Jats' common economic interests and their 'martial caste' identity were stressed by a succession of speakers. Both Khan Bahadur Mahomed Din and Captain Naunihal Singh MLA publicly called for Jats to enlist in the Army in ever increasing numbers to 'maintain their place of pride.' Khizr did not attend the conference, but he sent a letter expressing sympathy with its aims which was read aloud to the gathering.[61]

The Muslim press unanimously condemned the Jat meeting. Its criticism of the Jat and other 'tribal' associations gathered momentum as the tug of war intensified between the Unionists and the League. After its meeting in 1944, the Jat Mahasabha was roundly criticised as a tool of colonial interests which ignored the religious differences between Hindus, Muslims and Sikhs. 'Communal' ideals were trumpeted in word and print as more authentic foundations of local 'consciousness' than 'tribal' association. There was more at stake than just political competition between the Unionists and the Muslim League. Rather, two conflicting visions of Punjabi identity collided. One view saw this derived from religion in which individuals identified with symbols which by their very nature were exclusive. The other stressed a composite culture tied to local economic interests which included all rural communities.

Mian Mumtaz Daultana who became General Secretary of the Punjab Muslim League in April 1944 led the attack on 'tribal' interests and identities. He iconoclastically demolished the ideological position which his 'uncle' Sir Shahabuddin had helped construct. Shahubuddin who had paid for his 'nephew's' education,[62] had perhaps misplaced his generosity. Mumtaz's action, however was just part of a general revolt by the younger generation against the Unionist political tradition.

The ending of the Budget Session enabled Khizr to devote his energies to the war effort. This was the aspect of his Premiership which he most enjoyed. For it enabled him to tour the districts and

Inheriting the Crown

mingle with the rural members of the 'martial castes' with whom he felt at home. Whilst delivering war speeches, he could forget the burdensome boxes of paperwork, the sniping and clever debating points of his opponents and hark back to an earlier and less complicated era. Like the harbinger of the monsoon, however, storm clouds banked up on the horizon. With each day that passed, the odds lengthened that whilst Khizr would win the war, he might also lose the peace.

Notes

1 Major Shaukhat Hyat and Captain Azmat Hyat Khan were the two bridegrooms, whilst his daughter married Lt. Mazhar Ali.
2 *Civil and Military Gazette* (Lahore)29 December 1942.
3 *Ibid.*
4 *Civil and Military Gazette* (Lahore)29 September 1942.
5 For details of the Cripps Offer see, H.V. Hodson, *The Great Divide. Britain-India-Pakistan* (London, 1969) p. 90 & ff.
6 For an account of the disturbances see, F. Hutchins, *Gandhi and the Quit India Movement* (Cambridge Mass. 1973). Hutchins argues for the view that Indian independence was attained through revolution not an orderly transfer of power.
7 Nawab Sir Shah Nawaz Khan of Mamdot (1883–1942) came from the Ferozepur district. He had been handpicked by Sikander to lead the Unionist dominated reorganised Punjab Muslim League. His son Nawab Iftikhar Husain Khan succeeded him as League President. He aligned himself with the All-India leadership and led the opposition to Khizr from 1944–7.
8 *Tribune* (Ambala) 11 August 1940.
9 For British speculation on this consult, Punjab FR 10 September 1941 L/ P&J/5/244 IOR.
10 Glancy to Linlithgow 28 November 1941. Linlithgow Papers MSS.Eur.F.125 File 91 IOR.
11 Craik to Linlithgow 18 August 1940. Linlithgow Papers Mss.Eur.F.125 File 89; Linlithgow to Craik 1 March 1941. Linlithgow Papers Mss.Eur.F.125 File 90 IOR.
12 *Civil and Military Gazette* (Lahore)19 November 1941.
13 S. Oren, 'The Sikhs, Congress and the Unionists in British Punjab, 1937–1945' *Modern Asian Studies*, 8,3 (1974) p. 405.
14 This prompted Baba Kharak Singh to revive the pro-Congress Central Sikh League.
15 See, Oren *op.cit.* p. 411.
16 Baldev Singh officially entered the Government as the leader of the United Punjab Party which contained some Muslim and Hindu members as well as Sikhs. For a history of the Akali movement see, Mohinder Singh, *The Akali Movement* (Delhi, 1978).

17 *Civil and Military Gazette* (Lahore) 5 June 1942.
18 For further details of the Azad Punjab scheme see: N.N. Mitra (ed), Indian Annual Register (Calcutta, 1943) Vol.1 p. 294 & ff.
19 Tribune (Ambala) 27 September 1940.
20 Punjab FR for the second half of January 1943 L/P&J/5/246 IOR.
21 *Civil and Military Gazette* (Lahore) 14 March 1942.
22 Chhotu Ram to Azim Husain 4 January 1943. Courtesy of Azim Husain.
23 Hodson *op.cit.*, p. 271.
24 C. Baxter, 'Union or Partition: Some Aspects of Politics in the Punjab, 1936–45' in L. Ziring et al *Pakistan: The Long View* (Durham N.C. 1977) pp. 54–5.
25 A. Jalal, *The Sole Spokesman. Jinnah, the Muslim League and the Demand for Pakistan* (Cambridge 1985) p. 84.
26 Baxter *op.cit.*, p. 55.
27 Quoted in H.V. Hodson, *The Great Divide-Britain-India-Pakistan* (London 1969) p. 89. and in R. Coupland, *Indian Politics 1936–1942* (London 1943) p. 252.
28 The Punjab Governor acknowledged to the Viceroy that 'Khizr (was) in some respects in a weaker position than his predecessor'. But he blamed Sikander for 'leaving his successor an unpleasant heritage' as a result of his 'sometimes unnecessary surrenders' to Jinnah. Glancy to Linlithgow, 20 July 1943 *T.P*, IV p. 110.
29 *Civil and Military Gazette* (Lahore)30 December 1942.
30 Baxter *op.cit.*, p. 54.
31 Firoz Khan Noon, *From Memory* (Lahore, 1966) p. 187.
32 Interview with K. Rallia Ram, New Delhi 9 December 1993.
33 *Civil and Military Gazette* (Lahore)31 December 1942.
34 *Civil and Military Gazette* (Lahore)5 January 1943.
35 *Civil and Military Gazette* (Lahore)7 January 1943.
36 They were Faqir Chand, Jugal Kishore, Harnam Das and Mula Singh. *Civil and Military Gazette* (Lahore)24 January 1943.
37 Khizr was still deeply upset about Shaukat's actions when he met his younger brother in London early in the 1950s. There is some evidence for the viewpoint that the more politically astute Mian Mumtaz Daultana used Shaukat as his stalking horse. Interview with Sirdar Izzat Hayat Khan London 8 November 1993.
38 *Civil and Military Gazette* (Lahore) 9 March 1943.
39 *Ibid.*
40 *Civil and Military Gazette* (Lahore) 13 March 1943.
41 Glancy to Linlithgow 15 March 1943 T.P., iii, p. 809.
42 Mian Abdul Haye was the Minister of Education and was the' urban Muslims' Cabinet member. Raja Ghazanfar Ali was a Khokar Rajput from Pind Dadan Khan in the Jhelum district. He was the maternal uncle of the influential pir of Jalalpur, Pir Fazl Shah. Bashir Ahmad won the Ferozepore East seat for the Muslim League in the 1946 Punjab elections. Syed Amjad Ali came from a prosperous Shia mercantile family which had acquired extensive property in Lahore and Ferozepore.
43 *Civil and Military Gazette* (Lahore) 9 March 1943.
44 *Ibid.*

Inheriting the Crown

45 Punjab Provincial Muslim League, Vol. 162, pt.7 p. 2. FMA.
46 *Ibid.*
47 Maulana Zafar Ali Khan was President; Malik Barkat Ali and Mian Nurullah, Senior Vice-Presidents; Nawabzada Rashid Ali Khan, General Secretary; Syed Mustafa Shah Gilani, Secretary; Haji Abdul Karim, Financial Secretary, and Khan Rabb Nawaz Khan, Propaganda Secretary.
48 Jinnah had presided over a Pakistan Conference which the Punjab Muslim Students Federation had organised at Lahore in March 1941. The Conference created a rural propaganda committee. During the course of a twenty day tour it visited fifty villages in which it opened primary branches of the Muslim League.Report of Mohammad Sadiq: Sheikhupura Student Deputation 22 July 1941. QEAP File 1099/84 NAP.
49 S.Q.H. Jafri & S.A. Bukhari (eds) *Quaid-i-Azam's Correspondence with Punjab Muslim Leaders* (Lahore, 1977) p. 318.
50 The All-India Muslim League's investigation in October 1941 revealed that no Muslim League organisation existed at all in the following ten districts: Ambala, Hoshiarpur, Shahpur, Jhelum, Mianwali, Jhang, Kangra, Dera Ghazi Khan, Rohtak and Gujranwala. The total primary League membership of the seven city and six district branches, which were able to return reasonably accurate figures, was only just under 15,000. Ferozepore had the largest number of primary members 3,500; Montgomery was second with 3,200; next came Lahore with 2,000. Attock had the lowest district total with only 491 primary members. Only in Sind was the League weaker in terms of the number of primary members. Bombay had nearly double Punjab's number, U.P. eight times, whilst even the 'backward' region of Baluchistan possessed a thousand more. Conference of the Presidents and Secretaries of the Provincial Muslim Leagues October 1941, Vol. 326 pt.2, pp. 4, 32, 74, 87 and 95, FMA.
51 The estate with its headquarters at Jallalabad Mamdot was the largest in the East Punjab and covered around 88 square miles. It had been cleared of massive debts of Rs 357,000 during its administration by the Court of Wards in the first decade of the twentieth century.Khan Rabb Nawaz Khan to Jinnah 25 march 1943. QEAP File 579/46, NAP.
52 The constituency lay in the Lyallpur Canal Colony. Mian Nurullah represented the interests of Arains and others who had migrated there from the East Punjab.
53 The Arain group largely on factional grounds had decamped in 1939.
54 *Civil and Military Gazette* (Lahore) 16 March 1943.
55 *Civil and Military Gazette* (Lahore) 27 March 1943.
56 Glancy to Linlithgow 21 July 1943. Linlithgow Papers Eur.Mss.F.125/94 1943. pp. 5–2 IOR.
57 Khizr to Glancy, 20 April 1946, Glancy Papers, Rogate, Surrey. Cited in C. Dewey, *Anglo-Indian Attitudes. The Mind of the Indian Civil Service* (London, 1993) p. 218.
58 Sir Shahabuddin was a Virk Jat who was closely related to the Daultana family. He was a lawyer who had been involved in provincial politics since the early 1920s.
59 He was a leading member of the Ahmadiyah community. He represented

Khizr Tiwana, the Punjab Unionist Party and the Partition of India

Sialkot in the Punjab Assembly from 1926–35, before joining the Viceroy's Executive Council. Zafrullah Khan was a close political ally of Mian Fazl-i-Husain.

60 *Civil and Military Gazette* (Lahore) 28 March 1943.

61 *Ibid.*

62 Syed Nur Ahmad (C. Baxter ed) *From Martial Law to Martial Law. Politics in the Punjab, 1919–1958* (Boulder, 1985) p. 111.

Chapter 6

Leader in War and Peace

On the eve of Khizr's assumption of the Premiership, shortages of foodgrains were reported from thirteen districts, of fuel from ten, sugar from six and salt from four.[1] Unable to spend their increased income, cultivators made a virtue out of necessity and redeemed land. Shortages of consumer goods fuelled inflation. The Lahore Retail Price Index rose from a base of 100 in August 1939 to 371 in August 1945. It had climbed still further to 398 by the time of the 1946 elections.[2]

i

Khizr thus inherited a situation in which growing economic dislocation made his party's total commitment to the war effort increasingly unpopular. The new Premier soon discovered that his hands were tied by the central authorities. Wheat thus continued to be exported at the time of growing food shortages within the Punjab. When farmers encouraged by Chhotu Ram held back their stocks, despite the introduction of the requisitioning of grain the Unionist Ministry was pilloried at Westminster and by the Viceroy. Lord Hailey who had helped bring up Umar lashed out at his son's Government in the Lords,[3] whilst Linlithgow sent Khizr 'a pretty stiff letter' on 27 September 1943. The Viceroy followed this up the next day in a meeting both with Glancy and Khizr. The Punjab Governor had somewhat blotted his copybook by attempting to defend Chhotu Ram's actions on the grounds of political expediency.[4]

Linlithgow told both Governor and Premier that he must have 'early and categorical orders' sent to the Revenue Officers to 'get the wheat out' to famine stricken Bengal. He acknowledged that requisitioning would be unpopular, but demanded that this be faced.

Khizr Tiwana, the Punjab Unionist Party and the Partition of India

When Khizr lamented that it was very hard that the Punjabi cultivator should suffer in this way, the Viceroy brusquely dismissed this as an 'inadequate response.'[5] This attitude signalled the end in official circles of allowing the contentment of the Punjabi agriculturalists to take political precedence. Chhotu Ram was 'particularly sore' claiming that he had been treated with 'ignominity and ridicule' in London and New Delhi.[6] The contrast could not have been greater with the last 'crisis' of the Great Depression. Then the Government had cut canal water rates and reduced land revenue demands to assist the Punjabi farmers. Even more unprecedentedly it had imposed a protective duty on wheat to halt the slump in its prices.[7]

Khizr was well aware of the unpopularity of rationing. It provided his Muslim League opponents with a useful stick to beat the government. The Indianisation of the services which meant that Hindu and Sikh officials enforced this much resented policy in a number of Punjab districts still further served the League's interests. It was particularly galling to the more politicised agriculturalists that whilst they became subject to a range of centrally imposed regulations, the Hindu and Sikh businessmen were unhindered in their profiteering.[8]

Close on the heels of Khizr's humbling at the hands of the Government of India over grain requisitioning came another defeat, this time on the issue of price control of agricultural produce. Early in November 1943, the Punjab Assembly adopted without division an unofficial resolution to the effect that any attempt to control the price of wheat, 'would result in very keen resentment and discontent amongst the agricultural classes.'[9] Khizr, however, could not prevail upon the central authorities to prevent its reintroduction. He was even criticised for the one concession he had obtained, that this would not come into effect until after the 1944 rabi harvest. Opponents claimed that this three months' period of grace only assisted the large landowners.[10]

Khizr inherited not only mounting economic dislocation, but war weariness. Recruitment began to tail off during October and November 1942.[11] The major recruiting grounds were by this time almost completely exhausted and men were being enlisted in large numbers from the non-martial castes. Significantly the number of desertions rose to nearly three thousand by the end of March 1943.[12]

The formation of the National War Front was a response to this situation. Its members pledged to 'stamp out defeatism' and defy

Leader in War and Peace

'every peril threatening India's national honour and security.' In Khizr's words, the organisation did much to 'scotch alarmist rumours, to give publicity to authentic war news, to encourage enlistment and generally to maintain public morale and induce cooperation between all classes of the population in the Punjab's war effort.'[13] In April 1943, Khizr stepped up the National War Front's efforts in the Rawalpindi and Montgomery districts.[14] In the space of a week, he attended conferences in both areas.

A public meeting of the National War front was held on 12 April at the cattle fair grounds in Montgomery. Chhotu Ram chaired the gathering which was well attended. Much to Glancy's subsequent regret it did little to boost recruitment as many of those who came were curious bystanders.[15] Divisional delegates explained the aims and objects of the National War Front and gold watches were distributed to extra-assistant recruiting officers. A cheque for Rs 1 lakh was also subscribed for the Amenities of Troops Fund. The day before a sum of Rs 20,000 had been raised at a concert organised by the Deputy Commissioner Abdul Hamid. Khizr in addition to sitting through the gala performance laid on by Ram Gopal and his dance troupe had earlier attended a tea party organised by the Commanding Officer of the newly opened Recruits Reception Depot and had looked in on an especially arranged hockey match.[16]

Six days later, Khizr addressed the Rawalpindi Divisional National War Front Conference. A guard of honour mounted by the Civic guards and the Boy Scouts had awaited him. A row of rather antiquated military vehicles was provided for his inspection. Khizr, however put the occasion to rather better use, developing the themes in his speech which were to dominate the next eighteen months of his Premiership. He declared that he had no doubt about the transfer of power from Britain to India after the war, but that the martial castes who had made large sacrifices during it and who had laid the foundations of India's freedom should get their due share of the powers which would be transferred. 'I and my colleagues', Khizr declared in ringing tones, 'will try our utmost to secure for the martial classes a due place in the future India.' He concluded with the warning that in order to ensure success, the martial classes must stay united and distinguish between 'friend and foe.'[17]

ii

After Khizr's expulsion from the Muslim League and the emergence of Shaukat Hayat as a rival spokesman of the 'martial castes', the Punjab Premier devoted even more attention to tours of the recruitment centres. He realised that the military vote would play a key role in any future electoral contest with the League. He significantly made his first public criticism of the League's war policy in the speech following his open breach with Jinnah. 'Though some League workers in the Punjab said that the League stood for a different policy', he told his audience at Lahore on 5 July, 'it was clear beyond any doubt that the League's policy was bargaining and the League offered to cooperate only on certain conditions being fulfilled.' Khizr pointed to Sikander having to resign from the Defence Council at Jinnah's behest and contrasted this with the 'Unionist Party's wholehearted cooperation in the war effort without any conditions.[18]

Khizr increasingly turned in his speeches to the political and economic rewards which should be the due of the 'martial castes' at the end of the conflict. Late in October 1944, he made his first official visit to Kahuta, one of the leading recruiting centres in the Rawalpindi district. In his reply to the address presented by the District leaders of the National War front, Khizr described Kahuta as the 'best tehsil in the best district of the best province of India regarding recuitment to the Army.' He then publicly demanded for the first time the creation of separate and special constituencies for soldiers in the future constitution of India.[19] By January 1945 he had upped the stakes still further when addressing a Zemindara Conference held in a village some 15 miles from Lahore. The Punjab Premier called for two votes for every returned soldier and the 'allocation of an Island for such soldiers to provide for them a permanent homeland where they might be able to settle.'[20] He returned to the theme of ' rewarding'the Punjabi soldiers during a ten day tour of the Shahpur, Jhelum and Attock districts which commenced on 3 April 1945.

Khizr had in fact privately mooted the idea of political weightage for ex-service personnel in a meeting with Linlithgow in September 1943, shortly before the Viceroy's retirement. He had justified this suggestion of a special franchise by recalling that at the end of the last war, 'the Punjab soldier had got nothing and His Majesty's Government had devoted their attention to making concessions to people who had done nothing like as much.. and had nothing like as good a claim.'[21]

Linlithgow gave Khizr's idea short shrift, as did Sir James Grigg, the Secretary of State for War, when the Punjab Premier reiterated his

Leader in War and Peace

feelings in September 1944. He had again made the point that turmoil had followed the ending of the First World War,' because British Officers like Sir Michael O'Dwyer and Indian loyalists, who had worked devotedly to save the Empire, were not supported.' Khizr concluded his letter with a request that Grigg should see Brigadier Brayne on his behalf. Brayne who was on leave in England, was 'remarkable for his understanding of rural India and his unfailing sympathy for the man who handles the plough in peace and the rifle in war.'[22] This was of course yet another example of Khizr's naivety[23] in dealing with British officialdom. Thomas Brayne, although he possessed a famous father,[24] was a mere Brigadier in Khizr's own 19th Lancers Regiment. He was thus unlikely to carry any weight with the War Cabinet. Even more damaging, however, was the assumption which Khizr continued to hold down to 1947, that the interests of the British and the' loyalists' were identical.

iii

Khizr took his praises of the' martial castes' as far afield as the Paris Peace Conference which was held between 29 July – 15 October 1946. 'I want to tell you something about our soldiers', he told the assembled delegates, "for their courage and sacrifices are the reasons why we are(here) today. Not one of the two and a half million men in the Army was compelled to serve.. About a million men left their homes in the Punjab to serve in the war effort and three quarters of them served as active combatants. These men who know what it is to storm the heights of Cassino and to encounter the cunning Japanese in the jungles of Burma are not going to forget what they have done and seen. They, and others like them all over India, men of every caste and community, are the men this delegation represents.. If all the powers great and small lay their cards on the table and deal with each other openly and sincerely, then we shall give our soldiers a Peace that they will feel has been worth fighting for.'[25]

It had in fact been touch and go as to whether Khizr would attend at all. Shortly after a meeting with the Secretary of State, Lord Pethick-Lawrence at the India Office, Khizr received word of a Muslim League call for a vote of no confidence in his Coalition Ministry. After much indecision he telegrammed his Ministerial colleague Nawab Muzaffar Ali Khan Qizilbash[26] promising that he would return to Lahore for the debate. Nazar who was on vacation from Pembroke College, Cambridge accompanied his father to

Southampton where he caught the flying boat for Marseilles. Khizr, however rang his son that evening feeling rather unwell. Nazar successfully seized the opportunity to persuade his father to return to the U.K. and attend the conference.[27]

iv

From early 1945 onwards Khizr turned his attention from unsuccessful endeavours to secure special representation for servicemen to schemes for post-war rehabilitation. He was determined that there should be economic opportunities awaiting the large numbers of demobilised soldiers. This concern stemmed from his own family background and outlook. It also made sense politically, because of the significance of ex-servicemen in the Punjab's restricted electorate. With the approach of the 1946 Provincial elections, Khizr found himself, however, vying with Shaukat Hayat for the mantle of the true upholder of the soldiers' interests.

His erstwhile Cabinet colleague[28] at the inaugural meeting of the Punjab Muslim League campaign held outside Mochi gate, Lahore, launched into a blistering attack on the Unionist Government's 'professions of love for soldiers.' He ridiculed the fact that it had reserved only 75,000 acres of land for 10 lakh servicemen, 'out of which 20,000 had been earmarked for supporters of the Unionists in these elections.' 'How can this bureaucratic government',Shaukat declared in ringing tones, 'claim to be called a protector of the interests and rights of a soldier who went to the war to sacrifice his life, but on return only receives a few yards of land. Is this the price of his blood?'[29]

Khizr replied to these gibes when he announced during a visit to Sargodha that legislation would soon be introduced to give a 'jagir' of Rs 100 lasting a generation to every father who had sent at last three sons to the defence forces during the war. It would be increased by Rs 10 for every additional son.[30] This statement was, however, seized upon by the Muslim League as confirmation that whilst it was genuinely concerned about the soldiers' welfare, the Unionists were seeking only to 'scramble prizes for the recruit hunters.'[31]

The Working Committee of the Punjab Muslim League passed a resolution early in October 1945 which assured the 'brave Punjabi soldiers' of its 'whole-hearted support in all matters relating to post-war resettlement and welfare.'[32] Such vague assurances carried much less weight, however than its ability to turn disaffected **jawans**

Leader in War and Peace

against the Government by reminding them that they had returned home only to face unemployment.[33]

Rather late in the day in August 1945, Khizr's Government published an ambitious five year plan for post-war development. A sum of Rs 100 crores was earmarked for reconstruction work. This was to be spent on over 200 separate schemes ranging from massive irrigation projects to the development of fruit-growing and bee-keeping societies. Common to them all, however, was the aim of benefiting the ex-servicemen either by providing employment or improved services. In the later category, for example, the Plan proposed the construction of 59 rest-houses for the comfort of servicemen travelling on leave or business.[34] Facilities were to be provided to ex-servicemen for the purchase of improved seeds, agricultural implements and equipment at concession rates.[35] They were also to be provided with grants for the setting up of cottage industries, for training as teachers and vets[36] and for the establishing of sheep breeding units free of cost. Whilst sons of ex-servicemen were to receive free education up to B.Sc level at the Punjab Agricultural College, Lyallpur.[37]

The Plan advocated a massive public works programme not only to improve the Punjab's infrastructure but to alleviate unemployment. Amongst the smaller schemes were proposals to provide around 1500 jobs in constructing septic tank latrines[38] and 2,000 miles of village roads.[39] It was estimated that a further ten thousand jobs could be created for ex-servicemen by planting canal and road side trees.[40] The most important public works programmes were, however, irrigation projects. The Thal project was expected to irrigate 831,000 acres in the Mianwali and Shahpur districts. This would release land on which an estimated 85,000 former servicemen could be settled as tenants.[41] The Bhakra Dam, canals and Hydro-electric project, however dwarfed the Thal irrigation scheme. Indeed the project for a five hundred foot high dam which would store sufficient water to feed 200 miles of canals and generate 2 lakh kilowats of hydro-electric power was one of the biggest undertakings ever planned in British India.[42] The lengthy construction work was expected to provide upwards of 5,000 jobs for ex-soldiers.[43] A further two thousand construction jobs would be created by the Gurgaon irrigation project which was designed to serve a 400,000 acre area.[44]

If any further evidence of the Plan's commitment to the well-being of ex-soldiers was required this was provided by the decision to select 29 tehsils for concentrated development.[45] These tehsils were

105

earmarked for improved roads, water supply, schools, public health, medical treatment and for an expansion in the existing work of the Co-operative Department Societies. Significantly, they corresponded with the best recruiting areas.

It was fitting that Khizr, the leading representative of the military lobby should preside over a reconstruction programme which favoured its interests so strongly. Five hundred years of family history seemed to be climaxed in this moment. For Khizr it must have provided immense satisfaction. He would bequeath to his community an inheritance of which even Umar could be proud. The future, however lay, with another ex-soldier, Shaukat, who Khizr contemptuously regarded as a turn-coat.

The Five Year Plan failed miserably to stem the tide of the Muslim League's advance in the recruiting districts of Rawalpindi, Jhelum and Mianwali. This was partly because it had been announced too late, after the Muslim League was making headway in the Unionists' rural heartland. It also promised jam tomorrow, rather than bread today. The Bhakra Dam project, for example, had been discussed **ad nauseam** for twenty years. Even if it was commenced this time round, its benefits would be felt in the longer rather than the shorter term.

The Muslim League on the other hand offered cash on the nail in that it took up issues which were of immediate importance to the **jawans**. It expressed concern for example about the use of Indian troops to put down nationalist forces in Indonesia. More importantly, nearer to home it appointed a defence committee for the Punjabi Muslim officers who were involved in the I.N.A trials at Delhi. It also supported student demonstrations and protests in Amritsar and Jhajjar against the 'victimisation' of Captain Abdul Rashid of the 14th Punjab regiment whose sentence meant 'one hundred million Musslaman's humiliation.'[46]

This approach possessed an immediate impact in contrast with the Unionist Party's vague assurances. It is important to recognise, however, that the ex-servicemen were first and foremost caught up in the popular religious enthusiasm which surrounded the Pakistan demand. It was this which undermined the Unionists's standing not only amongst them, but other groups of traditional supporters.

Notes

1 Punjab FR for the first half of December, 1942 L/P&J/5/245 IOR.

Leader in War and Peace

2 *Annual review of Economic Conditions in the Punjab* Punjab Board of Economic Enquiry, No. 90 (Lahore, 1946), Table Xii, p. 62.

3 Wavell to Amery 16 November 1943*T.P* iv, p. 476.

4 For full details consult, I. Talbot, *Punjab and the Raj 1849–1947* (Delhi, 1988) p. 147.

5 Linlithgow to Amery, 29 September 1943, *T.P.*, IV p. 327.

6 Wavell to Amery 16 November 1943*T.P* iv, p. 476.

7 This measure was directed against imports from Australia which were forcing the price down.

8 For the Muslim League's use of wartime dislocation to further its popularity, consult, Talbot *op.cit.*, p. 163 & ff.

9 *Civil and Military Gazette* (Lahore) 6 November 1943.

10 *Civil and Military Gazette* (Lahore) 6 November & 19 December 1943.

11 Punjab FR for second half of January 1943 L/P&J/5/246 IOR.

12 Punjab FR for the second half of April 1943. L/P&J/5/246 IOR.

13 Khizr *op.cit.*

14 Recruitment had been disappointing in the Montgomery district which stood twentieth in the Punjab's order of merit, with only six districts ranking below it. *Eastern Times* (Lahore) 10 November 1942.

15 Punjab FR for the second half of April 1943 L/P&J/5/246 IOR.

16 *Civil and Military Gazette* (Lahore) 14 April 1943.

17 *Civil and Military Gazette* (Lahore) 18 April 1943.

18 *Tribune* (Ambala) 6 July 1944.

19 Cutting from *Hindu* (Madras) 26 October 1944 filed in F99/44–R Secretary of Governor General Reforms NAI.

20 *Civil and Military Gazette* (Lahore) 28 January 1945.

21 Linlithgow to Amery 1 October 1943*T.P* iv, p. 344.

22 Khizr to Sir James Grigg 18 September 1944 T.P v, pp. 224–5.

23 In September 1943, for example, he had provoked Linlithgow's ridicule when he had declared it 'would be such a help to the Punjab if he could only find out from His Majesty's Government what the future Indian policy was likely to be and make the Punjab acquainted with it so that the Punjab could spontaneously work in the right direction.' Linlithgow to Amery 1 October 1943*T.P* iv, p. 344.

24 Frank Lugard Brayne (1882–1952) his father was renowned for his work for village uplift in the Gurgaon district of the Punjab. For further details see Clive Dewey's excellent study, *Anglo-Indian Attitudes. The Mind of the Indian Civil Service* (London, 1993).

25 Draft Speech to Paris Peace Conference 7.8. 1946. This document was in the private possession of Nazar Tiwana in Chicago. It is now deposited with the Unionist Party papers at Southampton University.

26 Qizilbash (1908–1982) came from a leading Shia family of the Lahore district. He was a trained lawyer who had been educated at Cambridge.

27 Khizr returned by train and boat to England. This delighted Nazar who was homesick and had also wanted his father to appear on the world stage of the Peace Conference. Interview with Nazar Tiwana, New Delhi, 12 December 1993.

28 For the circumstances which surrounded Shaukat's dismissal see Chapter Seven below.

29 *Eastern Times* (Lahore) 29 September 1945.
30 *Civil and Military Gazette* (Lahore) 27 October 1945.
31 Shaukat had first made this claim during a Muslim League meeting at Sargodha on 3 June 1945. *Eastern Times* (Lahore) 8 June 1945.
32 *Dawn* (Delhi) 8 October 1945.
33 The Rawalpindi Employment Exchange had found work for only 1 in every 5 ex-soldiers who had registered with it by December 1946.Punjab FR 14 December 1946 L/P&J/5/249 IOR.
34 Government of the Punjab, *Five year Plan for Post-War Development Schemes* (Lahore, 1945) Scheme 231 p. 335. It was estimated that the cost of construction and endowment would run to Rs 70 lakhs.
35 *Ibid.*, Scheme No. 21 p. 73. The detailed proposals were as follows: (1) supply of improved seed to 50,000 ex-servicemen annually for three years at 25% concession; (2) supply to 50,000 ex-servicemen of a set of improved agricultural implements costing about Rs 500 each at 25% concession; (3) boring of 5,000 wells belonging to ex-servicemen to augment water supply where it is deficient at a concession of 25%; (4) sinking of 5,000 new wells where necessary on ex-servicemen's lands and the installation of Persian Wheels by contributing 25% of the cost; (5) supply of fruit plants to 25,000 ex-servicemen who may wish to plant a garden at 25% concession.
36 Provision was made for 15 grants for a four and a half year period to the value of Rs 50 a month to enable suitably qualified ex-servicemen to take up places at the Punjab Veterinary College, Lahore.
37 *Ibid.* Scheme 22 p. 75.
38 *Ibid.*, Scheme 181 p. 265.
39 *Ibid.*, Scheme 191 p. 278.
40 *Ibid.*, Scheme 18 p. 65.
41 *Ibid.*, Scheme 1 p. 27.
42 The Project planned to convert about five million acres of arid land in the Hissar, Rohtak and Gurgaon districts into rich arable land.
43 *Ibid.*, Scheme 4 p. 32.
44 *Ibid.*, Scheme 6 p. 37.
45 They were as follows: in the Rawalpindi division; Kahuta, Murree, Gujar Khan, Talagang, Pindigheb, Jhelum, Fatahjang, Chakwal, Pind Dadan Khan, Kharian, Rawalpindi, Khushab, and Isakhel; in the Lahore division; Sialkot, Narowal, Tarn Taran, Ajnala; in the Ambala division; Rohtak, Jhajjar, Rewari, Bhiwani, Hissar, Kharar; in the Jullundur division; Hamir, Palampur, Hoshiarpur, Jullundur and Jagraon.
46 *Dawn* (Delhi) 18 February 1946.

Part Three

The Passing of a World

Chapter Seven

Sailing in Two Boats

Trouble had been brewing between the Unionist Party and the Muslim League ever since the Delhi Council Session of March 1943. It had put Khizr on probabation to establish a vigorous Muslim League Assembly Party even if it jeopardised the running of his Ministry. The storm finally broke in April 1944. Jinnah and Khizr thundered at each other through the columns of the press following the collapse of their negotiations. The conflict became so intense that the Punjab Premier was unprecedently expelled from the All-India Muslim League.

The pyrotechnics appeared to stem from a seemingly innocuous disagreement over the interpretation of the Pact which Jinnah had 'signed' with Khizr's successor, Sikander in 1937.[1] Put at its simplest it boiled down to whether, the 'Muslim League group' established under its terms, in the Punjab Assembly, should in future adopt the the Muslim League label with the consequence that the Government should be named the 'Muslim League Coalition Ministry' instead of the Unionist Ministry.

So what was in a name to cause such conflict? Moreover, why did Jinnah suddenly object to an arrangement which had existed since 1937? It was accepted that Khizr was merely continuing the time honoured practice, whereby an Assembly Member could be simultaneously recognised as a Unionist and a Muslim Leaguer. Why was Sikander allowed to adopt this approach unchallenged, whilst Khizr was charged with 'sailing in two boats?'

The political label was of course only important because of what it implied. Behind the tussle over it, there existed two conflicting visions of the Punjab and its people. The Muslim League view was that religious community was the primary source of political identity. The Unionists, however looked to accommodation and cross-communal cooperation. After the 1940 Lahore Resolution, the Muslim League could not ignore such contradictions in the heartland of a future Pakistan State. Conflict over the interpretation of the Jinnah-Sikander Pact became inevitable. Jinnah bided his time until the beginning of 1944 because he realised that the outcome was crucial to the wider battle for Pakistan. He had been sent packing from Lahore by Mian Fazl-i-Husain in 1936 and was not prepared to repeat such humiliation.

The stakes were also high for Khizr. He realised that far more was at risk than the snuffing out of his own political career. For reasons of family history, upbringing and education, he was personally as well as politically committed to the Unionist vision. Moreover, because he was completely devoted to the Imperial war effort, he feared the consequences of the Muslim League rocking the boat in the 'sword-arm' of India. British officials, naturally shared these anxieties. 'It is of the greatest importance that until the end of the war against Japan there should be a stable administration in the Punjab,' the Viceroy Wavell noted to Glancy in April 1944, 'the dissolution of the Unionist Ministry and the substitution of a Muslim League Ministry such as Jinnah wants, will be a disaster. I very much hope that Khizr will look at the matter from this point of view and rally the Unionists.'[2]

The Punjab Governor shared his superior's reading of the situation. As early as April 1943, he had warned that, 'the main threat to our political tranquility comes from Jinnah and the Muslim League.'[3] He accordingly stiffened Khizr's resolve whenever he appeared to be feeling the strain of his protracted negotiations. Wavell with a certain amount of satisfaction reported to the Secretary of State that Khizr 'has from the first leant heavily on Glancy for advice and support.'[4]

Such British backing was not significantly evident, when Khizr crossed swords with the Muslim League during 1946–7. The Unionist Party had by this stage outlived its usefulness to New Delhi. Although Wavell and Mountbatten still found Khizr personally charming[5] and certainly much better company than Jinnah, his views were dismissed as irrelevant and anachronistic. The British shared with the Muslim League and Congress high commands, the belief that the' special pleading' of regional interests as represented by the Unionists should not be allowed to stand in the way of an All-India settlement. The greatest congruence of course existed between the interests of the British and the Congress. Both

Sailing in Two Boats

wanted a speedy transfer of power to a strong successor state. It was this fact, rather than Mountbatten's celebrated friendship with Nehru, which explains why the British leant so heavily on Jinnah to accept a 'moth-eaten' Pakistan. The British were reluctant to accept Partition at all, but the Muslim League's growth in prestige during the war meant that its interests could not be lightly cast aside. Khizr received short shrift, despite his unfailing loyalty, simply because he lacked the Quaid-e-Azam's 'nuisance value.'

i

Jinnah took his cue for pressurising Khizr from Sikander's son. In a speech at Sheikhupura on 15 July 1943, Shaukat Hayat publicly declared that he would carry out all the mandates of the Muslim League with a soldier's discipline, 'shirking no danger or sacrifice.' He further asserted that all elected representatives of Muslims in the Punjab Assembly were not only members of the League, but had the same loyalty towards it as members of any political party. Moreover, he declared that there could be no question of conflict between the League and the Ministry, as the latter had been formed by the leader of the Muslim League Party or in other words by the Muslim League itself.[6] The speech succeeded in its purpose of raising the political temperature. It followed on from the fledgling Minister's 'unpardonally indiscreet references to Pakistan' in earlier statements.[7] Khizr gently rapped his errant colleague over the knuckles. With hindsight he acknowledged that if he had instantly dismissed Shaukat it might just have nipped the growing Muslim League agitation in the bud.[8] In all probability, however, the momentum for Pakistan was already unstoppable.

Jinnah was astute enough to play the situation long. He noted the growing tensions within the Punjabi Muslim elite,[9] but did not immediately leap into the cockpit of the province's politics. Glancy, nevertheless, hoisted the storm cones in a series of reports to the Viceroy. In one such missive he lamented that, 'a preeminently Muslim Government, which, whatever its defects has carried on for so many years with a reasonable efficiency, should now (be in danger of) collapse through the machinations of the Quaid-e-Azam.'[10] Jinnah remained unconcerned, although he realised that the establishment of a clearly Muslim League Ministry in the Punjab could provoke such strong Hindu and Sikh opposition that Governor's Rule would have to be introduced. For he believed that

Khizr Tiwana, the Punjab Unionist Party and the Partition of India

this might help rally the Muslims to its support. Anyway his sights were set on a wider goal than merely running an effective administration in the Punjab. Glancy of course sought to avoid at all cost a Section 93 administration in wartime Punjab. He noted with misgiving that, 'One of the difficulties is the loose wording of the Sikander-Jinnah Pact.. the more I study the document the less I like it. Unfortunately it is easier for Jinnah to twist the Pact to suit his own convenience than for the Unionist Party; it contains no satisfactory annunciation of the doctrine that the Central Muslim League authorities are expected to refrain from interference in Punjab politics.'[11]

Khizr travelled to Bombay early in September 1943 in an attempt to resolve the ambiguities surrounding the Sikander-Jinnah Pact. The Quaid-e-Azam reconstructed at such length the recent attempt on his life by a Khaksar assailant, that 'Khizr did not succeed for a long time in getting Jinnah to come to the point.' Both men then restated their positions. Khizr that he intended to retain the Unionist Party name for his Ministry. Jinnah that the Unionist Party had ceased to exist when the Pact was drawn up. Khizr so upset the Quaid when he pointed out that he himself had been returned to the Assembly on the Unionist ticket, that the meeting nearly ended there and then.[12] Jinnah was clearly on the verge of a confrontation with the Unionist Ministry.

Khizr attempted to land the first blow by formally establishing a Muslim League Assembly Party in November 1943. The following two provisions in its constitution seemed to meet Jinnah's demands.

(1) The Muslim League Assembly Party shall be subject to the control and discipline of the central and provincial Muslim League Parliamentary Boards.
(2) In all matters relating to Muslim interests the members of the Party shall vote in accordance with decisions arrived at in the Party meetings, or when no such decision has been arrived at in regard to a matter, in accordance with the directions of the leader given through a whip.. (Only) in matters of common interest will the members of the Party vote in accordance with the whip issued by the larger combination, namely the Unionist Party[13]

Khizr in reality, however had gone little more than halfway to meeting the Quaid-e-Azam's requirements. The infant Muslim League Assembly Party remained firmly tied to the leading strings

Sailing in Two Boats

of its Unionist parent. The provision that the Punjab League Assembly Party should be under the control of the central and provincial parliamentary boards had only been added as an amendement after four hours protracted discussions. Moreover, the same meeting had unanimously ratified the Jinnah-Sikander Pact and voted to incorporate it in the Assembly Party's constitution. The door was thus still kept ajar for the Unionists to claim autonomy in provincial politics. The pro-Muslim League, *Eastern Times* editorialised that this situation was untenable. 'The Pact', it warned, 'will make itself a nuisance to everybody and then they shall be glad to get rid of it. It is never right in principle to live under the tyranny of a dead hand.'[14] Few were surprised when Jinnah journeyed to Lahore the following Spring determined to resolve the matter. Indian Muslim history not just Punjab politics hinged on the outcome.

ii

Jinnah sought to boost Pakistan's credibility by installing a Muslim League Government in the Punjab which attached itself closely to his High Command. He was prepared to offer Khizr its leadership, even if it meant disappointing stalwarts like Shaukat, Mian Mumtaz Daultana and the Nawab of Mamdot. If Khizr had been an opportunist, he could have carved out a comfortable niche for himself in the Muslim League hierarchy. But he was a man who stuck stubbornly to his principles. Although he abhored the thought of conflict, he was unable to meet Jinnah's demand to abolish the Pact as it symbolised the guarantees of the Muslim Unionists to their Hindu and Sikh colleagues and to the non-Muslim population at large.

Khizr received powerful support from the triumvirate of Allah Bakhsh, Chhotu Ram and Bertrand Glancy. Chhotu Ram, for example, locked horns with Jinnah for three hours on the issue of the Unionist Party label on the evening of 28 March.[15] Allah Bakhsh just under a month later actually stood in for an exhausted Khizr in a Sunday meeting with the Quaid-e-Azam.[16] Whilst Glancy was on hand to remind the Premier of his duty to hold the line for political stability in the interests of the war effort. Indeed, he stretched his constitutional powers to the limit to secure Shaukat's dismissal on 26 April to prevent him embarrassing the Government by resigning. Khizr was grateful for such backing as the negotiations with Jinnah coincided with renewed health problems and the shock of Umar's death.[17]

Umar had become ill, shortly after Jinnah arrived in the Punjab.

Khizr Tiwana, the Punjab Unionist Party and the Partition of India

The Quaid-e-Azam had timed his visit to coincide with the opening of the Budget Session of the Punjab Assembly. He stayed as usual at Mamdot Villa. His first public engagement was a a tea party hosted by Raja Ghazanfar Ali at the Assembly building on Monday 20th March. Jinnah seized this opportunity to move onto the attack. He called the Jinnah-Sikander Pact a misnomer, declaring that neither he nor the Muslim League had been a party to a 'pact.' The Unionist Party label was a 'false trademark', although the Muslim League Assembly Party could if it wished enter into coalition with the groups of Sir Chhotu Ram, Sir Manohar Lal and Sardar Baldev Singh.[18] The gloves were off with a vengeance.

The following day, Khizr met the Muslim League President privately for over an hour at the Nawab of Mamdot's residence. That evening he made the first of two visits in the midst of the negotiations to see his ailing father at Sargodha. Each was an physically tiring as well as emotionally exhausting round trip of over six hours drive via the bridge at Chiniot. Umar remained the stern family patriarch to the last admonishing Khizr to do his duty and telling him 'Don't ever be a coward.'[19]

Umar died suddenly on 24 March. Khizr immediately cancelled his scheduled talks with Jinnah. After stopping to pick up Nazar at Aitchison College, Abdul Ghani drove them both to Sargodha. Sultan Bibi followed in another car. The following evening, Umar was buried in the family graveyard at Kalra, next to his beloved polo ground. The funeral procession was accompanied by an immense crowd of tenants and well-wishers.

Khizr remained at Kalra during the period of mourning. On the fourth day after the burial, his private secretary Stuart Abbott arrived along with boxes of files and other office staff.[20] The establishment of a Prime Ministerial office at Kalra could however be only a very temporary affair as there was still no telephone connection to the house. Even so Khizr could not escape the tension of the Unionist Party-Muslim League controversy, as Chhotu Ram visited him with news of his conversations with the Quaid-e-Azam.[21]

Jinnah meanwhile cooled his heels in Lahore. Umar even in death had continued his lifelong advancement of his son's position. For a wave of sympathy swept the province which strengthened Khizr's hand.[22] Another unforseen consequence was that at least for a short time the Premier softened his attitude towards Jinnah. He was always an emotional man, easily moved to tears. The bereavement heightened this sensitivity. Khizr was genuinely touched by Jinnah's

Sailing in Two Boats

dignified stance and the generous tributes which he made to Umar. This feeling certainly played a part in the genuine attempt he made at compromise in the second round of the negotiations.

iii

Jinnah had tarried in Lahore until the beginning of the second week of April. In Khizr's absence he had held talks with both Baldev Singh and Chhotu Ram on 30 March. The two non-Muslim Ministers had consulted at length in order to coordinate their response.[23] The day earlier, Baldev Singh had fired a shot across the Quaid's bows, whilst presiding over a meeting at the Law College. He had told the cheering audience that at least 90 per cent of Sikhs were opposed to the principle of Pakistan. 'I have come to the conclusion', he continued 'that the division of the country is neither in the interests of the country, nor in the interests of the Muslims, nor in that of our rulers. The Muslims may decide anything they like, but the problem will remain unresolved.'[24]

Chhotu Ram used the platform of the annual Jat Mahasabha conference which was held at Lyallpur on 8 April to publicly restate the traditional Unionist view that economic interests were more important than religious community for the rural population. Such issues as control of prices, imposition of import and export duties on agricultural commodities etc. were those in which, he declared 'there could be no difference of opinion between the Jats and the other agriculturalist tribes.'[25]

Jinnah returned to Lahore on the 19th to a hearteningly enthusiastic reception at the railway station. Shaukat's increasingly vocal support also caused him satisfaction. [26] This left Glancy ominously noting to Wavell that, 'his retention in the Cabinet has little to recommend it.'[27] Khizr held the first of the renewed round of meetings on the following evening at Mamdot Villa. His parley with Jinnah continued for about two and a half hours. It revealed to a relieved Governor that Khizr had recaptured some of his old spirit. He approved that Jinnah had been forced to concede that he had earlier admitted at Delhi that the name 'Unionist' could be retained, although his attitude had since altered. Glancy also related to Wavell the repartee which had followed Jinnah's comment that for a Muslim to adhere to the Unionist Party as well as to the Muslim League was like keeping a mistress. 'To this Khizr adroitly responded that being a Muslim himself he was entitled to have two wives.'[28]

117

Khizr Tiwana, the Punjab Unionist Party and the Partition of India

Shaukat met Jinnah immediately after Khizr had departed. Later callers included the veteran khilafatist and journalist Maulana Zafar Ali Khan,[29] and Nawab Mushtaq Ahmad Gurmani, a leading landowner from the Muzaffargarh district who had been associated with the Unionist Party from 1930 and served as a parliamentary private secretary.[30]

During the days which followed, Khizr engaged in lengthy negotiations with Jinnah. The Quaid-e-Azam also met leading Muslim Unionists. On Friday 21st, he offered prayers at the Badshahi Mosque and later fatiha at Iqbal's grave, whose sixth death anniversay fell on that day.[31] Neither leader would divulge to the press what was taking place.[32] But Khizr has left an interesting fragment of his side of the discussions. This reveals the hitherto unknown fact that a new formula to replace the Jinnah-Sikander Pact was actually drafted and discussed and an amended draft produced which incorporated Jinnah's suggestions.

The draft included the six following points: a. The League Party is to be accepted as a primary party in the Punjab Assembly. Members of the Party owe allegiance to no other party and do not belong to the Unionist Party. b. The Muslim League Party in conjunction with other parties in the Assembly will carry out the programme of the Unionist Party as contained in the rules and regulations framed originally in 1936. c. The existing combination shall maintain its present name 'the Unionist Coalition'. d. The members of the Legislature who constitute the Muslim League Assembly Party will be governed by the rules and regulations already published with the exception of rule 11 (relating to the Jinnah-Sikander Pact) which is being replaced by the present agreement. e. Malik Khizr Hayat Khan Tiwana as leader of the Muslim League Assembly Party will select his Muslim colleagues in the Ministry from among the members of the Assembly in whom he has confidence. f. The Punjab Provincial Muslim League will hereafter not raise any matter about the working of the Muslim League Assembly Party except with the specific permission of the Leader of that Party or through the Assembly Party itself.[33]

This draft was probably the focus of the protracted discussions which occurred over the weekend of 22–24 April and lasted into the Monday. When the talks resumed again two days later, however, it was clear that a breakdown was imminent. So what had gone wrong? It is clear that Khizr was more eager for a compromise than Jinnah. Indeed, the latter was being constantly bombarded with advice from

Sailing in Two Boats

Shaukat and the Nawab of Mamdot not to let the Premier off the hook. In one such meeting which was also attended by Zia-ul-Islam the President of the Punjab Muslim Students Federation, everyone argued that the Quaid-e-Azam should break with the Unionists 'who were nothing but British stooges.'[34] The communally minded Hindu press's sudden love for the Unionists and its singing of Khizr's praises also strengthened Jinnah's resolve.[35] He decided that it was more important to free the Muslim League from the shackles of a Unionist Party associated with the creed of a united India than to maintain a Muslim led government in the Punjab. The Muslim League Assembly Party even in opposition could launch a powerful propaganda movement for Pakistan.

Khizr, however understandably feared that a crisis would follow the breakdown of the talks. This would not only damage the war effort and communal relations, but also split the Muslim community. Nevertheless, he could only go so far to achieve an agreement, as he recognised the need to keep onboard Chhotu Ram and the other non-Muslim Ministers. Indeed, he even argued along these lines to Jinnah, but it naturally cut no ice.

iv

Glancy had grown increasingly anxious as the negotiations proceeded. 'A disruption of the Unionist Party even in name', he gloomily wrote to the Viceroy, 'is bound to weaken the solidarity of the Punjab and to undermine the war effort.'[36] The Governor would not meet Khizr's request to give him an 'order' to stand up to Jinnah in the interests of the war effort,[37] but he did take the controversial step of dismissing Shaukat, at the very moment when it was becoming clear that the talks were failing. Glancy had cleared his action in a letter to Wavell a couple of days earlier. The correspondence is interesting because it reveals both the Governor's misgivings and the fine political judgement which lay behind the decision.[38]

Glancy's disquiet stemmed not from any sympathy for Shaukat, or from the knowledge that he was over-stepping the bounds of his authority.[39] But rather out of a respect for the Hayat family and the knowledge that the Muslim League would claim he had acted in an improper manner. The League did duly charge that Shaukat had been dismissed for his political activities. This was of course largely true. Glancy admitted to Wavell that, 'I should have preferred.. to have merely forced him to resign..but a mere resignation will not produce the desired effect so far as concerns the staunchness of a certain influential MLA.'[40] It thus seems unlikely that Glancy would have dismissed Shaukat in different circumstances. Moreover, he had long been aware of Shaukat's 'glaring act of injustice' which formed the basis for his dismissal. Significantly, he chose this critical moment to act on it.

The case concerned Shaukat's suspension and subsequent sacking, several months earlier, of Mrs Durga Dass. She was an Indian-Christian Inspectress of Schools employed by Lahore Corporation. William Kennedy I.C.S. had investigated the eight charges of corruption levelled against her and had found them based on false evidence. Shaukat had nevertheless dismissed her, recording on the file that she had been 'proved' guilty of corruption. This confirmed Glancy's judgement that Mrs Dass had been victimised because she had offended one of Shaukat's subordinates.[41]

Shaukat has provided his version of the dramatic cabinet meeting in which he was dismissed.[42] It naturally paints Khizr in a bad light. Shaukat's claim that Khizr was party to the Governor's decision from the beginning, appears unjustified. What does ring true, however, is the part of the narrative which portrays the Premier's attempts to smooth things over and arrange a private post-lunch meeting for Shaukat with Glancy. Khizr's exaggerated respect for the Governor is also certainly authentic. Shaukat records for example, Khizr's comment that he had not intervened during the Cabinet meeting, because 'His Excellency had been so kind to him.. The Prime Minister now said to me that His Excellency was upset because I had dared to answer back in Cabinet.'[43] Khizr is also depicted as true to character in offering not to publish the case, if Shaukat refrained from making a press statement. The latter refused, so the public was regaled with the conflicting versions of the events. By the time these hit the news-stands, however, Shaukat's dismissal was overshadowed by the dramatic collapse of the Khizr-Jinnah negotiations.

v

Khizr was sitting in the garden of his 22 Queen's Road residence on 27 April, when Jinnah phoned him with what amounted to a final ultimatum. After a brief conversation in which the Punjab Premier refused to renounce the Unionist Party name, the Quaid-e-Azam rang off, declaring Khizr was a 'mad man' and ominously warning that

Sailing in Two Boats

'You will regret this the rest of your life.'[44] When Khizr arrived at Mamdot House that afternoon, Jinnah dictated to his private secretary a letter which formally requested him to put in writing his reply to the following three points:

(1) that every member of the Muslim League Party in the Punjab Assembly should declare that he owes his allegiance solely to the Muslim League in the Assembly and not to the Unionist Party or any other Party;

(2) that the present label of the coalition should be dropped, namely the ' Unionist Party'; and

(3) that the name of the proposed coalition should be the Muslim League Coalition Party.[45]

The Punjab Premier incensed the Quaid when he refused to reply by the 9pm deadline and failed to acknowledge a second letter from Jinnah which the Nawab of Mamdot and Mian Mumtaz Daultana delivered by hand. Khizr had in fact instead spent the time polishing a press statement which in a preemptive strike provided his version of the events.[46]

The press release explained that the repudiation of the Jinnah-Sikander Pact would 'amount to a breach of faith' and that the Punjab Premier would not accept a demand, 'involving intereference in provincial affairs and the inner working of the (Pact) as this would be contrary to the accepted democratic principle that the wishes of the electorate and the legislature should prevail.' Khizr concluded his statement with a warning that, 'the disunity of different communities could only spell disaster, embitter non-Muslims and intensify communal hatred leading to bloodshed and disorder and serious interference with the war effort at a time when the Japanese aggressor was on the soil of India.'[47]

Jinnah responded in a speech to the Punjab Muslim League Annual Session which was held at Sialkot on 28th-30th April.[48] He denied that any assurance of non-interference in the internal affairs of the Punjab had been given in his 'Pact' with Sikander. He then thundered 'Bury this name Unionist. Perform its funeral ceremony.' Like a courtroom judge, he then directed the following questions to Khizr. 'Why don't you agree to it? What are your reasons? He proceeded to pronounce the judgement. 'You want to deceive the League. You never intended to fulfil your promise. You come to the League fettered and chained by it. When God wants to destroy a people, he makes them blind and they are led by a boy leader.'[49]

Khizr Tiwana, the Punjab Unionist Party and the Partition of India

This onslaught was followed by a series of resolutions which deplored, 'the whole attitude and actions' of Khizr and condemned Glancy's dismissal of Shaukat. The Premier and his Muslim colleagues were called upon to resign, if the Governor did not 'afford all facilities' to Shaukat 'to clear up his position.'[50]

Jinnah turned up the heat still further in an address to the Sialkot Muslim Student's Federation, immediately after the League Session. For the first time in public he referred to the Unionists as 'traitors' and declared that 'charges are to be framed against the culprit' (ie Khizr) who was responsible for disuniting the Punjabi Muslims.[51] This animosity was increased, when Baldev Singh and Chhotu Ram publicly issued a statement on 3 May that they would not join a Muslim League Coalition in the Punjab, unless there was an All-India political agreement. Both Jinnah and the Working Committee of the Punjab Muslim League dismissed this as an attempt by so-called 'substantial' Hindu and Sikhs[52] to be the arbiters of the programme and destiny of the 'Muslim Nation.' The Working Committee after a meeting at Montgomery resolved that, 'it resents as an insult to the national self respect of Muslims any attempt to impose labels or platforms on Muslims as a condition precedent for a Coalition. The Muslims cannot afford to join local, makeshift political parties and thus disrupt the very solidarity which we are trying to build up under the Muslim League for the attainment of our National goal.'[53]

In this atmosphere, Khizr's offer to refer the question of the Jinnah-Sikander Pact to the arbitration of a Muslim judge of the Federal Court or to a mutually agreed Muslim judge of any High Court in India, received short shrift. It had already been judged by the 'Muslim nation.'[54] It was now only a matter of time before he would be stripped of his formal membership of the All-India Muslim League. Khizr wisely went to Simla for a much needed rest, rather than accept the summons to appear before the Muslim League Council of Action to explain himself. Liaquat Ali Khan who was the presiding judge, duly set in motion the machinery for Khizr's expulsion. This was announced on 27 May.[55] It temporarily created an anomalous situation in which Khizr was the only Muslim member of the Cabinet who did not owe formal allegiance to the organisation. His colleagues, however, resigned shortly afterwards to forestall their expulsion. The breach between the Unionists and the Muslim League could not have been made clearer.

Sailing in Two Boats

vi

Khizr faced the twin tasks of shoring up the Unionist Party's strength in the Assembly and counteracting a Muslim League propaganda campaign. He knew that at the best an dozen or so Muslim members would desert to the League. As it turned out, the Muslim League Assembly Party boasted 27 members by the beginning of December 1944.[56] Two senior Unionists, who had been close associates of Sikander, Mir Maqbool Mahmood and Allah Yar Khan Daultana had resigned as Parliamentary Secretaries[57] on the day his talks with Jinnah had collapsed. Khizr was also disquieted by the fact that the titular head of the Mitha Tiwanas, Major Nawab Mahomed Mumtaz Tiwana, had called on the Quaid-e-Azam on 3 April and given him a cheque for Rs 5000 to organise the Muslim League in the rural areas.[58]

Khizr steadied the situation by appointing two new Ministers both of whom came from the Multan division in which the largest number of rural Muslim constituencies were situated.[59] Sir Mohammad Jamal Khan Leghari, the representative of the Tumandar constituency, replaced Shaukat as Minister of Public Works. Nawab Ashiq Hussain took up the new post of War Planning. Both men wielded immense authority in their respective districts. The former was a Baloch leader and large landholder in the Dera Ghazi Khan district.[60] The latter was a member of the leading Qureshi pir family of Multan. He was also the son-in-law of Sir Liaqat Hayat Khan, Sikander's elder brother. His appointment did not, however, forestall the defection of the Khattar faction. Wartime dislocation and changes at the All-India level were snapping the fragile bonds which held together the rural faction leaders. Khizr hardly required Glancy's advice that it was 'high time' to set up an effective grassroots political organisation.[61]

Khizr and his Ministerial colleagues dug into their own pockets to fund the relaunching of the Zamindara League. Baldev Singh and Ashiq Hussain both contributed Rs 25,000 to its coffers. Khizr topped this by Rs 500. Other generous donations of Rs 20,000 came from Jamal Khan Leghari and Allah Baksh.[62] A further Rs 52,000 was donated after Khizr and three of his Ministers[63] were weighed in silver at the Kaurali (Ambala district) birthplace of Baldev Singh.[64] Such a high proportion of the donations were significantly now being given by non-agriculturalists[65] that Chhotu Ram announced at Kaurali that the Zamindara League would throw open its doors to all

Khizr Tiwana, the Punjab Unionist Party and the Partition of India

who had sympathies for the poor agriculturalists and agreed with its programme. The money had not of course been forthcoming for the latter reason, but because non-Muslims saw the League as the best vehicle to prevent the creation of Pakistan. This questioned whether the Zamindara League would be able to take root in the soil of the West Punjab, where the Muslim League had launched an intensive propaganda campaign in June and July. Its star speakers included such scions of families traditionally associated with the Unionist party as Shaukat Hayat, Mian Mumtaz Daultana and Nawab Iftikhar Hussain of Mamdot.

Their desertion of the Unionist cause highlights the fact that Khizr's personal upbringing and beliefs were of crucial importance at this particular historical juncture. His sense of duty, lack of political ambition, cross-communal family and friendship relationships all inclined him towards the 'fool-hardy' course of opposing Jinnah. A more calculating individual would have grasped the offer of leadership of a Muslim League Ministry. General accounts of this period which invariably provide a disembodied view of the Unionist leader overlook the importance of personality. They are also inevitably silent about the fact that Umar's death with all its emotional impact, coincided with the Jinnah talks. It did matter that Khizr, not any other Muslim landowner was in charge of the Unionist Party's fortunes during the Spring of 1944.

Notes

1 Jinnah was to deny that the written agreement between Sikander and himself had the legal status implied by the word 'pact'. He portrayed it as simply a domestic arrangement within the Muslim League. Because of the controversy which surrounded the Pact it is helpful to reproduce in full the statement which Sikander and Jinnah agreed at the Muslim League Council meeting at Lucknow.(a) That upon his return to the Punjab, Sir Sikander Hayat Khan will convene a special meeting of his party and advise all Muslim members of the party who are not members of the Muslim League already to sign its creed and join it. As such, they will be subject to the rules and regulations of the central and provincial boards of the All-India Muslim League. This will not affect the continuance of the present coalition Unionist Party.(b) That in future elections and by-elections for the legislature, after the adoption of this agreement, the groups constituting the Unionist Party will jointly support candidates put up by their respective groups.(c) That the Muslim members of the legislature who are elected on or accept the League ticket will constitute the Muslim League party within the legislature. It shall be open to the

Sailing in Two Boats

Muslim League party so formed to maintain or enter into coalition or alliance with any other party consistent with the fundamental principles, policy and programme of the League. Such an alliance may be evolved before or after the elections. The existing combination shall maintain its present name, Unionist Party.(d) In view of the aforesaid agreement, the provincial League parliamentary board shall be reconstituted.Cited in, Syed Nur Ahmad, *From Martial Law to Martial Law. Politics in the Punjab 1919–1958* (Boulder, 1985) p. 147.

2 Wavell to Glancy 15 April 1944 *T.P* iv, p. 461.

3 Punjab FR 17 April 1943 L/P&J/5/246, IOR.

4 Wavell to Amery 16 May 1944 *T.P* iv, p. 968.

5 Wavell at least in Khizr's mind, politically let him down badly at the time of the Simla Conference, although he still wrote of him in glowing personal terms to George VI. He described him as, 'the most attractive character of the Indians present.. a great gentleman, straightforward and gradually acquiring political experience.' Wavell to H.M. King George VI 19 July 1945*T.P* v, p. 1277.

6 Glancy to Linlithgow 20 July 1943*T.P* iv p.111.

7 Punjab FR 6 August 1943 L/P&J/5/243 IOR.

8 Interview with Nazar Tiwana, London 20 June 1993.

9 Glancy was firmly of the opinion that 'the chief exponents of a Muslim League Government consist mainly of disgruntled or ambitious politicians . . . who would sell the Unionist fort for their own personal advantage.Punjab FR 2nd half of August 1943 & 17 April 1943. L/P&J/5/243 IOR.

10 Punjab FR 6 August 1943 L/P&J/5/243 IOR.

11 Punjab FR 17 April 1943 L/P&J/5/243 IOR.

12 Glancy to Linlithgow 16 September 1943 L/P&J/5/243 IOR.

13 *Eastern Times* (Lahore) 10 November 1943.

14 *Eastern Times* (Lahore) 11 November 1943.

15 The meeting ended inconclusively. *Civil and Military Gazette* (Lahore) 29 March 1994. 16 *Civil and Military Gazette* (Lahore) 25 April 1944.

17 In an anxious letter to Wavell of 14 April, Glancy noted that 'Khizr was looking below par' that he had recently undergone a minor operation and that his 'health was never particularly robust.' He also made reference to the 'depressing effect' which Umar's death had exerted upon him. Glancy to Wavell 14 April 1944.*T.P* iv, p.

18 *Civil and Military Gazette* (Lahore) 21 March 1944.

19 Khizr recalled these as his father's exact words. Interview with Nazar Tiwana, Chicago, 2 September 1993.

20 *Ibid.*

21 *Civil and Military Gazette* (Lahore) 4 April 1944.

22 Punjab FR 2nd half of March 1944 L/P&J/5/247 IOR.

23 *Civil and Military Gazette* (Lahore) 31 March 1944.

24 *Ibid.*

25 *Civil and Military Gazette* (Lahore) 9 April 1944.

26 Shaukat had shared a public platform with Jinnah at a meeting on 2 April held in the grounds of Islamia College. He had declared that the Punjab

Khizr Tiwana, the Punjab Unionist Party and the Partition of India

Premier and the Muslim Ministers were wholeheartedly for Pakistan. Jinnah had taken this as his cue to remind the audience that the Punjab held the key to Pakistan and it was here that they had to cultivate power in favour of the scheme. Speaking in Urdu he went on to say that those who raised the slogan 'Punjab for the Punjabis' were men with divided loyalties. *Civil and Military Gazette* (Lahore) 4 April 1944.

27 Glancy to Wavell 21 April 1944 *T.P* iv p. 906.

28 *Ibid.*, p. 907.

29 For the role he played in the Khilafat movement see, G. Minault, *The Khilafat Movement. Religious Symbolism and Political Mobilization in India* (New York 1982) pp. 156 & ff. Zafar Ali Khan through his editorship of Zamindar was an important opinion former amongst the educated urban Muslim population.

30 *Civil and Military Gazette* (Lahore) 21 April 1944.

31 *Civil and Military Gazette* (Lahore) 22 April 1944.

32 *Civil and Military Gazette* (Lahore) 23 April 1944.

33 This file was numbered no. 16 and formed of an undated typescript. It was probably written quite shortly before Khizr's death when he was planning an autobiography. The author consulted the file in Chicago in September 1978. It is not known whether this file was deposited with the Unionist Party Papers at Southampton University.

34 Zia Ul-Islam, 'A Historical Background of Majlis Karakunan-e-Tehrik-e-Pakistan' unpublished typescript n.d. p.1.

35 *Civil and Military Gazette* (Lahore) 26 March 1944.

36 Glancy to Wavell 14 April 1944 *T.P* iv p. 880.

37 Khizr made this request on or around the 13th April. When doing so he revealed a perception of future political developments which dispels the view of such critics as Syed Nur Ahmad Shah that he was blinkered and unable to cope with the changing situation. The extract below sets out Glancy's gloss on the reasons for his wanting an 'order' to stand up to Jinnah.

> He does not himself believe in Pakistan, but he thinks that the Pakistan slogan is bound to gain momentum and that it is likely to be a decisive factor in the next elections . . . He says he has no liking for politics and intends to retire when the war is over. he would not mind taking risks for himself alone, but he does not like the idea of jeopardising his followers. He believes there will be only two parties of importance in India in the near future – the Congress and the Muslim League . . . Jinnah he is convinced will employ Maulvis and Mullahs to work up fanatical feeling and will not hesitate to revert to other still more nefarious methods of attack.. He suggests that I should solve the problem for him by giving him an 'order' to stand up to Jinnah in the interests of the war effort.

Ibid., pp. 880–1.

38 In a highly revealing sentence, Glancy declared, 'I must admit that I do not altogether like this course of action, but larger issues are at stake – the tranquility of the Province and the continuance of the War Effort.'Glancy to Wavell 24 April 1944 *T.P* iv, p. 924.

Sailing in Two Boats

39 Glancy dismissed Shaukat under the terms of Section 52 of the Government of India Act.

40 The MLA was Sir Muhammad Nawaz Khan of Kot who came from the same Attock district as Shaukat. He was not only a large landowner, the Kot estate covered an area of 88 square miles, but the head of the Ghebas, a tribe which claimed alliance with both the Sials and the Tiwanas. He would have thus been a prize catch for the Muslim League.

41 Glancy to Wavell 24 April 1944 T.P iv, p. 923.

42 The full details are contained in Shamsul Hasan Collection, Punjab Vol.3 Quaid-e-Azam Correspondence with Shaukat Hyat Khan. Shaukat maintained that he had referred the signed allegations to a Special Enquiry Agency and accepted its recommendation that Mrs Durga Dass be suspended. He further established an open enquiry into the case so that she could defend herself and appointed Abdul Hamid as the Chief Officer to conduct this. Because of his death, before recording evidence from the final witness, William Kennedy completed the enquiry. Shaukat admitted that Kennedy exonerated her, but said that the decision was left to him as Minister of Public Works. His reading of the evidence together with the comments by Abdul Majid I.C.S. his deputy Secretary 'left no doubt, in my mind that the lady was unfit for municipal service.' Shaukat maintained that he told influential christian gentlemen who came to plead her case that he could not possibly uphold her conduct, but he did rule that she could not be deprived of her provident fund.

43 *Ibid.*,

44 Interview with Nazar Tiwana, Chicago 2 September 1993.

45 Jamil-ud-din Ahmad, *Speeches and Writings of Mr. Jinnah* vol 2 (Lahore, 1976) p. 42.

46 Glancy noted that Jinnah was furious and that 'charges and counter-charges, some of them apparently quite trivial were interchanged.' Glancy to Wavell 8 May 1944 T.P iv, p. 954.

47 Punjab FR for the 2nd half of April 1944 L/P&J/5/247 IOR.

48 From Khizr's viewpoint the Session was ominously well organised and attended. Shaukat received a rapturous welcome which even exceeded Jinnah's.

49 Jamil-ud-Din Ahmad, *op.cit.*, p. 46.

50 A copy of these resolutions were despatched to the Secretary of State for India.Daultana to Turnball (Private Secretary to the Secretary of State for India) 2 May 1944 T.P iv p. 945.

51 Jamil-ud-din Ahmad *op.cit.* pp. 47–50.

52 Jinnah declared that it was 'preposterous' that Chhotu Ram and Baldev Singh who represented only nineteen members of the Punjab Assembly should demand 'that we come to an All-India settlement or understanding.' Jamal-ud-din *op.cit.*, p. 51.

53 Punjab Provincial Muslim League vol. 162, pt. vii p. 71 & ff. FMA, Karachi.

54 Punjab FR for the 1st Half of July 1944 L/P&J/5/247 IOR.

55 The Council of Action's statement read as follows: The Premier, 'had contravened the policy and programme of the Muslim League and violated its Constitution, rules, aims and objects.' It had thus decided that

he should be 'expelled from the membership of the All-India Muslim League (and should) be ineligible to become a member in future until the Working Committee of the All-India Muslim League removed the ban against him.' Punjab FR for the 2nd half of May 1944 L/P&J/5/247 IOR.

56 Just under a third of these came from the disaffected Khattar section led by Shaukat.

57 Allah Yar Khan Daultana was Parliamentary Secretary to the Education Minister, Mir Maqbool Mahmood was a general Parliamentary Secretary.

58 *Civil and Military Gazette* (Lahore) 4 April 1944.

59 Twenty three of the seventy five Muslim rural seats were situated there. Rawalpindi division had the next largest with twenty, followed by Lahore with eighteen and then Jullundur with eight. Ambala brought up the rear with six seats.

60 The Leghari estate was 115,000 acres in extent. G.L. Chopra, *Chiefs and Families of Note in the Punjab* vol. 2 (Lahore 1940) p. 421.

61 Glancy to Wavell 7 June 1944 *T.P* iv, p. 1009.

62 *Tribune* (Ambala) 26 July 1944.

63 They were Manohar Lal, the Finance Minister, Chhotu Ram, the Revenue Minister and Baldev Singh, the Development Minister.

64 *Tribune* (Ambala) 26 September 1944.

65 Thirty per cent of the donations raised at this time in the Multan district came from non-agriculturalists.

Chapter Eight

'Pakistan Zindabad'

Khizr attempted to establish a grassroots Zamindara League organisation during the eighteen months which elapsed from the collapse of his talks with Jinnah and the beginning of the 1946 provincial election campaign. These efforts however coincided with the mounting Pakistan campaign. The Unionists found themselves swimming against the incoming tide.

Khizr could not isolate the Punjab from developments which questioned the traditional approach to politics in the province.[1] He felt betrayed by his fellow soldier Wavell at the July 1945 Simla Conference. Jinnah's successful assertion that the Muslim League was the sole representative of Muslim opinion sparked off a second damaging exodus of MLAs from the Unionist Party's ranks. Whilst the Muslim League was eroding the Unionist position in the West Punjab, the Congress made major advances in the east, following Chhotu Ram's death in December 1944. By the eve of the 1946 elections, the Unionist Party was disintegrating like a mud fort in a monsoon.

i

Attempts to revive the Zamindara League were intensified from the late summer of 1944 onwards. Paid propagandists were sent into the villages to popularise the Unionist Party's message.[2] The reports which they regularly despatched to Mian Sultan Ali Ranjha at the Unionist Party headquarters in Lahore make fascinating reading. The following extract, for example, comes from the November 1945 report of Bashir Husain, the Jhelum district organiser.

> The Zamindara League workers have been allotted different areas of the **tehsil**. They always keep close touch with the

Khizr Tiwana, the Punjab Unionist Party and the Partition of India

influential people of their areas. The workers themselves are people of influence and have a link of brotherhood in their respective areas. They keenly watch the activities of the opponents – when they come to know that some persons somewhere have been misguided by the adverse propaganda of the Muslim League, they try to disinfect them of all such influences.[3]

The approach of the elections put at a premium, knowledge of the 'tribal' composition of constituencies. Deputations were supposed to reflect the kinship allegiances of the voters. Thus Chaudhri Abdul Rahim MLA and Captain Mian Fateh Muhammad MLA were specifically added to the tour party at the time of the 1945 Hoshiarpur by-election because they were Gujars and 'Gujars form a considerable proportion of the voters.'[4]

Information on the Muslim League's supporters and sympathisers was especially valuable to a party which was beset by defectors, but which still controlled the machinery of government. Patronage could be witheld from such waverers as Chaudhri Faiz Ali, a Gujranwala Honorary Magistrate.[5] Allegations of official support for the Muslim League could also be verified.[6] The strong police presence at Muslim League meetings was of course designed to limit their attendance. The police also helped organise Zamindara League gatherings. Khizr during a flying visit to Mianwali, late in November 1945, intimated to the district's Zamindara league Organiser, that, 'if any occasion arose, I would be given police help in convening meetings. The District authorities (D.C.) would also help in such cases.'[7]

Such actions, however strengthened the claim that the Unionists merely represented the **zaildari-lambardari** class. When Hindu officials were involved as for example the Hoshiarpur D.C.[8] it seemingly confirmed the League's contention that the 'Khizri Muslims' were enemies of Islam.

Although rural notables and **biraderi** leaders had played important roles in the 1937 elections, the unique circumstances of the 1946 struggle undermined their influence. The Muslim League propaganda was designed to circumvent such intermediaries. A community based on faith was opposed to local 'tribal' allegiances.[9] 'Your vote is a trust of the community (**qaum**)', warned the **sajjada nashin** of the leading Chishti shrine at Ajmer, 'no question of someone's caste (zat) or conflicts of **biraderis** should at this time come before you.'[10]

The problems besetting the Ludhiana Zamindara League vividly

130

'Pakistan Zindabad'

illustrate the difficulties of a 'top-down' approach to political organisation. Despite supposedly 'vigorous' work in the district, it only boasted 167 rural members and 19 city members by the end of 1944.[11] Its propaganda secretary minced no words in explaining this pathetic situation. 'What (can) the League expect', he lamented, 'from office holders who are only in the field to further their names and their person with honours. In fact these office holders are political contradictions.'[12]

Not all the Unionists were so apathetic. Even allowing for exaggeration, the report of Chaudhri Taj-ud-din's tour of Hoshiarpur in January 1946 makes for impressive reading. During it, he addressed meetings in nineteen different places and reached an estimated total audience of well in excess of 36,000 persons.[13] The diaries of other Zamindara League workers indicate that this was unexceptional. Mohammad Shafi from the Lahore district, for example, toured seven villages during the course of a single week in August 1944, 'conversing with notables and peasant folk.'[14] Mohammad Aslam Khan sometimes addressed two meetings in a day and travelled by tonga to the villages surrounding Mianwali town. He also organised meetings near the **jama masjid**. He found it particularly profitable, however, to interview people who had come from the **mofussil** in connection with appeals to the Mianwali D.C.[15]

The diaries also lend useful insights into the activists' ideology. Their appeals were most frequently cast in terms of the 'good that had been done by the present Ministry through the so-called Golden Acts that were passed in the Legislature.' The Unionist Government was linked to the region's era of prosperity, when the rights of the agriculturalists found true representation. The activists also picked up Khizr's frequent allusions to the need for communal harmony and a stable Ministry. Surprisingly little attention was devoted to the shortcomings of the Muslim League. Just one speech by Mohammad Aslam Khan in Mianwali on 5 December 1945 seems to be the exception to this. He dwelt on the 'misdeeds' of the Frontier Muslim League Government of Aurangzeb Khan. 'The control of the Central authority over the Muslim League Ministries', he continued. 'is very meagre with the result that they become irresponsible and unscrupulous.'[16]

The propagandists' lauding of the 'Golden Acts' made little impact. Seven years had elapsed since their introduction. Moreover, during this time, the Unionist Government, through no fault of its own, had introduced intensely unpopular wartime controls and

131

restrictions. Most of all however, the Muslim League's Islamic appeals transcended 'bread and butter' issues. 'Wherever I went', reported a Jhelum Zamindara League activist, 'everyone kept saying **bhai** if we do not vote for the (Muslim) League we could have become **kafir**.'[17]

Khizr greatly feared the impact of such appeals on rural voters. He therefore directed the local Zamindara activists to cultivate the support of influential **pirs**. The drawbacks were ironically laid bare at the shrine of Baba Farid, where the Tiwanas had been converted to Islam some seven centuries earlier.

Agha Barkat Ali, the Montgomery district Zamindara League Organiser set up a camp during the 1945 **'urs** ceremonies at Baba Farid's shrine. On this as every other year multitudes flocked to the shrine famous for its 'gate of paradise.'[18] Pakpattan, however, was hell for the Unionist workers. Their pamphlets, gramaphone records and touring film van counted for little as the **dargarh** authorities refused to allow them to hold a meeting in the shrine. This privilege was only extended to the Muslim League. To add insult to injury the assembled **sajjada nashins** refused to sign the carefully prepared Unionist Manifesto which Agha Barkat Ali had brought with him. His comment to Mian Sultan Ali Shah that, 'the camp life had cost a lot of worries and we had to be very vigilant to avoid any undesirable incident'[19] puts the best possible gloss on a depressing experience.

It was shared by Unionist activists elsewhere. The Rawalpindi district Zamindara League organiser visited Muhra Sharif at Khizr's express wish, only to be rebuffed with the reply that **sajjada nashins** should not take part in politics. They did, however, overcome any scruples when it came to the Muslim League.[20] The Rawalpindi organiser visited Pir Taunsa on 18 September 1945. Here he played his trump card. 'It was in a way explained to His Holiness', he reported, 'that when the Muslim League will come in power the first act which will be passed will be **Auqaf** Bill which will take away all their properties and leave them almost destitute like the **mahants** after the Gurwara Bill.'[21] This was not in fact the first time that he had raised this spectre, but it left most **pirs** unmoved. Nor would they support the Unionists in return for the payment of **nazrana**. The belief that such a stick and carrot approach would succeed illustrates how much Unionist activists underestimated the religious stake which **pirs** and ordinairy Muslims invested in the Pakistan campaign.

'Pakistan Zindabad'

ii

The Punjab Muslim League continuously raised religious appeals and slogans. Its meetings were frequently held in mosques[22] and the Quran was paraded as the League's symbol. Pledges were made on it to support the Pakistan struggle. Student workers were primed to relate the Muslim League's struggle to Islamic history and to highlight the religious background to Pakistan. They were also advised to join in the prayers or lead them like 'Holy warriors'. Whilst their speeches were to be filled with emotional appeal and always to commence with a text from the Quran invoking God's protection and praising His Wisdom.[23]

The important role which **pirs** played in the Muslim League's advance is now widely recognised. Erland Jansson in his study of the Frontier, for example, has revealed how Pir Manki declared a **jehad** to achieve Pakistan and organised the religious leaders of the region in the **Anjuman-us-asfia**.[24] David Gilmartin has uncovered the role of the pirs in popularising the Pakistan movement in the Punjab.[25] He draws attention to the impact of the **fatwas** which they produced and circulated through the local press and by means of small leaflets and wall-posters. The significance of 'urs ceremonies in disseminating the Muslim League message has also been demonstrated by recent research.[26] The heightened religious emotions at these gatherings provided a fertile soil for the League's appeals. Moreover, returning devotees prepared the soil for the Muslim League workers who increasingly entered the villages in large numbers.[27]

The Punjab Muslim League commenced campaigning in the countryside in the summer of 1944. Important Pakistan conferences were held at Montgomery, Lyallpur, Multan, Sheikhupura, Sargodha, Jhang, Sialkot and Rawalpindi. Over 15,000 attended the meeting at Multan and 10,000 at Montgomery.[28] They included, as Nazir Ahmad Khan, the Muslim League organiser for Montgomery, reported '**Zaildars** and **Lambardars** the class that is generally under the Unionist thumb.'[29] Muslim League leaders were continuously surprised by the extent of their breakthrough. 'The League is spreading even to the rural areas with what is seen to the League leaders here (as) *unexpected* rapidity', Mian Bashir Ahmed wrote to Jinnah in November 1945, 'our workers have not yet reached the villages in adequate numbers and yet one hears of sensational conversions to the League.'[30]

This advance did not solely depend on the use of religious appeals, for Khizr also adopted them with minimal effect. The Muslim League's success was also rooted, firstly in its ability to link the Pakistan idea with popular aspirations and secondly in its growing influence elsewhere in India which created a bandwagon effect.

The Punjab Muslim League crystallised disatisfaction with the wartime economic dislocation and government intereference with grain supplies. It promised a better future, presenting the creation of Pakistan as a panacea for social and economic problems. Propagandists were directed when they visited a village to: 'Find out its social problems and difficulties to tell them (i.e. the villagers) that the main cause of their problems was the Unionists (and) give them the solution – Pakistan.'[31] The League gave a foretaste of the future by taking to the villages such scarce commodities as cloth and medical supplies.[32]

All-India political developments during the war years also boosted the League's standing in the Punjab. The Viceroy's August 1940 declaration and later the 1942 Cripps Mission lent credibility to its separatist demands. The Cripps Mission ended in failure, but the Muslim League emerged strengthened from it. Indeed, Jinnah at the time of his interview with Sir Stafford Cripps had been' rather surprised' to see how far the declaration went 'to meeting the Pakistan case.'[33]

The All India Muslim League's rising stock in the political market resulted not only from a genuine British desire to secure communal cooperation, but from the need to secure a counterweight to the non-cooperating Congress. Jinnah adroitly exploited to the full these fortuitous circumstances. The League grew in the 'sunshine of official favour' following the resignation of the Congress Ministries in October 1939 and the Congress's eventual slide into full scale confrontation with the Raj.

The incaceration of leading Congressmen following the 1942 Quit India movement created a power vacuum which the Muslim League filled. It formed Ministries in the Frontier and Bengal in the spring of 1943. The Bengal Muslim League enrolled 550,000 new members during 1944. Jinnah's new status and the League's breakthrough elsewhere increased the pressure on Khizr. The groundswell of support for Pakistan hampered the activities of the Zamindara League. In some instances it encouraged desertions to the Muslim League. The Rajput members from the Rawalpindi East and Gujjar Khan constituencies, Major Farman Ali and Raja Fateh Khan, both appear to have joined the League as a result of grassroot pressures.[34]

'Pakistan Zindabad'

Whilst, Shahzada Sadiq Bukhari, the Rawalpindi district Zamindara League organiser encountered open hostility in some of the villages, when he attempted to advocate the Unionist Party's cause.[35] Such experiences demoralised Zamindara League activists who became increasingly reluctant to work in Muslim areas.[36]

iii

The Congress simultaneously bit deeply into the Unionists' position in the Ambala division. Like the Muslim League its traditional support base had been restricted to urban middle class groups and it had lacked appeal in the rural areas.[37] Indeed, Chhotu Ram had boasted that the Unionists were the' real Congress.' But like the Muslim League it profited from both the wartime dislocation within the Punjab and the communal polarisation elsewhere in India. The Muslim agriculturalists gravitated towards the League, the Hindus to the Congress. Chhotu Ram's death on 9 January 1945 removed the last breakwater against the incoming Congressite tide.

Chhotu Ram had worked prodigiously to revive the Zamindara League, during the months which followed Jinnah's breach with the Unionists. He repeated the message he had earlier written in the tract, **Bachara Zamindar** (Helpless Peasant). 'Leave religion to the four corners of the temple, the mosque and the Gurdwara. Release yourselves from the bondage of the Maulvis, the Pandits and the Granthis. Do whatever you feel in observing your religious tenets but keep it strictly outside politics.'[38] He consoled Zamindara workers who were disheartened by the rising tide of communalism with verses from Iqbal, his favourite poet.

> Tundia badai mukhalif sa na ghabra aiy uqqab yah toh chalti hain tujhe udana kai-liya

> Do not get disheartened by the fury of the adverse winds, O Eagle These blow to enable you to fly still higher.[39]

The constant round of speaking engagements on top of Ministerial duties undermined the health of the sixty two year old Jat Minister. His final illness was hastened when he addressed a meeting in Jhang, early in November, whilst running a temperature.[40] Khizr mourned Chhotu Ram's loss as a friend and colleague. He was at the Jat leader's bedside when he died. Chhotu Ram's final words to him were, 'I am going may God help all.'[41] Khizr presented the Unionist

135

flag in which his body was wrapped for its journey by ambulance from Shakti Bhavan in Lahore to its cremation in the grounds of the Jat Heroes College at Rohtak. The Punjab Premier publicly declared that he regarded Chhotu Ram, 'Not only (as) an illustrious son of the Punjab and a valued colleague . . . (but) a cherished friend whose unfailing kindness and support I can never forget or replace.'[42]

All Punjabis recognised that Chhotu Ram's demise possessed profound political consequences. Jat farmers who flocked to Rohtak to pay their respects, declared, 'Hamare Raja mar gaye' ('Our King is dead'.)[43] Piyare Lal, the Unionist Party **bhajanik** mourned on Chhotu Ram's **tehrevin**,

> Lawaris kunbe ka khaiwa ab kaun uthaiga
> Dehat main ab Chhotu Ram kaun kahlaiga.

> Chhotu Ram's death has rendered the zamindarsorphans. Who will take his place in the villages?[44]

Wavell wrote back to London, 'Chhotu Ram's death is a very severe blow to the Unionist Party.'[45] He ominously added, 'Things may go badly with the Unionists in the Eastern Punjab, unless the Jats manage to sink their differences and follow Tikka Ram.'[46]

Tikka Ram had been promoted to the Cabinet after serving as a parliamentary secretary during both the Sikander and Khizr Ministries. He shared Chhotu Ram's legal background, but lacked the charisma and populist appeal of the Rahbar-i-Azam. Tikka Ram was not however, personally responsible for the Unionist collapse in the Ambala Division. Prem Chowdhry has recently demonstrated how high prices, shortages and economic controls alienated the Unionists' traditional supporters in this region.[47] The Congress cashed in by cleverly linking **azadi** with a period of abundance in such basic commodities as cloth, sugar and kerosene oil, as did the Muslim League in the West Punjab.

Police and government servants who always voted Unionist were won round by a combination of threats and promises. They had already been hit in the pocket by inflation which outstripped their wartime allowances. The problem of resettlement of demobilised soldiers, grievances over racial discrimination in pay and other facilities, but preeminently the impact of the Indian National Army issue, undermined the Unionists' influence amongst the military personnel who formed another traditional support group. Finally, the transformed All-India political climate contributed to the

'Pakistan Zindabad'

Congress triumph. The widespread belief that the Congress and Muslim League would be the new powers in the land, severely demoralised Unionist supporters.

iv

The Simla Conference dealt the Unionists the **coup de grâce**. Khizr to his dying day regarded Wavell's 'capitulation' to Jinnah at Simla as a major British betrayal. During the course of a prolonged visit to London in the Spring of 1945, the Viceroy Lord Wavell had secured Cabinet permission for a conference to be held whose purpose was to discuss the formation of an Executive Council. This was to consist entirely of Indians with the exception of the Viceroy himself and the Commander-in-Chief. The Council was expected to pave the way to an eventual constitutional solution. Wavell, significantly linked its success with the release of the remaining Congress **detainees.**

Khizr was immediately dismayed when he heard the broadcast of the Viceroy's proposals on 14 June 1945, just eleven days before the scheduled start of the conference. He later characterised the offer as 'so liberal that it made many of us shudder.'[48] He feared that a Congress-Muslim League bargain at the Centre would end his Ministry in the Punjab. This he thought would 'lead to chaos.'[49] Wavell indeed was concerned in the days prior to the conference that such misgivings would keep Khizr away. He therefore sought to reassure him on the basis 'that I have the interests of the Punjab and its soldiers at heart.'[50] This must have added to the Premier's subsequent sense of betrayal.

Khizr relied heavily as usual during the proceedings on the advice of Allah Bakhsh. He maintained a low profile and studiously avoided negotitations with Jinnah, although he had discussions with Maulana Abul Kalam Azad, the President of the Congress. His daily arrival by car elicited more interest from the onlookers than his speeches. His office as Premier of the Punjab entitled him to be driven by car in Simla. The hill station's strict ban on motor vehicles was not however waived for the visiting dignatories. These included not only Gandhi, Jinnah and representatives of the Sikhs and Scheduled Castes, but also the Chief Ministers of the Provincial Governments.

On the eve of the conference, Wavell met separately with Jinnah, Gandhi, Maulana Azad, Khizr and the Punjab Governor in order to take soundings on the composition of the Executive Council. This issue ultimately wrecked the conference. Jinnah adopted the position from which he refused to budge, that the Muslim League should nominate all the Muslim members. The Congress, however refused to accept this diminution of its status as a party with a national character. Khizr in a 'forceful but very friendly way' opined that the British should have left well alone. Glancy backed him up, by warning that the Ministry might resign, if the Unionist Party was not represented on the Executive Council.[51]

The conference proceeded in a series of fits and starts. More time was taken up by adjournments than the actual sessions. Wavell managed to get to base one, which involved the acceptance in principle of parity between the Muslims and Hindus other than the Scheduled Castes. In order to reach the second base, however, the thorny issue of how these representatives would be selected had to be tackled. The parties discussed the composition of their recommendations during the period between 29th June to 14 July. The Viceroy's task was to draw up a provisional membership after receiving them. Khizr's intervention ensured that the nominations would be secret and that Wavell would consult privately with the party leaders, 'before deciding whether to place his final proposals before the conference.'[52]

Jinnah used the lengthy adjournment to put out feelers to Khizr from his base in the Cecil Hotel.[53] It was especially bad news for the Punjab Premier that his kinsman, Malik Sir Feroz Khan Noon[54] gravitated towards the Muslim League, during this time. Indeed, Feroz was touted in some quarters as an 'independent' Muslim League nominee for the proposed Council. The stream of telegrams sent to the Viceroy by Punjab branches of the League endorsing Jinnah's stance further pressured Khizr.[55] Meetings were also held in the Badshahi and other mosques of Lahore on Friday 6 July in which resolutions were adopted claiming the Muslim League's exclusive right to nominate Muslim members.[56]

It was no surprise therefore that Khizr was still procrastinating about his list of nominations on 9 July.[57] Wavell during a pre-lunch session attempted to galvanise the Punjab Premier into action. Mohammad Khan Nawaz Khan of Kot Fateh Khan headed the list which Khizr eventually produced, no doubt in part as Wavell noted, because he was 'probably not disliked by the League.'[58] Wavell earmarked the Agriculture and Food Portfolio for the Unionist nominee. Khizr's second choices were his Ministerial colleague, Nawab Sir Jamal Khan Leghari, K.B. Shaikh Faiz Muhammad Khan who was a Parliamentary private secretary and Ghias-ud-din who was recently returned from a lecture tour of the United States.

'Pakistan Zindabad'

Wavell named the Unionist representative along with the four Muslim Leaguers he had drawn up in the absence of a response from Jinnah, during a meeting with the Quaid on the afternoon of 11th July. Jinnah refused to cooperate unless two demands were met, namely: (1) All Muslim members should be drawn from the Muslim League; (2) Any measure to which the Muslims objected could only be carried by a clear two thirds majority of the Council.[59] Wavell considered these conditions unacceptable, and without further ado declared that the conference had failed. He immediately informed Gandhi but Khizr and Azad had to wait until he received them the following morning.

During the final session of the now doomed conference, Khizr declared that he had put forward his claim, on the assumption that the 'main parties would come to an agreement.' He also quietly chided Jinnah's approach, maintaining that any party's monopolization of representatives would mean, 'disenfranchising other schools of thought.'[60] Jinnah had no time for such niceties, what was important for him was the massive boost to the Muslim League's fortunes which followed from his 'demonstration of imperious strength.'[61]

Khizr was shocked by the chorus of abuse which greeted him, following the conference's failure. He thought that Wavell's acceptance of the blame for its collapse would end the matter. The Muslim League, however, refused to pass up this opportunity. Members of its Punjab branch almost queued up to issue statements denouncing Khizr's role at Simla. Typical of their tone was the view expressed by K.B. Chaudhri Nazir Ahmad Khan, a member of the Punjab Muslim League Working Committee. In his opinion, 'it was in the Malik Sahib's interest that the Conference should fail' for its success would 'have had a serious and immediate repercussion on the fate of his Ministry in the Punjab.' 'The Unionist Party as such is a misnomer', his statement continued, 'There is no doubt that some self-seeking people who have everything to lose if they espouse the popular cause, have banded themseleves together under the misleading name of "Unionist" in the Punjab Assembly, but the Unionist Party as a parliamentary party has no branches.. no regular membership.. and in any case has no place in All-India politics.'[62]

The joint statement of the Nawab of Mamdot and Mian Mumtaz Daultana packed the biggest punch. It represented Khizr's action as a 'clear attack on the rights and solidarity of the Muslim "**Millat**".' He was charged with trying to weaken the League case and stultify the 'principles on which depends the future of the Muslim Nation in

India.'[63] Public meetings reiterated the view that Khizr had wrecked the Conference,[64] despite the skillfully drafted rebuttal which he had issued to the press.[65] This was no time, however for reasonableness and rational argument. Wavell summed up the situation when he noted, 'Khizr might have done better to say nothing, for he has little newspaper support and his original rejoinder has encouraged counter-attacks.'[66]

Many Punjabi Unionists, not least Khizr himself, felt that the Viceroy had let them down badly. Glancy conveyed this attitude to his superior with all the tact which he could muster. 'There is still a feeling of considerable resentment among the loyal section of the public', he reported some weeks later, 'which is summed up in the following quotation heard in one district "The enemies of England have nothing to fear and her friends have nothing to hope for.'[67]

The new atmosphere was brought home by the swelling of the opposition benches in the Punjab Assembly. Khizr was even deserted by his Parliamentary Private Secretary Syed Amjad Ali. *Dawn*[68] trumpeted the defection of Khizr's kinsmen to the League, they included Major Mohammad Mumtaz Khan Tiwana and Feroz Khan Noon who resigned from the Executive Council on 15 September in order to 'go back to the Punjab and help the Muslim League.'[69] Khizr now faced opposition from the senior members of both the Tiwana and Noon tribes.

Large numbers of Zamindara League workers also defected. The rot in the Jhelum district started right at the top, as its chief worker, Mohammad Iqbal divulged secrets to the Muslim League and obstructed operations until his final dismissal.[70] The situation was, however little better elsewhere. By the beginning of November 1945 the Presidents of the Ludhiana, Rawalpindi and Lyallpur branches of the Zamindara League had all decamped. Khizr could thus have hardly begun electioneering in less auspicious circumstances. The Muslim League from the outset appeared well placed to triumph in a poll which Jinnah sought to represent as a referendum on Pakistan.

Notes

1 There is an interesting parallel between the effect of external forces on the collapse of a consociational approach to communal conflict in 1940s Punjab and the descent into civil war in the Lebanon in 1975. In both situations, political accommodation had secured stability in highly segmented societies and this was ended largely by external pressures,

'Pakistan Zindabad'

rather than its own failings. In the case of Lebanon it was the intrusion of Palestinian-Israeli conflict and later intra-Arab conflict which brought on the collapse. Significantly, civil war followed the ending of consociationalism in both situations.

2 The workers were paid Rs 100 per month, as their numbers increased with the advent of the 1946 provincial election campaign, this was reduced to Rs 65. They could also claim travel expenses for activities outside their home district.

3 Monthly Report of November 1945 for the Jhelum district. Bashir Husain, District Organiser, Jhelum Zamindara League 5 December 1945 file D-48 Unionist Party Papers.

4 Raja Ghazanfar Ali Khan to Sultan Ali Ranjha 14 & 19 July 1945. Hoshiarpur By-Election File F-28 Unionist Party Papers.

5 Aminullah Khan to Sultan Ali Ranjha, 8 July 1945 File E-99 Unionist Party Papers.

6 See, for example, Sultan Ali Ranjha to K.B. Fateh Khan, Rawalpindi district Zamindara League Organiser, 6 October 1945 File D-40 Unionist Party Papers.

7 Diary of 28 November 1945, Personal File of Mohammad Aslam Khan, District Organiser Mianwali Zamindar League File E-171 Unionist Party Papers.

8 He had accompanied the Hoshiarpur Zamindara League Organiser on a lengthy village tour in January 1946. Report for January 1946 of Ch. Taj-ud-din Hoshiarpur district Zamindara League Organiser. File D-33 Unionist Party Papers.

9 This did not mean that the Muslim League entirely swept away local political loyalties. Nor that it did not seek to accommodate itself to the realities of biraderi influence in mobilising support. See, for example, I. Talbot, *Punjab and the Raj 1849–1947* (New Delhi, 1988) p. 209 & ff.

10 Cited in D. Gilmartin, *Empire and Islam. Punjab and the Making of Pakistan* (Berkeley, 1988) pp. 216–7.

11 Report on the working of the Ludhiana district Zamindara League for December 1944 File D-36 Unionist Party Papers.

12 Propaganda Secretary Ludhiana district Zamindara League to Secretary Ludhiana district Zamindara League n.d. Personal file of Ghazanfar Ali, Ludhiana Division Zamindara League Organiser File E-73 Unionist Party Papers.

13 Chaudhri Taj-ud-din District Organiser Hoshiarpur Tour Diary January 1946. File D-33 Unionist Party Papers.

14 Mohammad Shafi, Worker Lahore district Zamindara League Diary 2–27 August 1944. File E-75 Unionist Party Papers.

15 Diary Entries of Mohammad Aslam Khan, District Organiser Mianwali Zamindara League 14, 16 & 17 November 1945 File E-171 Unionist Party Papers.

16 *Ibid.*, Diary Entry 5 December 1945.

17 Gilmartin *op.cit.*, p. 218.

18 This was only opened once a year, on the final and most important day of the 'urs ceremonies, when it was believed that anyone who could squeeze through its narrow entrance was assured a place in Paradise.

Khizr Tiwana, the Punjab Unionist Party and the Partition of India

19 Agha Barkat Ali, Organising Director Montgomery district Zamindara League to Sultan Ali Ranjha 3 & 13 December 1945. File D-56 Unionist Party Papers.

20 As early as April 1943 the Muslim League had issued an appeal to the pirs of Muslim India to pray and exhort 'their followers to sacrifice their all in the cause of the attainment of a free and independent Muslim India.'G.F. Ansari to Jinnah, 25 April 1943 QEAP File 1101/105 NAP.

21 Zamindara League Rawalpindi Division Organiser to Sultan Ali Ranjha 10 October 1945. File E-105 Unionist Party Papers.

22 A grandiose proposal was once placed before the All-India Muslim League Working Committee to use 5,000 mosques in the 'Pakistan' areas as missionary sub-centres for the League. Muslim League Working Committee Meetings, 1943–7 Vol. 142 p. 23 FMA.

23 Punjab Muslim Students' Federation Election Board Pamphlet FMA.

24 E. Jansson, *India, Pakistan or Pakhtunistan? The Nationalist Movements in the North-West Frontier Province*, 1937–47 (Uppsala, 1981) p. 166.

25 D. Gilmartin, 'Religious Leadership and the Pakistan Movement in the Punjab'. *Modern Asian Studies*, 13, 3 (1979).

26 See, for example, I. Talbot, *Punjab and the Raj 1849–1947* (New Delhi, 1988) p. 211 &ff. The **Sajjada Nashin** of the shrine of Pir Sayed Mohammad Ghaus, for example, used the 'urs ceremonies at the shrine to appeal to his **murids** to support the Muslim League candidate in the Shakargarh constituency.

27 Much propaganda work was carried out by students. During the years before 1944, when tight Unionist control of the provincial Muslim League had limited its activities they had singlehandedly taken the Pakistan message to the countryside. Jinnah continued to closely patronise them, after his split with Khizr. During the peak of student activity during the 1945 Christmas vacation, there were 1550 members of the Punjab Muslim Students' Federation and 250 Aligarh students working on the Muslim League's behalf.

28 Report of the Punjab Provincial Muslim League's work for June and July 1944 submitted to the All-India Muslim League Committee of Action, 28 July 1944, SHC Punjab Vol.1.

29 Nazir Ahmad Khan, 'Thoughts on the Muslim League Speakers' Tour of Montgomery.' 10 January 1945 SHC, Punjab Vol. 3.

30 Mian Bashir Ahmed to Jinnah, 14 November 1945. SHC, Punjab Vol. 3.

31 Translation of a pamphlet issued by the election board of the Punjab Muslim Students' Federation FMA.

32 *Eastern Times* (Lahore) 28 August 1945.

33 Interview with Jinnah 25.3.42. P&J/10/4 Transfer of Power Records, IOR.

34 Report of the Organising Secretary Rawalpindi Division Muslim League. Punjab Muslim League 1943–4, Vol. 162, Part 7, p. 74 & ff. FMA.

35 Shahzada Sadiq Bukhari Tour Notes 28 May & 18 September 1945. Personal File of the Organiser of the Rawalpindi Zamindara League. Unionist Party Papers.

36 Mian Sultan Ali Ranjha to Sufi Abdul Haq Assistant Organiser Sargodha district 13 October 1944 File E-76 Unionist Party Papers.

'Pakistan Zindabad'

37 Prem Chowdhry's recent work has modified this view a little. She has shown that the Congress did acquire some support from lower class Jats and Untouchables from the 1920s onwards. But its continued leadership by the urban middle class groups confirmed in the public mind, Chhotu Ram's claim that it was the Party of the Banias.P. Chowdhry, 'Social Support Base and Electoral Politics: The Congress in Colonial Southeast Punjab' *Modern Asian Studies* 25, 4 (October 1991).

38 Cited in D.C. Verma, *Sir Chhotu Ram. Life and Times* (New Delhi, 1981) p. 175.

39 *Ibid.*, p. 167.

40 M. Gopal, *Sir Chhotu Ram* (Delhi, 1977) p. 149.

41 *Ibid.*, p. 150.

42 Cited in D.C. Verma, *Sir Chhotu Ram. Life and Times* (New Delhi, 1981) p. 196.

43 *Ibid.*, p. 217.

44 P. Singh (ed) *Chhotu Ram in the eyes of his contemporaries* (New Delhi, 1992) p. 62.

45 Wavell to Amery 23 January 1945 *T.P* v, p. 448.

46 Wavell to Amery 30 January 1945 *T.P* v, p. 489.

47 The following section draws heavily on her findings contained in Chowdhry *op.cit.*

48 Wavell to Amery 15 July 1945*T.P* Vol.v p. 1259

49 Wavell to Amery Telegram 27 June 1945 *T.P* v p. 1165.

50 Wavell to Glancy 8 June 1945 *T.P* v, p. 1104.

51 Wavell to Amery Telegram 24 June 1945 *T.P*, v, p. 1151.

52 Wavell to Amery Telegram 29 June 1945 *T.P* v, p. 1173.

53 See, for example, Jahan Ara Shah Nawaz, *Father and Daughter* (Lahore, 1971) p. 192 &ff.

54 Feroz was the most prominent member of the Noon clan. It will be recalled that the Noons and Tiwanas were factional allies and were inter-related by a complex set of marriage alliances. Feroz had served as a Minister in the Punjab Legislative Council, before serving first as Indian High Commssioner in London and then as a member from 1941 onwards of the Viceroy's Executive Council. He was thus a most valuable catch for the Muslim League and a dangerous rival for Khizr.

55 *Dawn* (Delhi) 5 July 1945.

56 *Civil and Military Gazette* (Lahore) 7 July 1945.

57 The Congress had presented a list some three days earlier. Jinnah in the event never produced a list.

58 Wavell to Amery Telegram 9 July 1945 *T.P* v, p. 1216.

59 Wavell to the Provincial Governors 11 July 194 5*T.P* v, p. 1227.

60 Minutes of the Final Meeting of the Simla Conference 14 July 194 5.*T.P*, v, p. 1246.

61 The phrase is H.V. Hodson's and comes from his authoritative description of the Simla Conference contained in, *The Great Divide – Britain-India-Pakistan* (London, 1969) Chapter 10.

62 *Eastern Times* (Lahore, 22 July 1945).

63 *Dawn* (Delhi) 22 July 1945.

64 A large public meeting, for example, took place in the **jama masjid** at

143

Simla, a previous political backwater on 16 July. *Eastern Times* (Lahore) 17 July 1945.

65 It read as follows: I am reluctant to add to the number of statements which are being issued by the leaders who attended the Simla Conference to explain its unfortunate failure and to justify their attitude, but I find myself compelled to take public note of the statement made by Mr. Jinnah at a press conference on July 14th. It is regrettable to note that inspite of Lord Wavell's appeal to all leaders to ensure that there were no recriminations, Mr. Jinnah has lost no time in indulging in unjust and unwarranted vituperations. In the course of his statement, he accuses me of disrupting the Punjab Muslims and attributes the failure of the conference largely to the Viceroy's insistence on including a Punjabi Muslim in his Executive Council. What are the real facts? Mr. Jinnah was obviously ill at ease about his position. He knows that the conference failed on issues more basic than the allotment of a single seat. It is clear from his own statement and those made by the Congress leaders that there are irreconcilable differences between them and Mr. Jinnah and that these were the fundamental cause of the failure of the conference. Because of his failure to reach a settlement with the Congress leaders Mr. Jinnah refused to submit a panel of names to the Viceroy. I must repeat that the differences between the Congress and the League were the cause of the failure of the conference – not the allotment of a seat to a Punjabi Muslim. The present negotiations failed on account of certain fundamental differences between Mr. Jinnah and the Congress – differences which have been evident during the Cripps negotiations and again during the Gandhi-Jinnah talks and therefore the failure can in no way be attributed to the claim for the inclusion of a Punjabi Muslim in the Executive Council. *Dawn* (Delhi) 16 July 1945.

66 Wavell to Amery 22 July 1945 *T.P* v, p. 1287.

67 Punjab FR for the 2nd half of July 1945 L/P&J/5/248 IOR.

68 *Dawn* published the following statement from Major Mohammad Mumtaz Khan Tiwana:

I have been a supporter of the Unionist Party as most of my relations were its main pillars and up until recently there was no clash between the Muslim League and the Unionist Party. But after the Jinnah-Khizar breakdown last year I came to the conclusion that at this critical juncture in the history of the Muslim **millat** complete solidarity among its ranks was extremely essential. The attitude of the Congress and the Unionist Party at the Simla Conference finally demonstrated that the Hindus were determined to keep the Muslims in perpetual servitude to an Akhand Hindustan and that the Unionists were playing into the hands of the anti-Muslim forces in the country. I have decided therefore to join the Muslim League. *Dawn* (Delhi) 4 October 1945.

69 *Dawn* (Delhi) 31 August 1945.

70 Bashir Husain District Organiser Jhelum Zamindara League to Sultan Ali Ranjha 16 January 1946 File D-48 Unionist Party Papers.

Chapter Nine

General Without An Army

The 1946 elections terminated the Unionist Party's twenty year dominance of Punjabi politics. Khizr, however remained in office at the head of a Coalition Government with his erstwhile Akali and Congressite opponents. The Unionist tail, moreover wagged the Coalition dog, as although it was the smallest component of the Government, it alone could claim Muslim support. The Muslim League, nevertheless, denounced the Ministry as illegitimate and lacking in any moral authority.

In many respects, Khizr's final year of power parodied the old Unionist system of power sharing. The Punjab Premier recognised this as such, in his frequent absences from the province and eagerness to restrict parliamentary sittings to reduce the risks of defeat. Yet, the Government maintained communal peace in the province, whilst conflict racked such areas as Calcutta, Noakhali, and Bombay. It was significantly, only after Khizr's resignation on 2 March 1947, that the Punjab began the slide into civil war.

i

Khizr went down fighting in the 1946 provincial elections. Early in September 1945, he had made a preliminary tour of Sargodha, Lahore, Gujranwala, Simla, Jullundur and Ludhiana. This was taken up by interviews with notables and prospective candidates.[1] It was followed up in December with a series of keynote speeches, during a tour in which Khizr addressed numerous village gatherings.

The Punjab Premier warned that a Muslim League victory would result in communal chaos and bitterness and frequent breakdowns of Ministries with intervals of Section 93 Administration.[2] He also attempted to turn the Muslim League election slogans to his advantage. The cry of 'Islam in danger' was misleading, he maintained.' It was not Islam, but certain politicians who were in danger.' The cry, 'betrayed the terrorstricken mentality of Muslim spokesmen and immature students' who were being used by the Muslim League to mislead the masses. In a devastating put down, Khizr declared that, 'Apart from the great harm being done to the studies and careers of these students, it was an insult to the intelligence of Muslim stalwarts in the Punjab that young students from the United Provinces with no knowledge of experience of life should come and preach to us that we were in danger in this Muslim majority province.'[3]

Khizr also pointed out that the Muslims could only achieve solid and rapid 'moral and material progress' in alliance with the non-Muslims on a basis of identity of common interests.[4] This argument formed the cornerstone of the Unionists' election manifesto which was published on 30 November. 'The objective of the Party continues to be to build a better, more contented and prosperous Punjab', it declared, 'The Party creed recognizes economic affinity as the strongest and surest basis of common action and so-called communal differences as relatively minor issues.' It then enumerated the Unionists' achievements since 1923 in the fields of the relief of agricultural indebtedness, restoration of mortgaged lands, and the improvement of the economic conditions of all classes. It pointed out that the Haveli and Thal irrigation projects held out the prospects of further increases in the income of the agriculturalist population.[5] The old magic of this Unionist economic appeal had, however, long worn off.

The Unionists' difficulties were vividly brought home during Khizr's election tour of the Jhelum district. He unsuccessfully interviewed 120 people in an attempt to find someone willing to oppose the Muslim League candidate, Raja Ghazanfar Ali Khan in the Pind Dadan Khan constituency.[6] No one would take on this task because they feared the displeasure of the powerful **pir** of Jalalpur, Pir Fazl Shah. He was Raja Ghazanfar Ali Khan's uncle and was a traditional adversary of the Unionists.[7] He wielded immense authority over his **murids** in Jhelum. Like other **pirs** he issued **fatwas** in support of the Muslim League couched in terms of loyalty to the **piri-mureedi** relationship.[8]

Khizr risked the wrath of Pir Golra in his continued struggle against the Muslim League. He was warned that he would become 'a fiend in Hell' if he separated himself from the Islamic movement.[9]

General Without An Army

Another leading Chishti, **sajjada nashin,** Pir Qamaruddin of Sial Sharif held a meeting on the outskirts of the Kalra estate in which he publicily challenged Khizr and Allah Bakhsh to come to terms with the Muslim League. 'I have never begged for anything in my life before', he declared, 'but today I have come out of my home to beg for votes, believing God is present here (the meeting was being held in a mosque) it is Islamic to ask for votes and "religious" to give them. The Muslim League is purely a religious movement in which all the rich, poor, sufis and scholars are participating. Not as a **pir** but even as a Muslim, I have repeatedly advised Nawab Allah Bakhsh who is my **murid** not to desert the Muslims at this critical time.'[10]

The Unionists responded by introducing religious appeals into their own propaganda. Khizr garnished his speeches with quotations from the Quran. At Gujrat he used the first verse of the Sura Fatiha to prove that the Unionists had greater Islamic justification than the Muslim League.[11] The Unionist Party also employed 'ulama from the Jamiat-i-ulema-i-Hind who opposed the Pakistan demand. Local Zamindara League workers pleaded that the fiery Ahrar[12] orators Sayed Ataullah Bokhari and Maulana Mazhar Ali Azhar be despatched to counteract the **pirs'** influence.[13] Such reformist 'ulama had always been highly critical of the religious leadership provided by the **pirs.** But they had also been previously opposed to the Unionists because of their close ties with the British. They were not the only strange allies to whom Khizr turned in his moment of crisis. He also enlisted the support of the Khaksars[14] who had been bitter opponents of Sikander.[15] They, nevertheless possessed the virtue of being outspoken critics of the Pakistan scheme. A lorry load of Khaksars was duly despatched to do election work in Khizr's Khushab constituency. They were also deployed in the Ferozepore district; the political base of the Nawab of Mamdot.[16]

The Unionist Party profited little from this strategy. There was a glaring inconsistency between its professed non-communal stance and the employment of 'ulama. Neither they, nor the Khaksars possessed the **pirs'** local moral authority. They were also less able to relate their messages to the actual experience and rhythm of life of their hearers. The poets and singers which the Unionists deployed with their propaganda lorries were more successful in this respect. But the key to the Muslim League's impact was not just its ability to anchor its message in the substratum of local rural Islam. It also stemmed from its linkage of the Pakistan ideal with popular aspirations.

ii

The election results were announced on 24 February 1946. They confirmed that the All-India parties had squeezed out the Unionists. For the first time since Fateh Khan, a leading representative of the Tiwana family was on the losing side. Khizr and Allah Bakhsh had in fact bucked the political trend and secured victories by some 2472 and 1223 votes respectively in the Khushab[17] and Sargodha rural constituencies.[18] But even these successes had been at a price.[19] Khizr had expended 8 lakhs of rupees to ensure his election.[20] Allah Bakhsh had also spent heavily. This was money which Khizr in fact could ill afford as Umar's extravagant life style had cut deeply into the family fortune.

The Unionist Party was reduced to a rump of 18 members in the 175 strong Assembly. Chhotu Ram's former Unionist citadel in the Ambala division had fallen to the Congress which captured 9/11 rural Hindu seats.[21] His old seat at Jhajjar went to the Congress as did the constituency of Tikka Ram. In all the Congress had won fifty one seats in the Assembly under the leadership of Bhim Sen Sachar. The Unionist Party's power had also disintegrated in the rural Muslim seats. The Muslim League captured all but 11 of these. It had made a clean sweep in the Ambala and Jullundur divisions which following partition would go to India. In the Multan and Lahore divisions, it had won twenty one and twenty two respectively of the twenty four seats. Only in the Rawalpindi division had it received a slight check. But even here, it bagged fourteen out of the twenty one seats. The Muslim League added two more seats after the elections, when Sir Jamal Khan Leghari and Major Ashiq Hussain crossed the floor from the Unionist Party.

The elections' other striking feature was the success of the Akali dominated, Panthic Pratinidhi Board which won twenty two seats. Its victories were achieved largely at the expense of the Communist Party. None of its twenty four candidates were successful. Stalwarts like S. Teja Singh Swatantra and S. Sohan Singh Josh were unseated by large majorities.

The Muslim League was the largest single party in the Assembly with seventy five seats. It could not, however command a majority. The League had done well enough to demonstrate Punjabi Muslim support for the Pakistan demand, but not to form a Ministry. The slogans and tactics which it had adopted during the campaign made it debatable whether it would be able to acquire coalition partners.

General Without An Army

Khizr was shocked by the extent of the Muslim League's advance. He had anticipated that the Unionists would capture upwards of twenty seats more than they had managed and would thus still retain the balance of power. The Ministerialists had in fact put up a respectable showing in terms of the percentage of the vote, although this had not been translated into seats under the first past the post system.[22] Khizr, despite earlier threats to quit politics still felt a calling to bring stability to the region. He remained the dutiful zamindar and loyal ex-serviceman, although family history and political logic pointed to accommodation with the Muslim League. Daultana and Mamdot in fact provided him with one last opportunity to do so, after the elections. They offered him the opportunity to head a Ministry, even if he remained aloof from the League. When Jinnah got wind of the proposal he immediately vetoed it.[23] But the episode reveals that Punjabi Muslims still possessed an independent outlook which jarred with the Quaid-e-Azam's All-India strategy. The final breach between Khizr and the Punjab League only occurred after he formed the coalition government which excluded it from office in the' cornerstone' of Pakistan.

Khizr's formation of a coalition government on 11 March between the Unionists, the Akalis and the Congress remains highly controversial. Liaquat Ali Khan and the Nawab of Mamdot both complained to the Viceroy that Glancy had endeavoured to keep the Muslim League out of office because of his partiality for the Unionists.[24] Khizr has also been condemned for entering the Coalition at the behest of Maulana Abul Kalam Azad and for shattering all hopes of a United Punjab by forestalling an agreement between the Muslim League and the non-Muslims.[25]

Whilst the Muslim League's frustration at its exclusion from power was genuine, none of these charges carry any weight. The Muslim League parlyed with the Akalis, before Khizr resumed office, but the negotiations broke down.[26] Moreover, Azad had been quite prepared to form a coalition government with the Punjab League, but again agreement could not be reached.[27] Glancy rather than 'procrastinating and using irrelevant arguments for some days'[28] to pave the way for Khizr to return, was in fact anxious to appoint a Ministry in 'order that the Budget Session might be completed by the end of the financial year.' The delay in fact resulted from the Nawab of Mamdot's protracted efforts to cobble together a majority. After checking the claims that Congress-Panthic-Unionist Coalition accounted for 94 members in the Assembly, Glancy invited Khizr to form a Ministry on 7 March. It is true that the Government represented an unholy alliance[29] far more than a consociational grand coalition, but it was the best that could be achieved in the circumstances.

iii

The three Muslim Unionists in the Cabinet included, Khizr, Mian Mohammad Ibrahim Barq and Nawab Sir Muzaffar Ali Khan Qizilbash. Barq, an obscure Arain politician from the Muzaffaragarh district was appointed by Khizr as the Minister of Education and Health. The Cambridge educated, Minister for Revenue, Nawab Sir Muzaffar Ali Khan Qizilbash, in contrast came from a leading Shia family of the Lahore district. The leading Congressman, Lala Bhimsen Sachar became the Minister for Finance, the post which Manohar Lal had held before his defeat in the elections. Chaudhri Lehri Singh, the Minister of Public Works, was the second Congressman in the Cabinet. The Akalis were represented by the wealthy industrialist, Sardar Baldev Singh who had of course been a member of Khizr's first Ministry. He was, however to serve only briefly as Development Minister before his promotion to the Centre to represent Sikh interests in the Interim Government and the complex negotitions which culminated in the 3 June Plan of 1947.

Khizr faced two immediate tasks. He had to survive the Budget Session of the Assembly and represent the Punjab's views to the Cabinet Mission. The Budget Session met between 2–30 March. Government speakers were frequently interrupted as the Speaker attempted to call the members to order. The Muslim League had in fact set the tone for the sitting even before the Coalition had officially come into existence, when it had organised a province wide **hartal** on 7 March and two days later had observed the celebration of 'Traitors day.'[30] During the course of the debates on the Budget, Muslim League speakers continuously denounced the Coalition as a 'fraud.' Chaudhri Mohammad Hassan addressed the Premier as Malik Sir Gaddar Hayat Khan and Shaukat called him a 'quisling.'[31] In such circumstances, Khizr could hardly be blamed for avoiding fresh legislation which would have risked parliamentary defeat, as well as presenting further opportunities for villification. The new Governor, Sir Evan Jenkins who had replaced Glancy on 8 April, was nevertheless, displeased with Khizr's 'ingenuity' in this respect.[32]

150

General Without An Army

Khizr met with Wavell and the Cabinet Mission of Pethick-Lawrence, Stafford Cripps and A.V. Alexander, just under a fortnight after the three man team had arrived in Karachi. Mamdot had already informed the Mission that an undivided Punjab should be included in Pakistan. Khizr minced no words when he maintained that the Pakistan issue would never have arisen in its present shape, if Jinnah 'had been officially asked to define what he wanted. Even now it was not too late.'[33] When Cripps pressed him concerning the effects of the establishment of Pakistan on the Punjab, Khizr explained that Muslims would be very pleased, 'if it included the whole of the province as now existed'. The Sikhs' relations with the new Government, however, would be 'very difficult' and they might not 'be dealt with peacefully.'[34] The Punjab Premier pessimistically declared that democratic institutions would not survive long after the British withdrawal. His comment that if there was to be any All-India Central Government at all, it should be a weak one, was also in keeping with long established Unionist traditions.

When Khizr was shown a copy of the Cabinet Mission's proposals[35] on 16 May, he further elaborated to Jenkins his solution to the constitutional deadlock. Khizr's answer was provincial autonomy and a weak federal centre. He argued for provincial autonomy on the basis that Punjabis possessed little in common with Sindhis and Pathans.[36] He thus had little expectation that the idea of Group Legislatures and Executives would work. When the Governor pointed out that the Group Constitution could be almost as light as the Central Constitution, The Premier acquiesced to the Cabinet Mission statement. It ran into the sand, however, when Nehru maintained that the Congress would not be bound by its safeguards for the Muslim majority areas. Jinnah responded by calling for 'direct action'. This precipitated the communal breakdown which made the creation of Pakistan inevitable. The Punjab had to pay the price of partition.

iv

These All-India developments compounded Khizr's problems in the Punjab. He appeared an increasingly isolated figure, in Jenkins' telling phrase, a 'General without an Army.' The Governor's initial impression of the Ministry was unflattering. He dismissed Ibrahim Barq as a nonentity with very 'little experience of any kind'. The Congress Ministers in his view were little better, they had no control

Khizr Tiwana, the Punjab Unionist Party and the Partition of India

over their rank and file and meddled in the affairs of the officials. Lehri Singh struck the Governor, 'as more of a Jat than a Congressman.' Whilst Sachar was 'a mild and well-meaning man' who was unfortunately 'opposed in principle to capital punishment.' Jenkins admitted that Khizr was 'as friendly and charming as ever', but believed that Sachar 'had no love lost for him' and indeed almost regretted that a deal with the League had' proved impossible.'[37]

Jenkins was one of the most able British Officers in India, so his views should not be dismissed lightly. Moreover, Khizr himself admitted to the Cabinet Mission that 'the present coalition was very different' from the old Unionist Government. But the Governor's criticisms must be set in the context of his strong belief that a League-Sikh agreement held the key to the Punjab's stability.[38] He also partly sympathised with the Muslim League's frustration at being shut out of office. Swaran Singh[39] who replaced Baldev Singh, as the Akali representative, on his move to the Centre has however provided a much more favourable picture of the functioning of the Cabinet.

Swaran Singh shortly before his death recalled how he forged a Pact with Sachar to reduce rivalries between the Congress and the Akalis concerning the contesting of by-elections. Each party agreed to support the other in the event of an election so that the Ministry's united front would not be undermined. He also reminisced about his good relationship with Qizalbash, and the support which Khizr provided when he first entered the Cabinet. The Punjab Premier put the young Sikh Minister at ease and demonstrated his confidence in him, by entertaining him to leisurely repasts in his favourite Davico restaurant on the Mall at Simla.[40] Khizr had in fact initially viewed with considerable disquiet the proposal that Baldev Singh should be taken for the Interim Government at the Centre.[41] All was inevitably not quite as rosy as Swaran Singh recalled. Khizr, for example, did not drop prosecutions against J.P. Narayan's supporters[42] following their demonstration at Lahore Railway Station on 29 December 1946, as Sachar wished.[43] But the Congress leader accepted his authority and impartiality in this as other contentious issues. This was as well as Khizr kept a tight personal control over all matters relating to law and order.

Qizalbash steered the Government through a motion for the adjournment of a special one day Assembly Session,[44] whilst Khizr was attending the Paris Peace Conference. Before crossing the Channel, Khizr had called on Pethick-Lawrence at the India Office. He had taken the opportunity to go over 'the familiar ground' that the

General Without An Army

Punjab should remain undivided. He had also held out the hope that 'with their experience of compromise between communities, Punjabis would be a conciliatory force inside the constitution making body.'[45]

Whilst Khizr was in Europe, a number of ominous developments had occurred in his home province. The Congress Socialists and the Communists had exploited a wave of labour unrest which saw strikes on the North-Western railway and in textile mills at Okara and Lyallpur. In the countryside there was agitation amongst tenants led by kisan organisations. Most threatening of all was the spread of armed volunteer movements. The RSS and the Muslim League volunteers stood at the forefront of this development. Shaukat turned his military experience to the organisation of a half million strong volunteer force.[46] Sikander's son thus continued to haunt his rival for the leadership of the' martial castes.'

During Khizr's absence, Jenkins had drafted a Punjab Public Safety ordinance without consulting the Cabinet. When Khizr learnt of this he encouraged the Governor to promulagate the ordinance under his discretionary powers contained under Section 89 of the Government of India Act. This short circuited discussion of a measure in a hostile Assembly.[47] A different Prime Minister would not have agreed so readily to this liberal interpretation of the Governor's discretionary powers. But the ordinance was effectively used to curb communal unrest in Rohtak in November 1946 and to nip in the bud trouble involving RSS and Muslim League volunteers.[48]

Wavell noted to the Secretary of State that it was 'to (Khizr's) credit and the credit of Jenkins, that the Punjab is remarkably steady at this time.'[49] The trouble in Rohtak had in fact been potentially very serious as it was connected with the communal disorders which were sweeping the western UP. The Ministry had also taken effective action against minor communal disturbances in Amritsar and Multan early in the summer. The Punjab stood out as a haven of peace, amidst the unprecedented disorders in Bombay, Calcutta, Noakhali, western UP. and the Frontier. The credit lay with the much vilified and ridiculed Khizr Ministry.

Events elsewhere in India confirmed Khizr in his 'diehard' views. He suggested to Jenkins that the meeting of the Constituent Assembly should be postponed as it could not avoid controversial issues and would thus add to communal hostility. The Punjab Governor agreed with him, but this had no effect on the decision to plough ahead at the All-India level.[50] Khizr nevertheless, expressed the opinion to the Viceroy that the British would be 'compelled by the course of events

Khizr Tiwana, the Punjab Unionist Party and the Partition of India

to stay in India.' He laboured the view to Jenkins that the only solution was a dismissal of the Interim Government and a 'reversion for some years to firm administration.'[51] The old Adam of Unionism was alive, despite the setback of the 1946 elections. This was in fact mere wishful thinking on Khizr's part. The domestic situation in Britain rendered such a course of action inconceivable. But the rapidity with which the Attlee administration was eventually to divide and quit left him incredulous.

Khizr visited Delhi in mid-November 1946 for discussions with Wavell, the Commander-in-Chief Field Marshall Auchinlek and Congress leaders. The communal polarisation at the Centre shocked him. He also passed onto Jenkins the suspicion that Congressmen had been in receipt of private communications from the India Office without Wavell's knowledge. Jenkins was sufficiently impressed by Khizr's shrewdness to report this impression to New Delhi, despite the absence of hard evidence.[52]

It was also at this juncture that Khizr raised the idea that in the last resort the Punjab should be declared a dominion and maintain direct relations with the crown after the British departure.[53] During an informal cabinet meeting, before the Punjab Governor opened the Thal irrigation project at Daudkhel on 7 January 1947, Khizr again returned to this idea. He justified it in terms of the impossibility for a provincial government to enter into any agreement with the current Centre. He remarked that whatever truth there was in Gandhi's assertion in 1942 that the Cripps offer was a 'post-dated cheque on a crashing bank' a similar assertion about any offer for the Central Government today would be entirely true. Jenkins was sufficiently alarmed to report this to Wavell although it all 'was very vague.' He displayed considerable anxiety about the extent to which Khizr was disseminating this view in private.[54] It of course threatened the very balkanisation of the subcontinent which the British sought to avoid for strategic and economic reasons. The Punjab Governor need not have worried, however, for Khizr was soon preoccupied with a much more pressing task; that of maintaining law and order in the face of a Muslim League direct action campaign designed to topple his Ministry.

v

Jenkins had in fact unwittingly precipitated the struggle. From the summer of 1946 onwards, he had urged Khizr to take action against the private armies which were mushrooming in the Punjab. The

General Without An Army

Public Safety Ordinance which had been introduced in November had curbed the open activities of the RSS and Muslim National Guards, but intelligence reports had revealed that they were clandestinely training for armed combat with knives and **lathis.** Khizr consequently decided to take action against them, with the full approval of Jenkins. This provided the pretext for the Muslim League's direct action campaign.

Khizr had no inkling of the Muslim League's response. He was in fact in Delhi on the morning of 24 January, when orders were issued banning the Muslim National Guards and RSS. Routine searches of the premises of both organisations passed off without incident everywhere in the Punjab except the Muslim League National Guards' headquarters in Lahore. The prominent Muslim politician, Mian Iftikharuddin[55] refused the police entry and telephoned to his colleagues to join him in courting arrest. Shaukat, Mian Mumtaz Daultana and four others hastily responded and were duly arrested for obstruction. They naturally refused the offer of bail.[56] The Muslim League had acquired its cause célèbre. It no longer mattered that the police search had unearthed over two thousand steel helmets.

Disturbances broke out in Lahore following the news of the arrests. The next evening an appalled Khizr returned from Delhi, to a city in uproar. A Muslim League meeting held that morning in the Assembly Chamber had drawn angry crowds. A further seven Muslim League MLAs were arrested after they had deliberately defied a ban on processions and meetings. They were joined by eight of their colleagues after police had been called to a demonstration in the late afternoon at the Mochi gate. The police used tear gas to disperse the crowds and arrested a number of female protestors. A company of British troops was despatched to the chief police station as a precaution.[57]

Khizr went straight to Government House for a 6pm conference with Jenkins, Qizalbash, the Home Secretary, the Inspector General of Police and Deputy Inspector General of Police CID. The Governor briefed him on the situation and reminded the Premier that it was 'easier to send people to jail than to get them out of jail in a cooperative frame of mind.' Jenkins was nevertheless highly satisfied that 'Khizr took the situation quite calmly.'[58] The Premier also provided the reassurances which Jenkins could transmit to his superiors, that he had never intended to make any arrests or attack the Muslim League as a party and that police dispositions and not political considerations had lain behind the timing of the action.[59]

Khizr Tiwana, the Punjab Unionist Party and the Partition of India

The emergency meeting modified the notification under the Punjab Public Safety Ordinance which specifically outlawed the flag along with the uniform and other emblems of the Muslim National Guards for, 'the description of the flag might as it stands, be taken as banning the ordinairy flag of Islam.'[60] Its other main outcome was the drafting of instructions to district officers concerning their response to any future disturbances.

The next day Khizr issued a conciliatory statement and withdrew the cases against the eight who had been arrested at the Muslim National Guards' Headquarters. He hoped that this action would drive a wedge between Muslim 'moderates' and' extremists'. Jenkins was concerned that such gestures were pointless, because the Premier had no direct personal contact with the League. He therefore met with the Nawab of Mamdot on 27 January with Khizr's consent.[61] Within hours of this parley, however, Shaukat and the other released Muslim Leaguers had taken out an unauthorised procession and made speeches which Jenkins in his measured prose described as 'not conciliatory.'

Khizr called a full cabinet meeting on the morning of 28 January. This decided to withdraw the ban on the Muslim National Guards and the RSS, whilst reemphasising the Ministry's commitment to maintaining law and order.[62] The Muslim League's initial grievance had been fully met. But the genie was now out of the bottle. Shaukat uncompromisingly declared that,'The Khizr Ministry must be made to go whatever the cost to the Muslim League.' He boasted that the opposition would 'put out 15 million Muslims to break the law.'[63] Khizr now had no alternative but to tough things out. Following a day of great tension, he ordered a police preemptive strike during the night of 28–9 January. All the important League leaders in Lahore, including the Nawab of Mamdot and Feroz Khan Noon were arrested and detained outside the city. A rigid censorship was introduced.[64] This action brought only a temporary respite from the regular round of demonstrations in Lahore. The agitation now also spread to the districts. The police stood firm, but Muslim opinion, both official and unofficial was solidly behind the Muslim League campaign.

Jenkins supported his Premier, although he tried to nudge him in the direction of a compromise before the Budget Session of the Assembly was due to convene on 3 March. The correspondence between Wavell and Pethick-Lawrence is, however noticeably cool towards Khizr. They were preoccupied by the need for an All-India

General Without An Army

constitutional settlement between the League and the Congress. The disturbances in the Punjab threatened to disrupt this. They were as prepared as the Congress or Muslim League High Commands to discount the short term interests of the Punjab to the greater prize of an orderly transfer of power. Secretary of State and Viceroy alike lamented that Khizr's action was ill-judged at a time when the League was on the brink of entering the Constituent Assembly.[65] Neither were worried that Khizr's days as Prime Minister were now ' numbered.' Indeed, the Secretary for State sanguinely believed that 'some of the Muslim Unionists would support a League Government rather than have a Section 93 Government.' He also reasoned that it was not impossible 'that the Sikhs might see an opportunity of offering support to the Muslim League in return for assurances about constitutional matters.'[66]

The Punjab Governor possessed a more realistic view of the communal consequences of the agitation. He knew that Khizr was personally preventing Sachar's Congress rival, Gopichand Bhargava[67] from involving Hindus in reprisals against the League campaign.[68] This danger had also been relayed to Jenkins during a meeting with Lehri Singh on the morning of 12 February. Master Tara Singh[69] never one to pour oil on troubled waters had moreover issued a statement, which was suppressed, that the Sikhs were in danger and must revive their 'army' under his command.[70]

Jenkins sombrely concluded that, 'the agitation has convinced Hindus and Sikhs that the League wants undiluted Muslim Raj.' 'It is quite impossible', he continued, 'for one community to rule the Punjab with its present boundaries. Long term alternatives are therefore reversion to Unionist principles..or partition which would create intolerable minority problems. Effect of agitation is to force second alternative on non-Muslims and to impair very seriously long-term prospects of the Muslim League and Muslims generally. The Muslim League are in fact wantonly throwing away the certainty of Muslim leadership in a United Punjab for uncertain advantages of a partition which the Sikhs will gradually now demand. But nobody has the brains to understand this.'[71] Jenkins might have added, on the Muslim League side. For Khizr had always known that the only alternative to some kind of consociational arrangement was partition which could spell disaster for the Punjab and its people.

It is in fact doubtful whether the Punjab League leadership could have halted the agitation at this time, even if it had wanted to do so. The direct action campaign had begun as a movement of students, politicians and their wives who had for the first time taken to the streets.[72] But wider sections of the Muslim population were increasingly drawn into the movement. There was a ten thousand strong procession in Lahore on 30 January. Ten times that number surged towards the civil lines in Amritsar a fortnight later. The crowd was only held back by baton charges and tear-gas.[73] A large procession of men and horses said to number thirty thousand moved through the Muzaffargarh home of the Unionist Minister for Health and Education on 18 February. The same day a huge crowd wound its way through Lahore. It was headed by a man on a donkey impersonating Khizr.[74] Such action must be understood in terms of a Punjabi rural society whose social and political life revolved around the principles of **izzat** (honour) and **beizzat** (insult). To insult and humiliate an enemy was to reduce his authority. Another interesting symbolic assault on the Government was provided by forty veiled women who had earlier forced their way into the Central Jail Compound in Jullundur where they performed a mock funeral of the Unionist leaders.[75] Mock mourning was also enacted outside Khizr's residence on a number of occasions. Crowds from Rohtak to Rawalpindi routinely chanted anti-Khizr slogans.

Clashes between the police and demonstrators became increasingly violent. In one incident in Lahore, five hundred rounds of tear-gas were fired.[76] On 13 February the police **lathi** charged processions as far afield as Sargodha, Ferozepore and Wazirabad.[77] Sixty protestors were seriously injured in clashes with the police at Gujarat, three days later.[78] The first death occurred in Simla. When the news spread, angry crowds gathered in many of the Punjab's towns on 8 February. The funeral of the first victim in Lahore shortly afterwards, attracted nearly a quarter of a million people. Craftsmen, butchers, traders and even **tongawallahs** swelled the numbers. Streets were blocked, schools were closed. All the Muslim shops in such leading bazaars as Delhi Gate, Kashmiri bazaar, Bazaar Hakiman, Dabbi bazaar and Bhati Gate bazaar went on **hartal** (strike).[79]

Hartals played an increasingly vital role in the Muslim League agitation. They not only paralyzed normal activity, but freed people to demonstrate. Muslim shopkeepers in Kasur, for example, closed daily between one and four to attend public meetings held in defiance of government orders.[80] The Punjab Muslim League Committee of Action commemorated the first month of the agitation with 'National Struggle Day.' Stoppages and strikes spread from Lahore to Amritsar, Multan, Kasur, Rawalpindi, Jullundur and Ludhiana.

General Without An Army

Their success eloquently attests to the growing multi-class involvement in the struggle. For a complete **hartal** could not be achieved without support from casual labourers, industrial workers, shopkeepers and artisans as well as the professional classes. In Lahore, even the small roadside tobacconists, **paanwallahs**, and tea stalls packed away their wares. The increasing frequency of **hartals** also of course risked communal conflict occasioned by attempts to force non-Muslim traders to close their businesses. Sikh resentment was also rising because of the growing number of incidents involving them. In Amritsar, for example, Muslims were singling out Sikh policemen for their attacks.[81] There was very little in any of this to cheer Khizr.

His anxiety was further increased by Attlee's announcement of 20 February 1947, that H.M.G. intended to transfer power by a date no later than June 1948. After an attempt to 'laugh it off' as the work of lunatics, he beame increasingly gloomy.[82] In later years, Khizr claimed that his despondency stemmed from the fact that Attlee had 'misled' him, assuring him just days before the announcement that the British did not contemplate a rapid departure from India. There is no record of this telegram. Whether or not Attlee had 'betrayed' Khizr, the decision to quit, radically altered the situation in the Punjab. Khizr wisely reckoned that repression would not facilitate a peaceful transfer of power. He accordingly agreed to settle with the League. Just six days after Attlee's announcement, a compromise was secured between the Government and the League. Khizr agreed to introduce new legislation to replace the Punjab Public Safety Ordinance. He also lifted the ban on public meetings and agreed to release all political prisoners except those convicted for offences under Section 325 of the Indian Penal Code. The continuation of the ban on processions was little more than a fig leaf to cover the fact that the Ministry had totally caved in to the Muslim League's demands.[83]

Khizr contemplated resignation during the final stages of his negotiations with the Muslim League. He discussed this in some detail with Jenkins, but decided to soldier on to avoid the 'very awkward' situation of the Governor being forced into a Section 93 administration.[84] He had no intention, however, of clinging onto power for the sake of it. Rather he intended to act as a 'bridge' between the Muslim League and the minorities. He made it known to his colleagues and Jenkins that he intended to see through the Budget Session of the Assembly which opened at noon on 3 March. The end came unexpectedly, when Khizr announced his resignation to a stunned Cabinet and Governor on the eve of the Session.

What lay behind his change of mind? Swaran Singh has provided a colourful anecdote purporting to pinpoint the event which finally forced The Unionist Premier to admit defeat. Khizr had cradled Ibrahim Barq's eight year old son in his lap, during a party at his colleague's residence. The boy's father perhaps to curry favour had exclaimed how lucky he was to be sitting with the Prime Minister. The lad to the embarrassement of all present blurted out, 'Oh you are Uncle Khizr, you are the one, all my friends say are coming in the way of the creation of Pakistan.' When Khizr later retold this incident to Swaran Singh, he added that Barq was a' nonentity' before he had made him a Minister, now even his son was so influenced by the League that he was personally blaming me for coming in the way of Pakistan. 'I could go on fighting with the Muslim League,' he continued, 'but if our children feel we are the villains of the piece, let us disappear and whatever happens, happen.'[85]

However one judges this anecdotal evidence, it is clear that a number of Khizr's close associates were urging him to call it a day. Qizalbash, his senior Muslim colleague in the Cabinet was anxious to mend fences with the Muslim League.[86] Allah Bakhsh, Azim Husain and Zafrullah Khan[87] who had come especially to Lahore, all advised him that he should no longer act as a 'buffer' between the Muslim League and the minorities. The Punjab Premier eventually shared their understanding that the Muslim League must face reality without further delay.

Once Khizr had decided to resign, he did not waver. He went to Jenkins and voiced this intention at 2.15 pm on 2 March. He then addressed a pre-arranged gathering of the members of the Coalition parties. Immediately afterwards he revealed his plans to his non-Muslim Cabinet colleagues. They were shocked that he was not going to see through the Budget Session as originally proposed. Late that evening Khizr again met Jenkins, prior to seeing the Nawab of Mamdot as a matter of 'courtesy' before issuing a resignation statement to the press.[88] It declared that the transfer of power was now a reality confronting the people of the Punjab. The Muslim League should face this on behalf of the Muslim majority and make arrangements on the future with the minority representatives as it saw fit. This would only be possible if the Muslim Unionists were no longer in the middle. The statement concluded that Khizr would be willing to assist the Muslim League in any way possible. It also,

General Without An Army

however reiterated his long held view that Punjabis would suffer a great loss if the province was divided and that 'his utmost desire was to maintain the integrity of the Punjab.'[89]

Jenkins saw the Nawab of Mamdot late on the morning of 3 March. He gave him an absolutely free hand to form a Ministry in the expectation that the Muslim League President would be able to report positive progress by Saturday 8 March at the latest.[90] The installation of a Muslim League led Coalition Ministry proved impossible. The Punjab entered its final months of British rule under a Section 93 administration, with the morale of its officials severely undermined.[91]

Mamdot failed to provide the reassurances which the Sikhs and Congress demanded, mainly because his hands were tied by the Muslim League High Command. Jinnah discountenanced a local arrangement in the Punjab which would in any way weaken his All-India demand for Pakistan. Moreover, Sikh resentment had almost boiled over during the Punjab Muslim League agitation. The mild mannered Swaran Singh had warned Jenkins, that the Sikhs 'must have a clear account of the Muslim League's plan for the future of the Punjab and of the position of Sikhs within this.. The Sikhs had no intention', he added, 'of being serfs under Muslim masters and felt they were strong enough to defend themselves.'[92] Tara Singh used far more intemperate language when he unsheafed his sword on the steps of the Punjab Assembly building, after hearing of Khizr's resignation. This action is conventionally taken as the catalyst for the violent demonstrations and riots which engulfed the Punjab in the following days.[93]

The Punjab had been a powder keg for many months. It is nevertheless significant, that within less than a week of Khizr's resignation, communal violence had reached alarming proportions and the Congress had demanded the partition of the province.[94] For the first time, violence spread from the cities to the countryside and took on the sinister undertones of 'ethnic cleansing'. Whole villages in the Jhelum, Attock and Rawalpindi districts were put to the sword. About 40,000 people, mainly Sikhs had taken refuge in hurriedly established camps. The outrage which many Sikh leaders felt at these assaults which were orchestrated by Muslim National Guardsmen and ex-servicemen[95] and condoned by Muslim League politicians[96] fed a desire for revenge which bred a civil war mentality. Barricades went up in some of the Punjab's towns. Muslim villagers stockpiled weapons smuggled in from the Frontier, whilst the Sikhs

Khizr Tiwana, the Punjab Unionist Party and the Partition of India

armed themselves from the neighbouring princely states. They harboured a burning desire for revenge and formed raiding parties of armed horsemen. The massacres which accompanied the transfer of power were rooted in the earlier outbreaks.

The March violence destroyed any lingering hopes that the Punjab might escape partition.[97] Three months later, the East and West Punjab sections of the Assembly met separately and voted for division. The violence also destroyed the British system of political control in the countryside centred around such loyalist political families as the Tiwanas.[98] The collapse of Unionist influence created political and administrative chaos. It was also accompanied by a communal hatred which wreaked untold suffering on hundreds of thousands of innocent Punjabi men, women and children.

Notes

1 *Civil and Military Gazette* (Lahore) 1, 18 & 20 September 1945.
2 Under Section 93 of the 1935 Government of India Act a Governor could directly rule a province, if no party could form a stable Government.
3 *Civil and Military Gazette* (Lahore) 3 January 1946.
4 *Ibid.*
5 See, *Hindustan Times* (Delhi) 23 December 1945; *Pioneer* (Lucknow) 1 December 1945.
6 Dawn (Delhi) 28 October 1945.
7 He had formed an independent political platform called Hizbullah, 'Party of God' in the 1930s. For details see, D. Gilmartin, *Empire and Islam. Punjab and the Making of Pakistan* (Berkeley, 1988) p. 69–70.
8 For details see. I. Talbot, *Punjab and the Raj 1849–1947* (New Delhi 1988) p. 211 & ff.
9 *Nawa-e-Waqt* (Lahore) 5 January 1946.
10 *Ibid.*
11 Khizr's point was that Allah is described in the Quran as Rabb-ul-Alameen, Lord of everything and everyone not just the Muslims. In this light the Unionist party's non-communalism was more Islamic than the Muslim League's communal rhetoric.
12 The Ahrar Party was an urban based communal organisation which had gained prominence in the Punjab in the early 1930s, during its agitations in defence of Kashmiri Muslim rights and against the heterodox Ahmadiyah community.
13 Sultan Ali Ranjha to Sultan Ahmad Ranjha 5 January 1946. File D-36 Unionist Party Papers.
14 The Khaksar movement had been founded in 1931 by Allama Mashriqi. Its members wore uniform and drilled with sharpened spades. The movement was strongest in the Punjab, when Sikander outlawed what he dubbed this 'fascist organisation', the scene was set for a bloody showdown in Lahore on 19 March 1940.

162

General Without An Army

15 For further details see, I.H. Malik, *Sikander Hayat Khan. A Political Biography* (Islamabad, 1985) ch.vi.

16 For further details see File D-99 Unionist Party Papers.

17 Khizr was returned for three constituencies in all.

18 Khizr had defeated his kinsman, Mohammad Khan Tiwana at Khushab, whilst Allah Bakhsh had won against Pir Qalandar Husain Shah who represented the Muslim League at Sargodha. K.C. Yadav, *Elections in Punjab 1920–47* (New Delhi 1987) pp. 113–4.

19 'Expenditure in the Punjab is virtually unlimited', wrote the election correspondent of the *Hindustan Times*, 'I gather that few candidates will spend less than £7,500 Rs100,000 and may spend twice as much. I should have doubted these figures had, they not been confirmed firstly by a banker whom the candidates importuned for loans and then by experienced British officials. It is customary for the candidate to entertain his supporters on the night before they vote at a lavish feast and he may also feed them as I have witnessed for myself, openly at the polls. Spirits.. are also freely dispensed. The competition for vehicles is so hot that candidates must spend vast sums to hire them. Votes moreover are bought outright on a vast scale. *Hindustan Times* (Delhi) 26 February 1946.

20 Interview with Nazar Tiwana, New Delhi 13 December 1993.

21 Unionist candidates had squeezed in with narrow majorities in Gurgaon North-West and Hansi.

22 The Unionists' percentage of the vote in the Hindu rural constituencies of the Ambala division stood at 32.72% as against the Congress's 52.13%. In the Muslim rural and urban constituencies, the Unionists polled 26.7% of the vote as against the Muslim League's 65.4%.Source: *Return Showing the Results of Elections to the Central Legislative Assembly and the Provincial Legislatures* (New Delhi, 1948).

23 For details see, A. Jalal, *The Sole Spokesman. Jinnah, the Muslim League and the Demand for Pakistan* (Cambridge, 1985) p. 151.

24 See for example, P. Moon (ed), *Wavell The Viceroy's Journal* (London, 1973) p. 220. This charge is also reflected in, Syed Nur Ahmad, *From Martial Law to Martial Law Politics in the Punjab, 1919–1958* (Boulder, 1985) p. 179.

25 Jalal *op.cit.* p. 151.

26 Governor of the Punjab's Note on the Formation of a Ministry 7 March 1946. T.P vi, p. 1136.

27 P. Moon (ed) *op.cit.* p. 222.

28 Ahmad *op.cit.* p. 179.

29 The Akalis for example had observed an Anti-Unionist Government day as recently as 3 August 1941.

30 Satya M. Rai, *Legislative Politics and Freedom Struggle in Punjab 1897–1947* (New Delhi 1984) p. 318.

31 *Ibid.*

32 Jenkins to Mountbatten 4 August 1947 48T.P xii, p. 513.

33 Note of a Meeting Between the Cabinet Mission, Field Marshall Viscount Wavell and Khizr Friday 5 April 1946 at 4pm. T.P vii p. 148.Khizr had in fact raised this issue during an interview with Linlithgow as early as May

Khizr Tiwana, the Punjab Unionist Party and the Partition of India

1943. The Viceroy had rejected his demand for a clarification from Jinnah with the words, ' Our attitude was that we must keep entirely out of this business, and take the line that..Pakistan or any other solution (is) a matter for consideration by Indians themselves at the post-war conference.Linlithgow to Amery 4 May 1943 *T.P* iii, p. 940.

34 *Ibid.*

35 The Cabinet Mission's plan was for a three-tiered federation, at the top there would be an All-India Union, below which there would be groups of provinces with their own executives and legislatures which would chose to act together for agreed topics. At the base there would be provinces.

36 Jenkins to Wavell 17 May 1946 *T.P* vii, p. 604.

37 Jenkins to Wavell 15 April 1946 *T.P* vii, p. 272.

38 Jenkins to Wavell 31 August 1946. Appreciation of the Punjab Situation at the end of August 1946 *T.P* viii, p.372.

39 Swaran Singh was a Jat Sikh lawyer from Jullundur. He was elected to the Punjab Assembly for the first time in 1946, and at the age of only twenty nine was the youngest member of the Government.

40 Interview with Sardar Swaran Singh, New Delhi, 11 December 1993.

41 Jenkins to Wavell 27 May 1946 *T.P* vii, p. 712.

42 At this stage in his career, J.P. Narayan was a fiery Congress Socialist.

43 Jenkins to Wavell 14 January 1947 *T.P* ix, p. 500.

44 The Session had been necessitated by elections to the forthcoming Constituent Assembly. The Ministry wound things up as quickly as possible in order to minimise the chance of defeat.

45 Pethick-Lawrence to Wavell 29 July 1946*T.P* viii, p. 141.

46 Jenkins to Wavell 20 May 1946 *T.P* vii, p. 400.

47 Jenkins to Colville 30 November 1946 *T.P* ix, p. 229.

48 *Ibid.*

49 Wavell to Pethick-Lawrence 27 November 1946 *T.P* ix, p. 197.

50 Jenkins to Wavell 8 November 1946 *T.P* ix, p. 24.

51 Wavell to Pethick-Lawrence 27 November 1946 *T.P* ix, p. 197.

52 Jenkins to Colville 30 November 1946 *T.P* ix, p. 229.

53 *Ibid.*

54 Jenkins to Wavell 14 January 1947 *T.P* ix, p. 501.

55 He was a member of the prominent Arain family from Baghbanpura, Lahore and was a former President of the Punjab Congress. He had joined the Muslim League amidst much fanfare in 1945 and had won the Kasur seat in the provincial elections.

56 This narrative is drawn from, Telegram of Jenkins to Pethick-Lawrence 26 January 1947 *T.P* ix, p.556.

57 Jenkins to Wavell 26 January 1947 *T.P* ix, p. 559.

58 *Ibid.*

59 Pethick-Lawrence in faraway London had jumped to the conclusion that Khizr's action looked suspiciously designed to 'influence Muslim opinion before the League Working Committee and thus ensure that the League did not come into the Constituent Assembly.' Pethick-Lawrence Telegram to Wavell 25 January 1947 *T.P* ix, p. 551.

60 Jenkins to Wavell 26 January 1947 *T.P* ix, p. 560.

General Without An Army

61 Jenkins to Pethick-Lawrence Telegram 27 January 1947 *T.P* ix, p. 565.
62 Jenkins to Pethick-Lawrence Telegram 29 January 1947 *T.P* ix, p.571 & ff.
63 *Ibid.*
64 *Ibid.*
65 See, for example, Pethick-Lawrence to Wavell 31 January 1947 *T.P* ix, p. 584.
66 *Ibid.*
67 Gopichand Bhargava (1889–1966) came from the Hissar district. He was educated at D.A.V. College, Lahore and Lahore Medical School. He had first entered Congress politics in 1919, when he was elected Secretary of the Lahore City Congress Committee. He was a close associate of Lala Lajpat Rai during the 1920s.
68 Jenkins to Wavell telegram 12 February 1946 *T.P* ix, p. 680.
69 Tara Singh (1885–1967) was a convert from Hinduism to Sikhism. He took the title 'master' from his time as a teacher. he was a founding member of the Akali Dal in 1920 and dominated the party.
70 Jenkins to Wavell telegram 12 February 1947 *T.P* ix, p. 680.
71 Jenkins to Wavell 3 February 1947 *T.P* ix, p. 655.
72 See for details, I. Talbot, 'The Role of the Crowd in the Muslim League Struggle for Pakistan' *The Journal of Imperial and Commonwealth History* 21, 2 (May 1993) pp. 307–334.
73 *Dawn* (Delhi) 15 February 1947.
74 *Dawn* (Delhi) 19 February 1947.
75 *Eastern Times* (Lahore) 29 January 1947.
76 *Dawn* (Delhi) 11 February 1947.
77 *Dawn* (Delhi) 14 February 1947.
78 *Dawn* (Delhi) 17 February 1947.
79 Eastern Times (Lahore) 11 February 1947.
80 *Dawn* (Delhi) 14 February 1947.
81 Punjab FR 2nd Half of February 1947 L/P&J/5/250
82 Jenkins to Wavell 3 March 1947 *T.P* x, p. 829.
83 Times of India (Bombay) 27 February 1947
84 Jenkins to Wavell 3 March 1947 *T.P* x, p. 829.
85 Interview with Swaran Singh, New Delhi 11 December 1993.
86 Jenkins to Wavell 3 March 1947 *T.P* x, p. 830.
87 He was a distinguished lawyer from the Punjab's Ahmadiyah community. He had been closely involved with the Unionist Party, before going to the Viceroy's Executive Council in 1935. From 1942–7 he was a judge of the Federal Court of India.
88 *Ibid.*
89 Cited in, Syed Nur Ahmad, *From Martial Law to Martial Law. Politics in the Punjab, 1919–1958* (Boulder, 1985) p.226.
90 Jenkins to Wavell 3 March 1947 *T.P* x, p. 832.
91 At the end of the Second World War, British morale had been higher in the Punjab than in those provinces in which officials had been subject to Congress attacks. But this slumped in the wake of the March 1947 disturbances. 'Every British official in the ICS and IP including myself', Jenkins wrote to Mountbatten in April 1947, 'would be very glad to leave (the Punjab) tomorrow. Six months ago the position was quite different,

Khizr Tiwana, the Punjab Unionist Party and the Partition of India

but we feel now that we are dealing with people who are out to destroy themselves and that in the absence of some reasonable agreement between them the average official will have to spend his life in a communal civil war. The Punjab is not now in a constitutional but in a revolutionary situation.' Note by Sir Evan Jenkins, 16 April 1947 *T.P* x, p. 282.

92 *Ibid.*
93 See, for example, Syed Nur Ahmad *op.cit.* p. 226.
94 Jalal *op.cit.* p. 239.
95 Jenkins to Wavell, 17 March 1947, R/3/1/176 IOR.
96 Jenkins to Mountbatten, 30 April 1947 *T.P* x, p. 506.
97 'The Muslims have little chance of maintaining a United Punjab', Jenkins noted on 11 March. 'The Sikhs will demand at least a deferred partition, and at worst an immediate partition of the province. They were not clear about the boundary, but it is clear that they will demand a good deal more than the Muslims have ever expected to concede. Note by Jenkins 11.3.47 R/3/1/176 IOR.
98 Khizr of course continued to act as the Governor's eyes and ears in his own district. During a meeting with Jenkins on 20 March he recounted how the attacks on non-Muslims in the Shahpur district had been organised. The Punjab Governor noted that, 'the Malik Sahib was very pessimistic and said that in the absence of a settlement at the Centre, there was in his opinion practically no hope of a stable government in the Punjab.' Note by Sir E. Jenkins 14 & 20 March 1947 *T.P* x, pp. 998 & 953.

Epilogue

The law and order situation continuously deteriorated during the weeks which followed the collapse of the Coalition Ministry. The British had barely restored order in the Rawalpindi and Multan divisions, when serious disorders swept the Gurgaon district. More than fifty villages were destroyed in the fighting between the Meos and Jats which spread over 1,000 square miles of countryside.[1] Initially only just over 300 troops could be spared, with the result that several areas temporarily slipped out of British control.[2]

Communal conflict raged in Lahore from April onwards, despite the imposition of martial law. By mid-July over 700 Hindu and Sikh homes had been burned down.[3] This followed the destruction of 4,000 Muslim shops and businesses in the walled area of Amritsar earlier in March.[4] The unreliability of the police in both cities cast a sombre shadow.[5] Jenkins also had the disquieting experience of having his telephone tapped and confidential information passed on to Muslim League politicians.[6]

Mountbatten interviewed Khizr on 3 May 1947 to sound out his opinion on the partition plan. The former Premier reiterated that the British should not be a party to any 'suicidal' vivisection of the Punjab. 'Once a division was announced', he declared, 're-unification would become almost impossible.' Khizr prophetically warned that the Sikhs would never join Pakistan and that a decision to split the Punjab would mean civil war. He concluded by arguing for the inclusion of the option of a free Punjab with an agreement or agreements with Hindustan and Pakistan about defence, in any referendum question on the province's future.[7]

During the following week, Khizr had a number of unofficial meetings with Jenkins at Barnes Court, Simla. He simultaneously issued a statement to the press offering to act as a link between the

Khizr Tiwana, the Punjab Unionist Party and the Partition of India

Muslim League and the minorities so that a Government could be formed. This came to naught, as Jenkins anticipated, 'since the Muslim League leaders have no sense at all, and Tara Singh is almost hysterical.'[8]

The Tiwana heartland did not escape the violence which followed Khizr's resignation. Muslim ex-servicemen faked a Hindu attack on a mosque in Khushab on the night of 10–11 March to provide a pretext for assaults on the town's large non-Muslim population. Despite the efforts of a local peace committee, there were widespread attacks on temples and property with an estimated loss of Rs 800,000. The violence spread from Khushab to the surrounding villages. The temple in Kund village, eleven miles away, was razed to the ground.[9] Although Khizr could no longer protect the minorities' interests at the provincial level, Hindus who had relatives at Kalra and the other Tiwana estates now sought refuge there, trusting that this would bring them security.[10]

The eventual Partition of August 1947, however destroyed the era of communal cooperation in the Tiwana properties of Kalra, Khizarabad, Mitha Tiwana and Khwajabad. In the absence of both Khizr and Allah Bakhsh, their Hindu and Sikh inhabitants suffered the same fate as minorities elsewhere in the Punjab. Sultan Shah, the **mukhtar** of the villages of the Khizarabad stud farm estate led out the Hindus on the pretext that they would be safely escorted to Sargodha. A mob assaulted them in a pre-arranged attack which left no survivors.[11] The bodies of women and children were later seen floating in the canal. Pir Mehr Chand Shah, the head **mukhtar** of Allah Bakhsh's estate[12] forcibly brought 60 Hindu villagers to a Sargodha mosque for conversion. They were later rescued by Gurkhas.[13] Family retainers also joined in the looting of the bazaar in Kalra village and the ransacking of the temple which Umar had constructed.

There were attacks on the Hindus and Sikhs throughout the Khushab **tehsil**. The wealthy Batras of Girot and Mitha Tiwana resisted for two days. Ultimately, twenty three members of the family were arrested on false murder charges. They were safely evacuated only after expending huge sums of money to buy off their accusers. Bhagat Ram Chand, for example, handed over Rs 35,000 in hard cash.[14] Mokam Singh a well known Sikh landowner of the **thal** suffered a more nightmarish fate. He led the resistance to the Muslim attack on Roda village. When the defenders' ammunition finally gave out, the settlement was overrun by a mob which beheaded him. His

168

Epilogue

severed head was transfixed to a spear and paraded as a war trophy from village to village.[15] News of the violence in the Khushab **tehsil**, spread as far as Nairobi. Glancy writing from there, commiserated with Khizr that 'all the Hindus and Sikhs have been frightened into leaving Kalra.'[16] Much personal suffering was hidden by such anodyne expressions. But what happened at Kalra was just a microcosm of the hate-filled violence throughout North India.

The most striking evidence of the passing of the old order at Kalra however, was the strange episode which occurred at the end of September 1947 involving Jiwan Khan, head of its **langar**. In the absence of any male members of the family he staged what amounted to a mini **coup d'etat**. He took over the running of the estate and forbade the retainers to allow the Tiwana women folk to leave. On the second day Fateh Khatun smuggled out a message for assistance through one of her maids who feigned pregnancy and required her husband to accompany her on a call of nature to the fields. The man walked the four miles to Jhawarian where he went by tonga to Chak Muzzafarabad. Once Ahmad Yar Tiwana was told of what he happened, he hurried off to Jhawarian **thana** police station where constables were sent to release Fateh Khan and the other ladies. No case was registered against Jiwan Khan because it would involve a loss of face. When Khizr later heard of the episode he generously forgave the retainer who escaped lightly with a fine.[17]

i

Khizr remained in Simla until independence. Shortly afterwards he travelled to Europe from Bombay. The ostensible reasons for his departure were to visit his son at Cambridge and to accompany Allah Bakhsh who needed hospital treatment for his throat cancer. Khizr naturally also wanted to put as much distance as possible between himself and vengeful Muslim League politicians.

Khizr initially lived with Nazar at Montello House, 77 Holbroke Road Cambridge. Early in 1948, Nazar quit his studies at Pembroke College in order to watch over the family property.[18] His father moved to the Athenaeum Court Hotel in Piccadilly which thereafter became his residence whenever he was in London. He was joined by Fateh Bibi and Malik Ghulam Muhammad Khan and Muhammad Ali from the Kalra entourage. Khizr's sense of political' betrayal' did not embitter his personal relationships with old India hands. True to his upbringing he continued to feel comfortable in the company of such former officials as Stuart Abbott, Sir Evan Jenkins, R.A. Butler and Lord Linlithgow. He also met Churchill who was then the celebrated Leader of the Opposition.

Khizr continued the correspondence with Glancy which had commenced soon after he had left Government House.[19] 'I think you are wise to keep out of the Punjab for some time', Glancy wrote to his former Premier in January 1948, 'until crazy boys like Mumtaz (Daultana) have time to cool down.'[20] He also advised Khizr against following him to East Africa. 'The Indians here are not your class at all', Glancy declared, 'they're mostly Kathiarwaris and Gujaratis and Ismailis from Bombay and a certain number of Khatri Sikhs. You'll had few friends among them and I'd think you'd be badly bored.'.[21]

Shortly before Khizr left London for Pakistan, Glancy counselled, 'I should say your best plan is to lie low in Kalra for the present and decline to be involved in any form of party politics.'[22] The former Premier of the United Punjab did not in fact enter Pakistan until October 1949. He then arrived on his favourite Pan-Am airline at Karachi under the assumed name of Dr. Khan.[23]

Khizr was in fact the only member of the erstwhile Coalition Ministry not to pursue an active political career in the post-independence era.[24] Why did he not make his way in Pakistani politics, unlike other Muslim Unionists?[25] He of course had more of a Unionist past to live down. For as Premier, he had come to symbolise the 'treachery' of the Unionist party in Muslim League propaganda. The campaign against the Ministry had become increasingly personalized from 1944 onwards. But the main reason for his life taking a diametrically opposite path to say Qizalbash's after independence, lay both in his own diffidence and the factional political alignments of the Shahpur district.[26]

Umar it will be recalled, had pushed his son into politics in 1937. Khizr was never consumed by the pursuit of power, nor was he a political animal. He also stuck stubbornly to his principles which he would not compromise for the sake of expediency. Moreover, he was dispirited by the declining family fortune and did not want to divert his energies away from its restoration. The attempt to establish the Shahpur textile mill, however ended in financial ruin. Indeed, the enterprise's collapse shortly after his death probably provided the motive for the murder of his fourth wife Rehana who had taken over its management.[27]

Khizr thus turned his back on the few opportunities to re-enter public life which came his way. He could for example in 1953 have

Epilogue

entered Mohammad Ali Bogra's 'cabinet of talents' which included the former' renegade' Congress Premier of the Frontier Dr. Khan Sahib.[28]

Khizr's political re-emergence would in any case have been difficult because of the factional political scene in Shahpur. Once the mass mobilisation of the Pakistan movement subsided, politics in this as in other districts reverted to their former patterns. If Unionism could claim to have survived Pakistan's emergence, it was in the return of a local politics dominated by powerful landholders and **biraderi** networks. The uneasy relationship between Khizr and Feroz Khan Noon after the events of 1945–7 complicated the re-establishment of a powerful Noon-Tiwana faction. The greatest obstacle, however, was provided by the alliance between the Qureshis, the Tiwanas' long time local rivals and the Daultanas.

Mian Mumtaz Daultana had placed himself at the head of the Muslim League campaign from 1944 onwards. He demonstrated a similar singlemindedness in his efforts to hound the Nawab of Mamdot out of office from 1948 onwards. Shaukat assisted him in this as in his earlier anti-Unionist campaign. Daultana feared Khizr as a potential opponent, he therefore used his Ministerial powers to discourage his political come-back. Apart from the general Unionist skeleton in his cupboard, Daultana held over Khizr a threat of investigation into alleged 'misappropriation' of Zamindara League funds.[29] Petty harassments included the withdrawing of all arms licences for the Kalra employees.[30] During a tour of the Sargodha district in November 1950, Daultana publicly announced that the Kalra Great Canal along with smaller Tiwana canals would be taken over by the Government.[31] This threat was finally enacted in 1954. Khizr was not compensated for the loss of his private canals in contravention of Section 47 of the Punjab Minor Canals Act of 1905. Nazar was still engaged in litigation regarding this at the time of writing.

ii

Kalra never recovered its former prosperity or sense of community. Like other big landlords, Khizr circumvented Land Reforms by redistributing the property amongst relatives, whilst retaining overall control. On one occasion only half in jest he had told his grandson Omar that his increasing conjugal distractions were prompted by the need to save the ancestral patrimony. The fourth marriage he had declared 'is for land reforms. The more issue I produce, the less land I need to surrender.'[32] He also repurchased various tracts of land which had been resumed and 'leased' back about 7,000 acres of land at Khizarabad from the Punjab Government on horse and cattle breeding terms. Notwithstanding these responses to the Land Reforms, Khizr was increasingly confronted with the need to maintain an expensive lifestyle on a limited resource base. 'My estate is now a head supported by a skeleton' he colourfully remarked when reflecting on this plight.[33] But although he still produced the most magnificent animals for the annual Lahore Horse Show, he had lost the interest in the estate which he had displayed in the 1930s. This was evidenced by his failure to mechanise production unlike much smaller landowners. He was also increasingly absent from Kalra on overseas visits.

Khizr's constant travelling[34] in his later years was partly occasioned by the need to visit his son Nazar and his family who had settled in America. He was in San Francisco in both 1952 and 1953 to be on hand at the birth of his grandchildren Yasmin and Omar. It was also a symptom of an increasing restlessness and unease. This was brought on by a growing sense of failure not only as a politician and farmer, but as a husband and father.[35] It was in an attempt to confront these feelings that Khizr decided to write an autobiography in the final weeks of his life. He had acquired a tape recorder to dictate his memoirs just three days before his death.[36]

Khizr died not in his native Kalra, but in distant California. He was staying at a ranch near Chico in Glen County which he had first visited with his third wife, Zeinab,[37] a decade earlier. Indeed, one of their four daughters was born there. The ranch belonged to Fazal Mohammad from Jullundur. He had settled in California in the 1920s and made his fortune in rice farming. He had become friendly with Khizr and had at one stage broached a business deal in which they would exchange land. The deal which concerned 60 squares in the Sheikhupura district had not been completed before Fazal Muhammad's death.[38] The rancher's widow had remarried Ghulam Hassan, a retired Pakistan Army Major and former recruiting officer from Khizr's own Sargodha district. Ghulam Hassan was however, away during Khizr's final fateful stay at the ranch.

Local Indian and Pakistani acquaintances visited him during this time, as did his American friends Gene and Becky Stirling who had retired to Florida from California. He regaled them as he had done on other occasions with the view that before the end of the century some

Epilogue

kind of new geo-socio-political order would emerge in the subcontinent which would transcend the 'artificial' partition of 1947. It would restore the common cultural and economic ties which had been sundered in the name of religion.[39] Roughly three years before this final visit to America, Khizr had met his grandson Omar in New York and expressed similar views during lengthy discussions with him. 'I still think a Punjabi Muslim has more in common with a Punjabi Hindu or Sikh', he had declared on one occasion, than with a Bengali (or any non-Punjabi really and I think the separation of East Pakistan proved that.'[40]

Khizr intended to travel back to Chicago with Nazar, before calling in at the University of Columbia to seek assistance with his autobiography. Soon after Nazar's arrival at Chico, however he was troubled by nightmares and in a premonition of his death insisted that if anything happened to him, he should not be buried in the Muslim graveyard in Sacramento. He retired early as usual to his bedroom on the evening of 19th January. Sometime between 1 and 2 o'clock the following morning, he died of a massive heart attack. He was seven months short of his seventy-fifth birthday. In accordance with his wishes, Khizr's body was buried four days later in the family graveyard at Kalra.

The throng of mourners was much smaller and less colourful than at the time of Umar's funeral. Kalra had long been bereft of the Sikhs in their bright turbans and the Hindus in their checked lungis. Around five thousand men and women had gathered in the polo ground wrapped up against the cold of a winter Punjabi morning. Khizr in the full plenitude of his power had acted as the chief mourner at Umar's funeral. Thirty years later the role fell to Nazar who had remarkably carved out a fresh life for himself as a Chicago City librarian. He still wore his check American sports jacket beneath his overcoat.

Pir Ghulam Moinuddin of Golra's presence provided some continuity with the past, although the more superstitious would have preferred not to have been reminded through it, of his father's dire warnings to the Unionist Premier in 1946. A more reassuring link with Khizr's former career was symbolised by the guard of honour mounted by a contingent from the 19th Lancers regiment. Messages of condolence were fittingly received from Indira Gandhi, Zulfikar Ali Bhutto and Lord Louis Mountbatten. Khizr's coffin was draped not in the Pakistan flag, but the Kalra tricolour designed by Umar.

Khizr Tiwana, the Punjab Unionist Party and the Partition of India

Notes

1 Punjab Governor to the Viceroy and the Governors of the U.P., Sind and N.W.F.P., 1 June 1947 R/3/1/90 IOR.
2 Punjab FR for the 2nd Half of May 1947 L/P&J/5/250 IOR.
3 Report by John Eustace, Deputy Commissioner, Lahore n.d., R/3/1/9 IOR.
4 *Civil and Military Gazette* (Lahore) 18 March 1947.
5 Punjab FR 13 August 1947 L/P&J/5/250 IOR.
6 Punjab FR 14 March 1947 L/P&J/5/250 IOR.
7 Record of an Interview between Mountbatten and Khizr 3 May 1947. *T.P* x, p. 589& ff.
8 Jenkins to Mountbatten 15 May 1947 *T.P* x, p. 835.
9 K. Singh. *The Partition of the Punjab* (Patiala, 1972) p. 679.
10 *Ibid.*, p. 685.
11 Singh *op.cit.* p. 685.
12 When Allah Bakhsh died, Pir Chand became Kalra's general manager. He was a notorious drunkard and womaniser.
13 Singh *op.cit.* p. 686.
14 Singh *op.cit.* p. 688.
15 *Ibid.* p. 687.
16 Glancy to Khizr 24.11.47 MS 210/7 Tiwana Papers.
17 Interview with Nazar Tiwana, Chicago September 1993.
18 Khizr was probably the only person who stood to lose property in both India and Pakistan because he was declared an evacuee. An order was served on 16 squares of land in village chak 28/22 Okara tehsil Montgomery district. Khizr's houses in Simla and Delhi were declared as abandoned property. He secured an informal arrangement with Nehru that he could retain ownership of the Hardinge Avenue property. After Nehru's death this was taken over by the Delhi Municipal authorities and subsequently demolished. Nazar pursued compensation for this through-out the early 1990s.
19 Glancy had written the following to Khizr at the end of December 1946. 'I think it is wonderful how you have succeeded in maintaining peace in the Punjab with all the massacres elsewhere. Long may it remain so, but I know very well that your task is becoming more difficult every day. I wonder whether any of your former supporters who deserted you in the hour of trouble have shown any signs of remorse? Glancy to Khizr 30.12.46 MS 210/7 Tiwana Papers Southampton University.
20 Glancy to Khizr 16.1.48. *Ibid.*
21 Glancy to Khizr 26.3.48 *Ibid.*
22 Glancy to Khizr 14.10.49 *Ibid.*
23 Petty harassments of Khizr and his tenants, together with more serious threats to his property fuelled a growing persecution complex. Although British representatives in Lahore sympathised with his plight, he received shorter shrift in London. J. O. McCormick of the Commonwealth Relations Office minuted for example, 'Sir Khizr surrounds himself with an interesting "cloak and dagger" atmosphere in which assailants appear to crouch behind every bush.' J.O. McCormick 11.5.51. Do. 134.20

174

Epilogue

Record of Conversations with Khizr regarding the confiscation of his property. 13 February 1948–17 April 1957. Dominions Office & Commonwealth Relations Office PRO.

24 The advancement of the non-Muslim Coalition Ministers does not of course contain any surprises. Sachar was Chief Minister of the Indian Punjab from 1949–56, before ending a distinguished career as a High Commissioner to Ceylon and State Governor of Andhra Pradesh. Lehri Singh was an East Punjab Cabinet Minister for a number of years and was later involved with the movement for a separate Haryana State. Swaran Singh had the most distinguished career of all. From 1952–77 he was a central cabinet minister holding the important posts of defence and external affairs in addition to a number of other portfolios.

25 Qizalbash like other Muslim Unionists made a political come-back through the emergence of Feroz Khan Noon as Chief Minister of the Punjab in 1953. He was a founding member of the Republican Party in 1956 which contained many former Unionists. He rose to become the Chief Minister of West Pakistan in 1958. Qizalbash re-entered politics following the Ayub era as Minister of Finance in the Yahya Cabinet. A distinguished career was crowned with his being appointed ambassador to France in 1972. Ibrahim Barq achieved less elevated status after 1947, although he did secure election to the West Pakistan Assembly (1962–5).

26 Zeinab, however during an interview with the author in December 1994 in Lahore maintained that Khizr had not entered Pakistan politics on her express advice.

27 Khizr had married Rehana in 1963. It was his fourth and her fifth marriage. She came originally from a middle class Punjabi family. In 1970 she gave birth to 'twin' sons, Morhar Hayat and Samar Hayat. The former was killed as a teenager in a car crash. Rehana was reportedly murdered by family retainers in 1976, although no case was lodged. Interview Nazar Tiwana, New Delhi, 10 December 1993.

28 Khizr turned down this offer because he had been appalled by the political deterioration in the country as evidenced by corruption, party squabbles and the cynical use of religion in the 1952 anti- Ahmadiyah campaign. Interview with Nazar Tiwana Chicago 1 September 1993.

29 R.L.D. Jasper Office High Commissioner Lahore to Oliver High Commissioner Karachi 10 January 1950 D0.134.20 *op.cit.*

30 Jasper to Graffety Smith High Commissioner Karachi 3 May 1951 *Ibid.*

31 Lahore Weekly Report 7 November 1950 *Ibid.*

32 Omar Hayat Tiwana, 'Requiem for a provincialist. Sir Khizr Hayat Tiwana 1900–1975.' *The Friday Times* (Karachi) 19–25 January 1995 Special Supplement Page ll.

33 *Ibid.*

34 In addition to his trips to America, he visited England in 1951, 1956, 1963, 1969 and 1974.

35 Nazar's decision to settle permanently in the USA with his family in 1965 distressed Khizr. His third marriage to Zeinab had ended acrimoniously and involved him in a legal suit.

36 Interview with Nazar Tiwana Chicago 3 June 1991.

37 Zeinab was half English, her father came from a leading UP **taluqdar**

Khizr Tiwana, the Punjab Unionist Party and the Partition of India

family. This was her third marriage. Her first husband had been an Army Officer the second an American General Motors Manager who was posted to Karachi.

38 Interview with Nazar Tiwana, New Delhi 11 December 1993.
39 N. Tiwana, 'Unionism in the British Punjab: A Personal Memoir' p. 5. Paper presented to the International Conference on Punjab Studies, Coventry University, June 1994.
40 Omar Hayat Tiwana *op.cit.*

Conclusion

This work at its simplest is a record of a life. Like all biographical writing it has represented history in microcosm. It has filled in the fine detail on the broad brush approach of my earlier portrayals of the system of collaboration between the Punjabi landed elites and the British authorities.[1] To tell the story of any individual's career, it is necessary, however, to describe the stage on which it is played out. Biographical subjects cannot be disembodied from their environments. This study has thus described both the social and economic background of the British Punjab, and the history of Khizr's forbears.

Biographers have tended to divide between those who view individuals as significant only because of the times in which they lived, and those who maintain that they can alter the course of history. Thomas Carlyle took the latter understanding to its logical extreme, when he declared that 'no great man lives in vain. The history of the world is but the biography of great men.'[2] Khizr could be viewed in this light as a great heroic failure, who attempted to make history in the face of exceptional difficulties. A social determinist on the other hand would depict him bobbing up and down helplessly on the tide of elemental economic forces. The reality was of course less clear cut. It did matter that he, rather than another Unionist landlord was leading the Punjab in 1944. At the same time he was caught up in the tide of events over which he possessed little control.

Khizr was undoubtedly influenced by his times, his education and his social upbringing. The kind of world into which he was born opened up the possibility of political power and influence. Land ownership held the key to power in the Punjab and the Tiwanas held the most land in its western districts. The Punjab's communal composition also decreed that only a Muslim could hold office as Premier. This is why it was Khizr not Chhotu Ram who succeeded

177

Sikander. Khizr's background, however, also limited what he was likely to do with this power. He saw it as his duty to maintain the rural traditions of loyalty, military service and the elevation of the 'backward tribes'. In this sense, he was the archetypal product of the British co-option of the Punjabi landed elite. But Khizr was more than an identikit 'agriculturalist.' If he had been, he would have no doubt like many of his former Unionist colleagues carved out a successful career in the Pakistan Muslim League or Republican Party. To discern a fuller picture, we must consider the interplay between the individual and his environment.

It has been difficult to uncover the man himself, his character and personality. The paucity of personal memoirs has meant that Khizr's individuality has had to be teased out through an examination both of what he did and the recollections of others. The picture which has emerged is that despite his glamour and public self-assurance, he was an emotional and insecure individual who was prone to self-doubt. This is evidenced both in his indecision and reliance on the psychological reassurance he could receive from stronger personalities. Chhotu Ram, and Allah Bakhsh both exerted immense political influence over him. The latter was truly his **eminence grise.**

His father was, however the most significant factor in Khizr's life. The towering personality of the 'General' kept his son in awe even in adulthood. Khizr never questioned Umar's call to political arms in 1937, although he harboured no personal ambitions. Once he entered public life, he was driven by the need to live up to his father's standards. He could not bear to disappoint him. This stiffened his resolve when facing Jinnah. Ever the dutiful son, he took to heart Umar's dying words to display courage in the face of the Quaid-e-Azam's assault on the Unionist citadel.

Khizr was above all, a devoted and highly principled person. He was devoted to his father, to Kalra and to his regiment and ministerial colleagues. In many respects he was too loyal to the British connection as it blinded him to the changing political realities of the war years. It came as a great shock that the British could discard their Unionist allies as a child would a rag doll. Khizr's own principles and code of conduct would not allow him to opportunistically jump on the Muslim League bandwagon. His failure to do so flew in the face of Tiwana family history. It was to cost him dear.

A less principled individual with the same social background would have swapped the Unionist leader's noose of laurels, for the

Conclusion

Muslim League's crown. Punjabi politics would then have taken an entirely different trajectory. It is of course open to doubt whether the sufferings of August 1947 could have been avoided, even if a Muslim League Ministry had taken office in 1944 and been forced to terms with the minorities. The balance of evidence is that any Punjab Muslim League Ministry would have been severely constrained by the All-India situation and the bidding of its high command.

Khizr's public career, ended in abject failure. He could not even protect his loyal Hindu and Sikh workers at Kalra. Instead he scuttled to a self-imposed exile in Britain, when India finally achieved self-rule, 'at the midnight hour.' What then is the justification for treating his life as more than a side-show in South Asian Muslim history? Is it merely mischievous to take out the Unionist skeleton from the Punjab's cupboard?

History has always been written by the victors, although we can learn equally as much from those who' lost'. In the South Asian context, the towering personality of Abdul Ghaffar Khan immediately comes to mind in this respect. Khizr's lasting significance lies not in his tenure of power as the Punjab's Premier, nor in his ultimately unsuccessful tussle with Jinnah and the Muslim League. What is important is not what he did, but what he stood for. He acted in both public and private life as if communal differences were irrelevant. Other Punjabi landholders shared this outlook, but it was rooted much more deeply in Khizr's personality and family tradition. This work has uncovered for the first time his warm friendships with non-Muslims and the existence of the Hindu and Sikh branches of the family. It was this background, reinforced by the Aitchison experience which led Khizr to reject the view that religious and political identities were coterminous.

Khizr believed that Partition would sunder the fabric of Punjabi society and destroy a whole way of life. He regarded the Muslim League's demands as based on the hatred of the non-Muslim. He maintained that there was nothing in the Koran that made the creation of Pakistan a sacred act. On the contrary the Partition demand was profoundly un-Islamic in the true sense of the word. Khizr's personal distaste for Jinnah arose from what he saw as the latter's hypocrisy in using religion for his own political interests, when he possessed only a rudimentary knowledge of Islam himself and did not practice it in a ritual sense.

Khizr's attachment to political accommodation was overturned in the fevered days of the end game of Empire. But this approach remains highly significant for the contemporary Indian Subcontinent which has witnessed a recrudescence of communal hatred and violence.[3] It is no coincidence that this has accompanied an abandonment of political power-sharing and the revival of sectarianism in both India and Pakistan. In the South Asian context it is necessary to reach out beyond the confines of community to establish a stable and prosperous political system.

Khizr was not a political thinker. With his educational background this is hardly surprising. Nor was he a democrat other than of the most conservative kind. But he still provides an example of the type of leadership required to develop a successful power-sharing system. His natural tolerance and flexibility enabled him to intuitively arrive at the conclusion that the Unionist system was the only possible means to maintain peace in the Punjab's divided society. He sustained the consensual framework which had been established by Chhotu Ram, Mian Fazl-i-Husain and Sikander, in the much more difficult political circumstances after 1944. Indeed, he reached beyond his predecessors in an endeavour to heal the breach between the urban and rural communities. It was at his suggestion that the Zamindara League for the first time opened its doors to non-agriculturalists.

Ironically, Khizr's legacy lies not in his self-conscious espousal of the slogan ' Punjab for the Punjabis'. This is anachronistic, at least in the Punjabi dominated Pakistan State.[4] where in Iftikhar Malik's words there is 'a bleak absence of a sustained debate on a coherent Punjabi identity revolving around cultural, territorial or historical symbols.'[5] A fact which probably explains why Nazar was permitted to bring home his body, whilst Chaudhri Rahmat Ali still lies in his Cambridge exile.[6] Khizr's claim to be a serious political figure lies rather with his style of statecraft. He arrived at this intuitively as a result both of his upbringing and the impact of the Colonial State. His coalition building approach linked with concern for widespread diffusion of power is acutely relevant to contemporary South Asia. The principles which he espoused of decentralisation of power, cross-communal cooperation, power-sharing and proportionately in political representation and government appointments lie at the heart of a consociational system. It could be strongly argued that in their continued absence India and Pakistan will undergo further communal and ethnic travail.

Khizr practised consociationalism without grasping its intellectual underpinnings. His career, nevertheless demonstrates the long held

Conclusion

belief of its theorists that leadership is a crucial variable in its functioning.[7] Khizr's qualities of honesty, flexibility, and tolerance are in short supply in present day Indian and Pakistani politics. Their absence has greatly exacerbated the damage to community relations caused by centralising drives intended to dragoon diverse societies into uniform nation states.[8] In order to provide hope for their long suffering peoples, the present rulers of India and Pakistan would do well to go back to the future and seriously consider Khizr's consociational approach to politics.

Notes

1 See, for example, I. Talbot, *Punjab and the Raj 1849–1947* (Delhi 1988).
2 T. Carlyle, *Heroes and Hero Worship. i The Hero as Divinity* (London, 1841).
3 For details of communal disturbances in the 1980s see, I. Talbot, 'Politics and Religion in Contemporary India' in G. Moyser (ed), *Politics and Religion in the Modern World* (London, 1991) pp. 136–62. In the aftermath of the destruction of the Babri mosque at Ayodhya in December 1992, there were over 1,200 deaths in one month. Bombay saw its worst violence since Partition in January 1993 when more than 600 people were killed in communal rioting. See, R.L. Hardgrave, 'India: The Dilemmas of Diversity' *Journal of Democracy* 4,4 (October 1993) pp. 54–68.
4 The Punjab is not only the most populous province of Pakistan and is the most agriculturally and industrially developed, but Punjabis have disproportionately dominated the State's bureaucracy and Army. It is now a commonplace finding that two thirds of the Pakistan Army is recruited from inhabitants of a 100 mile radius of Rawalpindi. Clive Dewey amongst others has pointed to the important economic multiplier effects stemming from this in addition to its political consequences. It is in no way surprising that Punjabis have replaced **muhajirs** as the most enthusiastic proponents of Pakistani nationalism. Khizr's anxiety in 1946–7 that Partition would kill the goose which laid the golden egg for the martial castes has from this perspective been gloriously refuted. For an analysis of the Punjab and Pakistani Militarism see, C. Dewey, 'The rural roots of Pakistani Militarism', in D.A. Low (ed), *The Political Inheritance of Pakistan* (London, 1991) pp. 255–84.
5 I.H. Malik, 'Understanding Punjab's Political Economy: Imran Ali's Interpretation' *International Journal of Punjab Studies* 1,1 (1994) p. 117.
6 By his death, Khizr was no longer so controversial as he had once been. Ironically, his leading political opponents, Shaukat and Daultana had both been under a darker cloud in the 1960s.
7 This idea was recently restated in, A. Lijphart, *Power-Sharing in Southern Africa* (Berkeley, 1985).
8 For further details see, S. Mahmud Ali, *The Fearful State. Power, People and Internal War in South Asia* (London, 1993).

Glossary

amir	commander, chief
anjuman	association
biraderi	brotherhood, a patrilineal kinship group
darbar	court of a king
fatwa	ruling of religious law
gaddi	throne, seat of authority
hajj	pilgrimage to Mecca
halal	lawful, animal slaughtered according to Islamic law
jagir	a revenue free land grant for military or political service
jagirdar	holder of a **jagir**
jatha	band
jhatka	animal slaughtered by single blow
kafir	unbeliever, non-Muslim
Khalsa	the pure used in reference to Sikh community
lambardar	village headman
langar	free kitchen
malik	property owner used as title of respect
murid	disciple of a **pir**
pir	A Muslim saint, **sufi** guide
Quaid-i-Azam	'The Great Leader'. Title given to Mohammad Ali Jinnah
sahukar	moneylender
sajjada nashin	literally one who sits on the prayer rug; custodian of a **sufi** shrine
sufi	Muslim mystic. The word is derived from the woollen garment worn by early mystics
tahsil	a revenue subdivision of a district

Glossary

tumandar	title given to Baloch chief in the Punjab
'ulama	Muslims learned in Islamic religious sciences
'urs	celebration of the death anniversary of a sufi saint
zail	a group of villages, each in charge of a semi-ocial **zaildar**
zamindar	landholder responsible for paying land revenue to the government

Select Bibliography

Private Papers

Chelmsford Papers, India Office Library, London MSS.EUR E264.
F.L. Brayne Papers, India Office Library, London, MSS.Eur F152.
Halifax Papers, India Office Library, London, MSS.Eur C125.
Linlithgow Papers, India Office Library, London MSS.Eur F125.
Mian Fazl-i-Husain Papers, India Office Library, London MSS.Eur E352.
Mountbatten Papers, University of Southampton, MB1/D255.
Quaid-i-Azam Papers, National Archives of Pakistan, Islamabad.
Syed Shamsul Hasan Collection, Karachi, Pakistan.
Tiwana and Unionist Party Papers, Hartley Library, University of Southampton.

Government records

Dominions Office & Commonwealth Relations Office, Public Record Office, London.
India Office Library, London.
National Archives of India, New Delhi.
Do. 134.20. 13 February 1948–17 April 1957. Record of Conversations with Khizr regarding confiscation of his property.
Records of the Political and Secret department, 1928–47, L/P&S/10, L/P&S/ 12, L/P&S /20.
Records of the Public and Judicial Department, 1929–47, L/P&J/6; L/P&J/ 7 and L/P&J/9.
Records of the Military Department, 1940–2, L/Mil/14.
Records of the Home Department (Political) of the Government of India, 1927–45.
All-India Muslim League Records
All-India Muslim League Committee of Action Meetings 1944–7.
All-India Muslim League Working Committee Meetings 1932–7.
The Punjab Muslim League.

184

Select Bibliography

Theses

Brief, D., 'The Punjab and Recruitment to the Indian Army 1846–1918.', M.Litt., thesis Oxford University 1984.

Published Sources

N. Mansergh, E.W.R. Lumby and Penderel Moon (eds), *Constitutional Relations Between Britain and India: The Transfer of Power 1942–7* (ll volumes 1970–1982). The first four volumes have been edited by N. Mansergh and E.W.R. Lumby, and the remaining seven by N. Mansergh and Penderel Moon:

Volume I: *The Cripps Mission, January–April 1942.* London, 1970.
Volume II: *'Quit India', 30 April–21 September 1942.* London, 1971.
Volume III: *Reassertion of authority, Gandhi's fast and the succession to the Viceroyalty, 21 September 1942–12 June 1943.* London, 1971.
Volume IV: *The Bengal Famine and the New Viceroyalty, 15 June 1943–31 August 1944.* London, 1973.
Volume V: *The Simla Conference, Background and Proceedings, 1 September 1944–28 July 1945.* London, 1974.
Volume VI: *The post-war phase: new moves by the Labour Government, 1 August 1945–22 March 1946.* London, 1976.
Volume VII: *The Cabinet Mission, 23 March–29 June 1946.* London, 1977.
Volume VIII: *The Interim Government, 3 July–1 November 1946.* London, 1979.
Volume IX: *The fixing of a time limit, 4 November 1946–22 March 1947.* London, 1980.
Volume X: *The Mountbatten Viceroyalty, Formulation of a Plan, 22 March–30 May 1947.* London, 1981.
Volume XI: *The Mountbatten Viceroyalty, Announcement and Reception of the 3 June Plan, 31 May–7 July 1947.* London, 1982.

Official Publications

Government of India, *Census Reports and Tables.* Decennial series. Punjab Reports 188–1941.
Government of India, *Return Showing the Results of the Elections in India 1937*, Delhi, 1937.
Government of India, *Return Showing the Results of Elections to the Central Legislative Assembly and the Provincial Legislatures 1945–6*, New Delhi, 1948.
Government of the Punjab, *Gazetteer of the Shahpur District* Lahore, 1918.
Punjab Legislative Assembly Debates (1937–46)
Punjab Press Abstract. Annual Series (1923).
Report of the Punjab Provincial Banking Enquiry Committee (1942).
Report of the Administration of Estates under the Charge of the Punjab Court of Wards. Annual Series (1893, 1910, 1911, 1921 & 1928).

Khizr Tiwana, the Punjab Unionist Party and the Partition of India

Newspapers

Civil and Military Gazette, Lahore, 1936–47.
Dawn, Delhi 1943–6.
Eastern Times, Lahore, 1943–6.
Hindustan Times, Delhi, 1937 & 1944.
Leader, Allahabad, 1937.
Nawa-i-Waqt, Lahore, 1945–6.
Pioneer, Lucknow, 1937.
Star of India, Calcutta, 1943–6.
Tribune, Ambala, 1936–44; 1944–6.

Annuals

The Indian Annual Register, Mitra, N.N. (editor), Calcutta, 1944–7.

Interviews

Interviews with, Nazar Tiwana, various 1991–4; Azim Husain 1991–2; Narinder Saroop July 1991; Stuart Abbott December 1990; C.H. Barry August 1991; Swaran Singh December 1993; Bansi Lal December 1993; Izzat Hyat Khan November 1993 & December 1994; K.V.F. Morton, December 1990, Bikram Singh May 1991; Brigadier John Woodroffe, August 1993; Justice Kalwant Singh Tiwana, December 1993; Pran Neville, December 1993; Alan Campbell-Johnson, November 1993; Rajeshwar Bhali, December 1993; Zeinab Tiwana, December 1994; Omar Tiwana, December 1994; Shahjehan Ayub, December 1994.

Correspondence with, Arthur Lall, May 1991; Roger Howroyd January 1993; Syed Amjad Ali, December 1991; Azim Husain, October 1991.

Printed secondary works cited

Ahmad, Jamil-ud-Din, *Speeches and Writings of Mr. Jinnah* 2 vols. Lahore, 1976.

Ahmad, Syed Nur, *From Martial Law to Martial Law Politics in the Punjab 1919–1958* Boulder, 1985.

Ahmed, A.S., ed., *Pakistan. The Social Sciences Perspective* Karachi, 1990.

Aijazuddin, F.S., *Aitchison College Lahore 1886–1986. The First Hundred Years* Lahore, 1986.

Alam, A., *The Crisis of Empire in Mughal North India. Awadh and Punjab 1707–1748* Delhi, 1986.

Alavi, H., 'Kinship in West Punjab Villages.' *Contributions to Indian Sociology* new ser., 6 (December, 1972)

Ali, I., *The Punjab Under Imperialism 1885–1947* Princeton, 1988.

Ali, T., *Can Pakistan Survive?* Harmondsworth 1983.

Banga, I., *Agrarian System of the Sikhs: Late Eighteenth Century and Early Nineteenth Century* New Delhi, 1978.

Barrier, N.G., *The Punjab Alienation of Land Bill of 1900* Durham, 1966.

Baxter, C., 'The People's Party versus the Punjab Feudalists', in Korsen, H. (ed) *Contemporary Problems of Pakistan* Leiden, 1974.

186

Select Bibliography

—— 'Union or Partition: Some Aspects of Politics in the Punjab 1936–1945'in Ziring, L. et al (eds.) *Pakistan the Long View* (Durham, 1977).

Bayly, C.A., *Rulers, Townsmen and Bazaars. North Indian Society in the Age of British Expansion 1770–1870* Cambridge, 1983.

Campbell-Johnson, A. *Mission with Mountbatten* London, 1985.

Caryle, T., *Heroes and Hero Worship i The Hero as Divinity* London, 1841.

Chandra, B., *India's Struggle for Independence* Delhi, 1989.

Chopra, G.L., *Chiefs and families of Note in the Punjab* 2 vols. Lahore 1940.

Chowdhry, P. *Punjab Politics: The Role of Sir Chhotu Ram* New Delhi, 1984.

—— 'Social Support Base and Electoral Politics: The Congress in Colonial Southeast Punjab.' *Modern Asian Studies* 25, 4 (October 1991)

Corr, G.H., *The War of the Springing Tigers* London, 1975.

Coupland, R., *Indian Politics 1936–1942* London, 1943.

Darling, M., *Rusticus Loqitor* Lahore, 1929.

—— *The Punjab Peasantry in Prosperity and Debt* Reprint, Columbia, 1978.

—— *Wisdom and Waste in the Punjab Village* Lahore, 1934.

Dewey, C., *Anglo-Indian Attitudes. The Mind of the Indian Civil Service* London, 1993.

—— 'The rural roots of Pakistani Militarism' in Low, D.A. (ed) *The Political Inheritance of Pakistan* London, 1991.

Edwardes, H., *A year on the Punjab Frontier in 1848–9* 2 volumes London, 1851.

Ewing. K., 'The Politics of Sufism: Redefining the Saints of Pakistan.' *Journal of Asian Studies* 42, 2 (February 1983).

Fox, R., *Kin, Clan, Raja and Rule* Berkeley, 1971.

—— *Lions of the Punjab: Culture in the Making* Berkeley, 1985.

Gilmartin, D., *Empire and Islam. Punjab and the Making of Pakistan* Berkeley 1988.

—— 'Religious leadership and the Pakistan Movement.' *Modern Asian Studies* 13, 3 (1979).

Gopal, M., *Sir Chhotu Ram: A Political Biography* Delhi, 1977.

Grewal, J.S., *The Sikhs of the Punjab* Cambridge 1990.

Gupta, H.R., ed., *Panjab on the eve of the First Sikh War 1844* Hoshiarpur, 1956.

Hardy, P., *The Muslims of British India* Cambridge, 1972.

Hodson, H.V., *The Great Divide. Britain-India-Pakistan* London 1969.

Jalal, A., *The Sole Spokesman: Jinnah, the Muslim League and the Demand for Pakistan* Cambridge, 1985.

Jones, K., *Arya Dharm* Berkeley, 1976.

Josh, B., *Communist Movement in the Punjab* Lahore, 1979.

Kanwar, P., *Imperial Simla. The Political Culture of the Raj* Delhi, 1990.

Lijphart, A., *Power-Sharing in Southern Africa* Berkeley, 1985.

—— *The Politics of Accommodation: Pluralism and Democracy in the Netherlands* Berkeley, 1968.

Malik, I.H., *Sikander Hayat Khan (1892–1942) A Political Biography* Islamabad, 1985.

Khizr Tiwana, the Punjab Unionist Party and the Partition of India

Malik, I., *The History of the Punjab 1799–1947* Delhi, 1983.

Mehr. G.R., (ed), *General Sir Umar Hayat Khan Tiwana Sawaneh Hayat awr unki Khandani Tarekh ka Pas-e-Manzar* Lahore, 1965.

Minault, G., *The Khilafat Movement, Religious Symbolism and Political Mobilisation in India* New York, 1982.

Moon, P., (ed), *Wavell. The Viceroy's Journal* London, 1973.

Moore, R.J., *Churchill, Cripps and India, 1939–1945* Oxford, 1979.

Narendranath, R., 'The Punjab Agrarian Laws and their Constitutional Bearings.' *Modern Review* 65, 1939.

Naqvi, H.K., *Urban centres and Industries in Upper India 1556–1803* Bombay, 1968.

Nawaz, J.A.S., *Father and Daughter* Lahore, 1971.

Nizami, K.A., *The Life and Times of Shaikh Farid-u'd-din Ganj-i-Shakar* Lahore, 1976.

Noon, F.K., *From Memory* Lahore, 1969.

Oren, S., 'The Sikhs, Congress and the Unionists in British Punjab, 1937–1945.' *Modern Asian Studies* 8, 3 1974.

Page, D., *Prelude to Partition: The Indian Muslims and the Imperial System of Control 1920–1932* Oxford, 1982.

Philips, C.H., and Wainwright, M., (eds), *The Partition of India: Policies and Perspectives, 1935–1947* London, 1970.

Pirzada, S.S., (ed), *Foundations of Pakistan: All-India Muslim League Documents, 1906–1947* 2 vols. Karachi, 1970.

Pocock, J.G., *The Spirit of a Regiment. Being the History of the 19th King George V's Own Lancers 192–1947* Aldershot, 1962.

Rai, S.M., *Legislative Politics and Freedom Struggle in Punjab 1847–1947* New Delhi, 1984.

Ram, C.T., *Sir Chhotu Ram: Apostle of Hindu-Muslim Unity* Rohtak, n.d.

Rizvi, G., *Linlithgow and India: A Study of British Policy and the Political Impasse in India, 1936–43* London, 1978.

Singh, Chetan, *Panjab in the Seventeenth Century* Delhi, 1991

Singh, K., (ed), *The Partition of the Punjab* Patiala, 1972.

Singh, K., *Partition and Aftermath. Memoirs of an Ambassador* New Delhi, 1991.

Singh, M., *The Akali Movement* Delhi, 1978.

Singh, P., *The Punjab Chiefs' Association*, Lahore, 1911.

Talbot, I.A., 'British rule in the Punjab, 1849–1947. Characteristics and Consequences.' *The Journal of Imperial and Commonwealth History*, 19, 2 (May 1991).

—— 'Deserted Collaborators: The Political Background to the Rise and Fall of the Punjab Unionist Party, 1923–1947.' *The Journal of Imperial and Commonwealth History*, 11, 1 (October 1982)

—— *Punjab and the Raj 1849–1947* New Delhi, 1988.

—— 'The Growth of the Muslim League in the Punjab 1937–1946' *Journal of Commonwealth and Comparative Politics*, 20, 1 (March, 1982).

—— 'The role of the crowd in the Muslim League Struggle for Pakistan', *The Journal of Imperial and Commonwealth History*, 21, 2 (May 1993).

Select Bibliography

Trotter, L.J., *The Life of John Nicholson* London, 1897.

Uprety, P.R., *Religion and Politics in Punjab in the 1920s* New Delhi, 1980.

Wikeley, J.M., *Caste Handbook of the Indian Army: Punjabi Mussalmans* Calcutta, 1922.

Willcocks, Sir James, *With The Indians in France* London 1920.

Wolpert, S., *Jinnah of Pakistan* New York, 1984.

Yadav, K.C., *Elections in Punjab, 1920–1947*, Tokyo, 1981.

Zaheer, S., *Muslim Lig aur Yunyunist Parti: Punjab men Haqq o Batil ki Kashmakash* Bombay 1944?

Zaman, M., *Students' Role in the Pakistan Movement* Karachi, 1978.

Index

Abbott, Stuart, 116, 170
agricultural tribes, 6, 53, 57–8; and
  1900 Alienation of Land Act, 6,
  57–8, 77
Aitchison College Lahore, 36–8, 48,
  49fn, 50fn, 51, 79, 88
Akalis, 7, 85–6, 95fn, 149–50, 152
Ali, Barkat, 73
Ali, Imran, 2, 29, 34fn, 63fn
Ali, Tariq, 2
Alienation of Land Act (1900), 6,
  57–8, 68, 72, 77; and definition
  of agriculturalist tribes, 53, 58;
  and Unionist Party ideology, 58,
  72–3
Amritsar district, 73
anjumans, 60
Arains, 57, 92, 97fn, 150, 164fn
army recruitment, 4, 25, 28, 30, 38,
  52–3, 85, 101–6, and martial
  castes, 4, 38, 41–2, 44, 52–3,
  101–3
and Shahpur district, 38
and Umar, 38
Attlee, Clement, 5, 159
Awans, 2, 18–19, 21, 38, 67

Badshahi mosque, (Lahore), 83,
  118, 138
Baloch, 2, 21, 45
Barq, Ibrahim, 150, 160, 175fn
Barry, C.H. 37
Batras, 45, 168
Baxter, Craig, 82fn, 87

Brayne, Thomas, 103, 107fn
British colonial policy, 4, 6–7, 12,
  26, 28, 30, 34fn, 38, 41–2, 51–4,
  58, 61, 84, 93, 100, 103, 112-13,
  134, 137–40, 149–50, 153–4,
  156–7, 159

Cabinet Mission (1946), 151–2,
  163–4fn
canal irrigation, 2, 59, 76, 105;
  colonies, 31, 34fn, 53–6, 74, 89,
  106–9; commercialisation of
  agriculture, 7, 53–4; land grants,
  2, 12, 28, 30, 52, 55, 105; private
  canals, 29, 30–1, 34fn, 171
Chand, Roop, 38
Chinarthal, 14, 31fn
Chico, 172
Choudhry, Prem, 136, 143fn
Churchill, Winston, 83–4, 170
communal award (1932), 61
Congress (Punjab), 43, 68–9, 90,
  135; and rural population, 73,
  136–7; and the Sikhs, 73, 85;
  coalition with Unionists, 2, 149,
  151–61; opposition to Unionists,
  2, 84, 151–61; opposition to
  Unionists, 2, 84, 136–7
consociational democracy, viii, 7,
  9fn, 69, 80fn, 150, 179–80, 181
Court of Wards, 30, 47

Darling, Malcolm 70
Daultana, Mian Mumtaz, 94, 124,

Index

139, 155, 171; and 'tribalism', 94

Dyarchy, 42, 58, 64fn

elections, 58, 60; 1937, 61–2, 67–9, 130; 1946, 129–35, 145–8; and Muslim League, 133–5, 145–8; and Unionist Party, 129–132, 145–8

Edwardes, H., 25, 93

Farid, Baba, 15, 132
fatwas, 133
Fox, Richard, 19

Ghani, Abdul, 45, 116
Gilmartin, David, 53, 133
Glancy, Bertrand, 70–1, 88, 93, 96fn, 99, 101, 112–13, 114–15, 119–20, 122–3, 125fn, 126fn, 127fn, 140, 149–50, 169–70, 174fn
Golra, pirs of, 3, 9fn, 146, 173
Government of India Act (1935), 58, 61
Gujars, 19, 23, 130

Hadali, 18, 30
Hailey, Malcolm, 30, 47, 99
Hamoka, 18
Hayats, 26, 52, 119
Hindus, 4, 5, 12, 15, 37, 41, 48, 56, 77, 119; and the Congress, 73, 136, 148; and the Unionist Party, 51, 57, 59, 60, 71–2, 92, 94
Husain, Azim, 75–6, 82fn, 160
Husain, Fazl-i-, 52, 57, 61–2, 70, 75–6, 180; and Muslim League, 62, 112; as a 'communalist' 58–9, 60

Iftikharuddin, Mian, 2
Ikram, S.M., 4fn
Iqbal, Muhammad, 60, 83, 118
Islam and Khizr and Unionist Party, 3–4, 132, 147, 162fn, 179; and Muslim League, 133–4, 145–8

jagirs and jagirdars, 17, 21–2, 23, 26, 28, 33fn, 104

Jats, 41, 57, 69, 71, 94; and Sir Chhotu Ram, 59, 71, 135–6
Jenkins, Evan, 150–2, 153–7, 159–61, 165fn, 166fn, 167, 170
Jhawarian, 47–8, 169
Jinnah, Muhammad Ali, 1, 6, 13, 62, 68, 85, 87, 91–2, 111, 112–13, 116–18, 119, 133, 137–9, 144fn, 151, 179; breakdown of talks with Khizr, 120–22, 129; Pact with Sikander, 73–4, 90–1, 111, 114–15, 118, 124–5fn; tensions with Khizr, 1, 8, 111, 114; tensions with Sikander, 84–5

Kalra, 3, 29, 30, 43–4, 46, 47–9, 54–5, 78, 116, 168–9, 171–4
Khan, Ghazanfar Ali, 68, 90, 96fn, 116, 146
Khan, Jiwan, 169
Khan, Muzaffar, 87–8
Khan, Shaukat Hayat, 96fn, 102, 104, 107fn, 113, 115, 119–20, 122, 124, 126–7fn, 153, 156
Khan, Sikander Hayat, 8, 61–2, 69–70, 74, 80, 83–4, 87, 89; and agrarian legislation, 71–3; and Pact with Jinnah, 73–4, 90–1, 111, 114–15, 118, 124–5fn; and relations with Jinnah, 62, 84–5; and relations with Khizr, 70; and relations with Sikhs 85–6
Khizarabad, 56, 168
Khushab, 21, 32fn, 45, 67, 148, 168

Lahore, 18, 19, 23, 24, 25, 36, 37, 44, 60, 71, 77–8, 104, 116–17, 129, 145; and anti-Khizr agitation, 155–9; and communal conflict, 160, 167
Lahore Resolution (1940), 87, 112
Lal, Manohar, 69, 116, 128fn
Latifi, Daniyal, 2
Lawrence, John, 26, 27, 36
Leghari, Jamal Khan, 123, 138, 148
Linlithgow, 2nd Marquis of (Victor, Alexander, John, Hope), 99–100, 102

191

Ludhiana, 145, 158
Lyallpur, 54, 55, 106, 133, 153

Mahmood, Mir Maqbool, 62, 64fn, 123, 128fn
Majithia, Sunder Singh, 69, 72, 80fn, 81fn
Mamdot, Iftikhar Husain Khan, 92, 95fn, 97fn, 116, 119, 121, 124, 139, 149, 156, 160–1
martial castes, 4, 17, 28, 38, 41–2, 44, 52–3, 101–3
Mianwali, 17, 130, 131
Mitha Tiwana, 18–19, 24, 26, 31, 168
moneylenders, 12, 45, 56–7, 59, 64fn, 72–3, 81fn, 168
Montgomery, 56, 133
Morton, K., 44
mosques, 133, 147
Mountbatten, Lord louis, 112, 167, 173
Mughal Empire, 5, 13, 20
Multan, 15, 19, 26, 133
Muslim League (Punjab), 62, 69, 73, 85, 87, 89, 92, 94, 97fn, 102, 104, 106, 116, 119, 123–4, 148–9, 150, 155; and 1946 elections, 133–5, 145–8; and Pakistan demand, 133–5, 145–8; and pirs, 68, 133, 146–7; and Sikander-Jinnah Pact, 73–4, 90–1, 111, 145–15, 118, 124–5fn
Muslim League National Guards, 153, 155–6, 161
Muzaffargarh, 158

Nehru, Jawaharlal, 2, 68, 80fn, 113, 174fn
Noon, Malik Feroz Khan, 87–8, 138, 140, 143fn, 156, 171
Noons. See Tiwanas and Noons
Nurullah, Mian, 92, 97fn

O'Dwyer, Michael, 8fn, 42, 54, 93, 103

Pakistan, 1, 2, 85, 87, 92, 93, 112, 113, 126fn, 133, 134, 140, 147, 151, 160, 161, 167, 170, 173, 178, 180, 181; and Muslim League strugle, 133–5, 145–8; and support of pirs, 68, 133, 146–7
Pakpattan, 15, 22, 132
Parmar, Jagdev, 13
Pethick-Lawrence, Lord Frederick William, 152, 156–7, 165fn
pirs, 3, 9fn, 15, 132, 146, 173; and Pakistan movement, 68, 133, 146–7; and Zamindara League, 132
Punjab Five Year Post-War Plan, 105–6, 108fn
Punjab National Unionist Party. See Unionist Party
Punjab Village Panchayat Act (1939), 75

Quaid-e-Azam. See Mohammad Ali Jinnah
Qureshi, Nawab Muhammad Hyat, 67

Rajputs, 4, 13, 15, 18, 19, 21, 44, 52, 56, 57, 134
Ram, Chhotu, 51, 58–9, 69, 81fn, 82fn, 86, 87, 88, 92, 99–100, 101, 148; and agrarian legislation, 72–3; and Jats, 51, 59, 71, 94, 117; and Khizr, 70, 75, 115–16, 135, 178; and Zamindara League, 123, 135–6; death, 135–6
Ram, Tikka, 136, 148
Ranjha, Sultan Ali, 129
Revolt of 1857, 25–8, 42, 52
Roktak, 87

Sachar, Lal Bhimsen, 148, 152, 157, 175fn
Sargodha, 44, 47, 54, 116, 133, 145, 148, 168
Sarkesa, 30, 45
Shah, Pir Mehr Chand, 168
Shahpur, 2, 12, 17, 26, 27, 29, 31, 38, 44, 49, 54–5, 67–8, 76, 102, 105
Shankar, Rai, 13, 30

Index

Sheikhupura, 113, 133
Sikander-Jinnah Pact, 73–4, 90–1, 111, 114–15, 118, 124–5fn
Sikhs, 4–5, 20–4, 25, 37, 41, 47, 52, 60, 85–6, 100, 115, 137, 152, 157, 161; and Pakistan, 113, 117, 151; and Unionists, 69, 85–6
Also see Akalis
Singh, Baldev, 86, 95fn, 116, 117, 123, 150, 152
Singh, Mohan, 37, 38, 46
Singh, Ranjit, 7, 21–3, 41–2
Singh, Swaran, 152, 160, 161, 164fn, 175fn
Singh, Tara, 85, 157, 161, 165fn, 168
Simla, 44, 79, 139, 152, 167, 169
Simla Conference (1946), 6, 42, 137–40, 143fn

Tatta Tiwana, 16, 18
Tiwana Family: Tiwana, Allah Bakhsh, 67, 70, 77, 92, 123, 147, 148, 160, 163fn, 169, 174; and relations with Khizr, 46, 78, 115, 178
Tiwana, Fateh Khan, 23–6
Tiwana, Kalwant Singh, 14, 16, 31–2fn
Tiwana, Khizr Hayat Khan, 1, 2–4, 6, 13, 15, 16, 36, 40, 42, 48–9, 51, 63, 67, 72, 74–7, 83–4, 86, 88–90, 92–5, 99–106, 123–4, 129, 146–51, 166fn, 167–70, 180; and relations with Jinnah, 1, 73–4, 90–1, 111–22, 134, 151, 179; and relations with Sikander Hayat Khan, 70; and relations with Chhotu Ram, 70, 75, 115–16, 135, 178; and relations with Allah Bakhsh Tiwana, 46, 78, 115, 178; and relations with Umar, 3, 7, 43, 46, 63, 170, 178; and Simla Conference (1946),

137–40; anti-Khizr agitation, 1, 154–60; death, 173; education 37–8, 49fn, 180; family life, 2–3, 77–80, 140, 172–3, 175fn; personality, 43, 46, 70, 87, 152, 170, 177–8, 181
Tiwana, Nazar, 29, 46, 79, 103–4, 107fn, 116, 169, 172–3
Tiwana, Rai Melo, 15–17
Tiwana, Sadhu Singh, 14–16, 32fn
Tiwana, Sahib Khan, 26–30, 33fn
Tiwana, Umar Hayat Khan, 3, 7, 18, 29–30, 44–6, 55–6, 62, 67, 69–70, 71, 77, 88; and relations with Khizr, 3, 7, 43, 46, 63, 170, 178; army service, 38–41; death, 12, 116; education, 30, 36, 43, 49fn 53–4, 65–70; personality, 82–3, 85–7
Tiwana Lancers, 27–8, 38, 40–1, 173
Tiwanas and Noons, 20, 26, 61, 67, 69–70, 80fn, 140, 143fn, 171

'ulama, 147
Unionist Party, 1–2, 13, 62, 71, 93, 123, 129, 144fn; and elections (1946), 130, 145–8; and local power, 67–9; and Sikander-Jinnah Pact, 73–4, 90–1, 111, 114–15, 118, 124–5fn; coalition with Akalis and Congress, 2, 149–60; formation of, 51, 58–61
Unity Conference (1937), 77
'urs, 133, 141fn, 142fn

Wavell, Lord Archibald Percival, 6, 112, 136, 137–40, 151, 153–4, 156–7
Warcha, 20
Woodroffe, John, 40–1

zails and zaildars, 58, 130, 133
Zamindara League, 71, 123–4, 129–35, 140, 141fn, 171